A Bilingual Introduction to
Corporate Finance

第2版

対訳 英語で学ぶ
コーポレート
ファイナンス
入門

本合暁詩
Akashi Hongo

中央経済社

Preface

Welcome to Corporate Finance. The person who grabs this book must be interested in learning corporate finance, particularly someone who wants or needs to learn corporate finance in ENGLISH.

I deliver lectures related to corporate finance in English in various universities including Temple University, Japan Campus (TUJ) where I serve as a full time faculty member. In addition to foreign universities like TUJ, the number of Japanese universities offering English programs have recently increased as they become more aggressive to recruit foreign students from outside Japan.

A lecture provided in English can be an efficient approach because students learn the contents of a lecture (such as corporate finance) and English simultaneously. However, it is difficult for Japanese students who are not necessarily fluent in English to follow the pace of the lecture, and sometimes can be a big burden for them to read a thick English textbook.

Understanding complex terminologies in the area of business or finance is not easy even in Japanese. Students who are not native English speakers may face a higher hurdle to study them in English. For example, students need to understand what is "Kabushiki (Equity in Japanese)" before understanding what is "Equity".

The situation requires the lecture to use a standard (and often expensive!) textbook from western countries, referring to Japanese books as supplemental materials. Obviously, that arrangement increases the financial burden on students, and deteriorates learning efficiency.

In order to solve this problem, the initial edition of this English-Japanese bilingual textbook was written and published. Following the same style, this second edition deploys the full text in two languages, English on the left page, and Japanese on the right page with complete translation. **This one book offers a reader an English textbook and a Japanese textbook at the same time.**

はじめに

　コーポレートファイナンスへようこそ。本書を手にしている方は，コーポレートファイナンスを特に「英語で」を学びたいと考えている，あるいは学ぶ必要があると感じている方でしょう。

　私は，常勤教員として勤務するテンプル大学ジャパンキャンパスをはじめとするいくつかの大学において，ファイナンスの講義を英語で行っています。テンプル大学は米国の大学なので当然ですが，最近では，海外留学生の受け入れに積極的になってきた大学を中心に，英語で提供される講義がずいぶん増えてきました。

　英語での講義は，その講義の内容（たとえばコーポレートファイナンス）と，英語そのものを，両方一度に学べるという，とても効率的な学習方法に見えます。しかし，英語が必ずしも堪能ではない日本人学生にとっては，英語で進む講義のペースについていくのはなかなか難しく，また英語の分厚いテキストを読みこなすのは大変な負担となることが珍しくありません。

　特に，日本語でも難しいビジネスやファイナンス分野の専門用語を英語で理解することは，日本人学生にとってさらに高いハードルとなりえます。たとえば，「株式」とは何かがわからない中で，「Equity」という英語が出てきても，まず「株式」を理解しなければ「Equity」の意味をとらえられないからです。

　そのため，欧米でスタンダードな（往々にして結構高い！）英語のテキストを使用しつつも，参考図書として日本語の書籍を紹介していました。しかし，これは学生への費用的な負担を増してしまいますし，何よりも学習効率がよくありません。

　このような問題意識から，英語・日本語の対訳を完全装備した日英バイリンガルテキストである本書の初版は生まれました。第2版となる本書も，日本語の文章に英単語を重ねたり，用語解説のみ英語を加えたりということではなく，見開きの左ページを英語，右ページを日本語とした完全2カ国語の教科書です。**読者の皆さんは，この1冊で日本語と英語の教科書を同時に手に入れることができます。**

This book is organized in five parts including 16 chapters, starting with part 1 which provides an overview of corporate finance and management. Part 2 discusses how to measure the price of financial assets such as bonds and stocks, and the value of investments. Part 3 introduces risk which is essential to estimating value, discussing the definition of risk and how it affects the expected return and the cost of capital. Part 4 focus on financial decisions including discussion about raising and returning cash. Part 5 covers how to deal with unexpected risks in business activities such as changes in foreign exchange rates and the price of commodities.

The biggest change in this second edition is the addition of part 5: Hedging Risk and Derivatives. Throughout the book, texts and figures have been revised and enriched, and the flow improved. The major change in the flow is in part 3, separating the discussion about the portfolio theory as an independent chapter handling advanced topics (chapter 9. Detail Discussion about Portfolio Diversification) where students can skip without any problem about coherency in the book. Also, numerical data has been updated. The part focusing on valuation has been taken out due to the page limit. However, You can look forward to the upcoming book named "Bilingual Introduction to Valuation" which will be comprehensively concerned with the topic.

This book being described in two languages must pack as much content as two books. Therefore, it is unavoidable to carve contents down nearly to the essentials. Nevertheless, this book contains sufficient topics and will work not only as an introduction textbook for undergraduate/graduate students but also as a robust reference for business persons who need knowledge of corporate finance in English. This book is highly recommended to a person working with non-Japanese colleagues working in non-Japanese companies dealing with many overseas transactions.

Well, we do not have a lot of space, so let's begin the lecture now.

本書は 16 章からなる 5 部構成となっています。経営とコーポレートファイナンスを概観する第 1 部に続き，第 2 部では企業が資産を適切に使うために，債券や株式などの資産価値や投資の価値をどう算定するのかを議論します。価値を計測するためにはリスクの把握が欠かせないため，第 3 部ではリスクの定義と表わし方，そしてそれがどのように企業の期待リターン，資本コストに影響を与えるのかを学びます。第 4 部では，企業が資金を調達・返還するという資本政策について議論します。そして，最後の第 5 部では，為替や商品価格の変動など，企業活動を行ううえで予期できないリスクへの対処に関して考えます。

　第 2 版での初版からの一番の大きな変化は，第 5 部「リスクヘッジとデリバティブ」を加えたことです。また，第 1 部から第 4 部では，コンテンツを充実させつつ説明の流れをよりスムーズになるよう試みました。特に第 3 部のポートフォリオ理論に関しては，上級トピックとして章を切り出し（「第 9 章　ポートフォリオ分散効果の詳述」），この部分は必要に応じて飛ばしても全体の理解には影響を与えない構成にしています。もちろん説明に使用する数値データ類はアップデイトしました。一方で，初版では含めていた「企業価値評価」に関しては残念ながら紙面の関係でそっくり削除していますが，このトピックは大幅に内容を加えて再編集し，別途『英語で学ぶバリュエーション』として出版する予定です。ご興味ある方はこちらにご期待ください。

　2 カ国語で記述される本書においては，2 冊分の内容を詰め込むことになります。分量をコンパクトにする必要があるため，極力エッセンスに絞った内容としていますが，大学生・大学院生の入門テキストとしてだけではなく，社会人の方にもお使いいただける教科書になっていると思います。海外との取引が多い方，上司・同僚・部下が日本人ではない方，外資系企業に勤務する方など，英語で Corporate Finance の知識が必要な方には特におすすめです。

　さて，スペースに余裕はあまりありませんので，さっそく講義を始めましょう。

Table of Contents

Preface / 2

Part 1 What Is Corporate Finance?

Chapter 1 Introduction: Finance and the Value of a Company — 20

Topics and Persons Concerned in Corporate Finance / 20
Financing, Capital and Return / 22
Goal of Company / 24
What Is the Value of a Company? / 26
Value of Debt and Equity / 28
Role of Financial Markets and Financial Institutions / 32
The Market Is Efficient / 36

Chapter 2 Accounting and Finance — 38

Accounting Figures and Financial Statements / 38
The Income Statement / 40
The Balance Sheet / 42
ROA and ROE / 44
PER and PBR / 46
Cash Flow / 48
Free Cash Flow / 50
Calculation of FCF / 52

目次

はじめに／3

第1部　コーポレートファイナンスとは何か

第1章　イントロダクション：ファイナンスと企業価値 — 21

コーポレートファイナンスの議論と関係者／21
企業の資金調達／23
企業のゴール／25
企業価値とは／27
負債価値と株主価値／29
金融市場と金融機関の役割／33
株式市場は効率的／37

第2章　会計とファイナンス — 39

会計数値と財務諸表／39
損益計算書／41
貸借対照表／43
ROAとROE／45
PERとPBR／47
キャッシュフロー／49
フリー・キャッシュフロー（FCF）／51
FCFの計算／53

Part 2 — Measuring Value

Chapter 3 | Time Value of Money ——— 60

Value Depends on the Time ／ 60
Discounting to Present Value ／ 62
Funds Necessary for the Future ／ 66
Present Value of Multiple Cash Flows ／ 66
Inflation and Present Value Calculation ／ 68

Chapter 4 | Valuing Bonds ——— 70

Bond Value ／ 70
Value of Perpetuity ／ 74
Value of an Annuity ／ 76
Value of a Perpetuity with Growth ／ 78
Default Risk and Credit Risk Premium ／ 80
Credit Rating ／ 80
Appendix ／ 84

Chapter 5 | Valuing Equity ——— 86

Dividend Discount Model ／ 86
Growth Rate and PER ／ 90
The Relation Between ROE, Expected Return and PBR ／ 92

Chapter 6 | NPV and Other Investment Criteria ——— 94

Net Present Value ／ 94
Calculation of NPV ／ 96
Internal Rate of Return ／ 98
Payback Period ／ 102

第2部　価値の測定

第3章　時間価値 — 61

時間によって異なる価値／61
現在価値への割引／63
将来のために現在必要な資金／67
複数のキャッシュフローの現在価値／67
インフレーションと現在価値の計算／69

第4章　債券の価値評価 — 71

債券の価値／71
永久年金の価値／75
有期年金の価値／77
永久成長年金の価値／79
社債の債務不履行リスクと信用リスク・プレミアム／81
債券格付／81
参　考／85

第5章　株式の価値評価 — 87

配当割引モデル／87
成長率とPER／91
ROE，期待リターンとPBRの関係／93

第6章　投資の評価手法 — 95

正味現在価値（NPV）／95
NPVの計算／97
内部利益率法（IRR）／99
回収期間法／103

More Complex Choices / 104
Terminal Value / 108
Incremental Cash Flows / 112

Part 3 Risk and Cost of Capital

Chapter 7 Risk and Return — 116

Calculating Return / 116
Expected Return and Risk / 118
The Risk-Free Rate and the Risk Premium / 122
Market Return / 124
Estimate Market Risk Premium / 126

Chapter 8 Portfolio Risk and CAPM — 128

Portfolio Risk / 128
Effect of Diversification / 132
Two Types of Risk / 132
The Risk Measure for a Diversified Portfolio: Beta / 136
Beta for a Japanese Company / 140
CAPM / 142
Security Market Line / 146

Chapter 9 (Advanced Topic) Detail Discussion about Portfolio Diversification — 148

Covariance and Correlation / 148
Return, Variance and Standard Deviation of a Two-Asset Portfolio / 152
Investment Opportunity Set of a Two-Asset Portfolio / 154
The Efficient Frontier / 160
The Efficient Frontier with Risk-Free Assets / 162
Contents of Beta / 166

より複雑な案件選択の例／105

ターミナル・バリュー／109

追加的なキャッシュフローに注目／113

第3部　リスクと資本コスト

第7章　リスクとリターン ―― 117

リターンの計算／117

期待リターンとリスク／119

リスクフリー・レートとリスク・プレミアム／123

市場リターン／125

市場リスク・プレミアムの推定／127

第8章　ポートフォリオリスクとCAPM ―― 129

ポートフォリオのリスク／129

分散投資の効果／133

2種類のリスク／133

分散投資におけるリスク指標　ベータ／137

日本企業のベータ／141

CAPM／143

証券市場線／147

第9章　ポートフォリオ分散効果の詳述（上級トピック）― 149

共分散と相関／149

2資産のポートフォリオのリターン，分散，標準偏差／153

2資産のポートフォリオの投資機会集合／155

効率的フロンティア／161

無リスク資産がある場合の効率的フロンティア／163

ベータの中身／167

Chapter 10 — Weighted Average Cost of Capital — 168

Expected Return = Cost of Capital / 168
Weighted Average Cost of Capital / 170
Cost of Equity and Cost of Debt / 172
Tax Savings Effect of Debt / 174
Calculation of WACC / 176
Business Cost of Capital and WACC of the company / 178
Cost of Debt < Cost of Equity / 178

Part 4 Financing Decisions

Chapter 11 — Financing and Company Value — 182

Debt and Equity / 182
Variation of Corporate Financing / 186
Capital Structure Doesn't Matter / 188
Debt Changes Business Performance / 190
Effect of Debt Leverage / 192

Chapter 12 — Optimal Capital Structure — 198

Capital Structure and Cost of Capital / 198
Tax Contributes to Company Value / 202
Costs of Financial Distress / 208
Theory and Practice for Financial Choices / 210

Chapter 13 — Payout Policy — 214

Dividends / 214
Share Repurchases / 214
How Do Companies Decide on Payout? / 216

第10章 | 加重平均資本コスト ─────────── 169

　　期待リターン＝資本コスト／169
　　加重平均資本コスト／171
　　株主資本コストと負債コスト／173
　　負債の節税効果／175
　　加重平均資本コストの計算／177
　　事業の資本コストと加重平均資本コスト／179
　　負債コスト ＜ 株主資本コスト／179

第4部　資本政策

第11章 | 資金調達と企業価値 ─────────── 183

　　負債と株主資本／183
　　さまざまな資金調達手法／187
　　企業の資本構成は意味がない？／189
　　負債によって変わる業績／191
　　負債によるレバレッジ／193

第12章 | 最適資本構成 ─────────── 199

　　資本構成と資本コスト／199
　　税金が企業価値に与える影響／203
　　企業の倒産コスト／209
　　資金調達を巡る理論と実際／211

第13章 | 資金還元 ─────────── 215

　　配　当／215
　　自社株買い／215
　　資金還元の決定規準／217

Dividend Signaling / 218
Share Repurchase Signaling / 220
Share Repurchases Do Not Affect Share Price / 220
Share Issuance Does Not Affect Share Price / 226
Share Price Impact of Signaling / 228
Shareholder Special Benefit Plans / 230

Part 5 Hedging Risk and Derivatives

Chapter 14 Foreign Exchange and Cross-border Investments — 234

Foreign Exchange Rates / 234
Change in Exchange Rates / 236
Hedging Risk with Forward Contracts / 238
Setting Forward Exchange Rates / 240
Interest Rate Parity and Purchasing Power Parity / 242
Coping with Competitive Advantages / 246
Investment Decisions for Cross-border Projects / 248

Chapter 15 Futures and Swaps — 252

Approaches to Hedge Risks and Derivatives / 252
Forward Contracts / 254
Futures Contracts / 254
Characteristics and Mechanics of Future Trading / 256
Hedging with Forward and Futures / 258
Swaps / 260
Currency Swaps / 262

Chapter 16 Options — 266

What Are Options / 266

配当のシグナル／219
自社株買いのシグナル／221
自社株買いしても株価は変わらない／221
増資でも株価は下がらない／227
シグナルによる株価の変化／229
株主優待制度／231

第5部　リスクヘッジとデリバティブ

第14章　外国為替と海外投資 ── 235

為替レート／235
為替レートの変化／237
先物為替予約によるリスクヘッジ／239
先物為替レートの決定／241
金利平価と購買力平価／243
競争優位性に及ぼす影響への対処／247
海外の投資案件の評価／249

第15章　先物取引とスワップ ── 253

リスクのヘッジ方法とデリバティブ／253
先渡取引（先渡契約）／255
先物取引（先物契約）／255
先物取引の特徴／257
先渡，先物によるリスクヘッジ／259
スワップ／261
通貨スワップ／263

第16章　オプション ── 267

オプションとは／267

Payoff to Option Buyer / 268
Payoff to Option Seller / 270
In the Money vs. Out of the Money / 270
Profit for Options Trade / 272
Options vs. Stock Investments / 274
Hedging Risk with Options / 278
Option Values / 280
Determinants of Option Value / 282
Put Option Value / 286
Black-Scholes Model / 288

Postface / 290

Index / 292

オプションの買い手の利益／269
オプションの売り手の利益／271
イン・ザ・マネーとアウト・オブ・ザ・マネー／271
オプション取引の損益／273
オプションと株式投資の比較／275
オプションによるリスクヘッジ／279
オプションの価値／281
オプションの価値に影響を与える要因／283
プット・オプションの価値／287
ブラック・ショールズ・モデル／289

あとがき／291
索　引／292

Part 1
What Is Corporate Finance?

- As an introduction of this book, this part overviews topics covered in the field of corporate finance and introduces basic concepts such as the role of corporate finance, the value of a company, and capital.

- Next, financial statements in the accounting frameworks including the income statement and the balance sheet as well as select financial ratios will be reviewed. This part concludes with the introduction of free cash flows (FCF) which is widely used in finance. The definition and calculation of FCF will be covered.

Chapter 1　Introduction : Finance and the Value of a Company

Chapter 2　Accounting and Finance

第1部
コーポレートファイナンスとは何か

★

- 本書の導入となる第1部では，コーポレートファイナンスの取り扱うトピックを概観し，コーポレートファイナンスの役割と企業価値，資本といったファイナンスの基礎概念を学ぶ。

- また，損益計算書や貸借対照表といった会計の枠組みでの財務諸表やそれに基づく財務指標を概観し，ファイナンスにおいて広く使われるフリー・キャッシュフローの定義と計算方法を学ぶ。

第1章　イントロダクション：ファイナンスと企業価値

第2章　会計とファイナンス

Chapter 1
Introduction: Finance and the Value of a Company

> **Points!**
> - ✓ Corporate finance deals with "Raising," "Using," and "Returning" cash and everybody is involved in those activities
> - ✓ The value of a company is determined by the present value of the cash flows in the future
> - ✓ Investors provide capital to a company through a financial market and a financial institution, and a company tries to maximize its capital

● Topics and Persons Concerned in Corporate Finance

"Finance" is often associated with banking, funding, lending, raising funds and grants; however, it simply refers to the process of raising cash from some source. You call it "Corporate Finance" or "Business Finance" when "Finance" is conducted by a corporation or company, and as a business activity.

A company raises cash because it uses. Therefore, corporate finance covers how a company raises the cash that is necessary for its operations, how the company uses this cash in order to create value, and finally the redistribution of the cash earned from operations to the company's investors.

Figure 1.1 | Three Activities of Corporate Finance

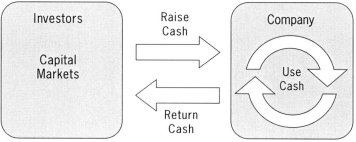

第1章 イントロダクション：ファイナンスと企業価値

> **ポイント！**
> - ✓ 資金を「調達する」,「使う」,「返す」ことを取り扱うコーポレートファイナンスは誰にでも関係している
> - ✓ 企業価値は，将来のキャッシュフローの現在価値によって決まる
> - ✓ 投資家は金融市場と金融機関を通じて企業に資本を提供し，企業は投資家から調達した資本の価値を最大化する

● コーポレートファイナンスの議論と関係者

ファイナンスは，金融，財源，融資，資金を調達する・助成するという意味をもっており，簡単にまとめると「お金をどこかからもってくる」ということである。これを企業が経営のために行うので「企業財務」や「経営財務」，英語で「コーポレートファイナンス」などと呼ばれる。

企業がお金を集める理由はそのお金を使うためである。したがって，コーポレートファイナンスにおいては，事業活動に必要な資金を投資家からどのように「調達し」，企業の価値を高めるために調達した資金をどのように「使い」，そして稼いだ資金をどのように投資家に「還元する（返す）」のかをめぐって議論がなされる。

図表 1.1　コーポレートファイナンスの3つの活動

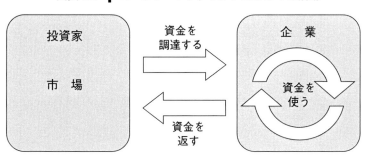

Among three activities, "Raising" and "Returning" cash are dealt by a limited staff in finance division in a company. Although they are experts on those activities they are not central figures in corporate finance. It is "Using" cash that has a significant impact on the value of a company, not "Raising" and "Returning" cash. Many business persons seldom raise or return cash as a business activity, but use cash as day to day business activities.

Each business person who uses cash and earns money every day, leading to create value for a company, is a main character of corporate finance.

◯ Financing, Capital and Return

There are multiple ways a company can raise cash (capital). For example, a company can raise cash from investors by issuing shares and making these investors shareholders of the company. Shareholders receiving a share of a company's common stock are granted voting rights at the shareholders meeting, and partially own profits and assets of the company. Shareholders get a return in the forms of dividends paid by the company and proceeds from sales of the shares in the future.

Another approach to raising cash would be for the company to borrow money and in return pay interest on the borrowed amount. Companies can borrow through banks or issue corporate bonds in the capital market. These banks and bond investors are referred to as creditors. Creditors get a return in the forms of interests paid by the company and repayment of the principal.

Cash financed by share issuance is equity capital while cash financed by bond issuance and bank loan are categorized as debt capital. Financial assets that can be traded in public market such as shares of stock or bonds are called securities.

この3つの活動のうち「調達する」と「返す」を企業の中で担当するのはごく一部の財務部門の人達である。彼らはこれらの活動を専門にしているが，コーポレートファイナンスにおける中心人物ではない。なぜなら，企業価値に大きな影響を与えるのは「調達する」でも「返す」でもなく，「使う」ことだからである。そして，ビジネス・パーソンの多くは（お金を調達したり返したりということは行っていないが）日常的な企業活動の中でお金を使っている。

　企業が価値を創造するために，日々，企業のお金を使い，稼いでいるビジネス・パーソン1人ひとりこそがコーポレートファイナンスの主役なのである。

● 企業の資金調達

　企業が資金（資本）を調達するためにはいくつかの方法がある。企業が株式を発行して投資家から資金を集めると，投資家は株主となる。株主は株式を受け取り，株主総会における議決権を得て，企業の利益と資産を部分的に所有することになる。株主は企業が支払う配当と将来の株式の売買によってリターンを得る。

　また，企業は利息を支払うことを条件に資金を借り入れることもある。銀行からお金を借りることもあるし，社債という債券を発行して市場から資金を集めることもある。この場合の貸し手は債権者となる。債権者は企業が支払う利息と元本の返済によりリターンを得る。

　株式発行により調達した資金は株主資本，債券発行や銀行借入により調達した資金が負債である。なお，株式や債券といった市場で取引される金融資産のことを有価証券と呼ぶ。

Figure 1.2 | Financing, Capital and Return

Financing	Investor		Capital	Return
Share Issue	Shareholders		Equity	Dividends · Sales Proceed
Bond Issue	Bond Holders	Creditors	Debt	Interest · Principal
Bank Loan	Bank			

◉ Goal of Company

A company is a separate legal entity from its shareholders, run by top management boards approved in the shareholders meeting. Shares of listed companies are traded in stock markets and owned held by a broad base of shareholders, and tastes, assets held, time horizons, investment opportunities, tolerance for risk, all varies by each shareholder. However, any investors will be happy if the value of investment increases. Therefore, maximizing the value of a company can be a common objective of a company.

The company is expected to make efficient use of the capital (equity and debt) it raises in order to maximize the value of the firm. Rational investors would not invest their capital in a company that they didn't think would create value. Therefore, a company that does not create value will have great difficulty in raising cash. A company that works to maximize its value should generate profits. These profits are then redistributed to the shareholders and creditors (investors) in the form of dividends and interest payments.

図表 1.2 ｜ 企業の資金調達と投資家のリターン

資金調達	投資家		資本	リターン
株式発行	株式投資家・株主		株主資本	配当・株価の値上がり益
債券発行	債券投資家	債権者	負債	利息・元本
銀行借入	銀行			

● 企業のゴール

　企業は，企業の所有者である株主とは異なった法的主体であり，株主総会で承認された経営陣により経営される。上場している企業の株式は証券取引所においていつでも売買されており，極めて多くの株主に分散して所有されている。そして，それぞれの株主の趣味趣向，所有する資産，投資する期間，投資機会の多寡，リスクの回避度合いなどは一致していない。しかし，どんな投資家にとっても，投じた金額の価値が増大することは望ましいことである。そのため，企業価値の最大化は投資家共通のゴールとなりうる。

　企業は調達した資金（株主資本＋負債）を活用して，その価値を最大化するために努力することが期待される。合理的な投資家は価値を大きくできないと考える企業に投資は行わない。つまり，そのような企業は資金が集められないということである。企業の価値を最大化するためには稼ぐことが必要である。企業は投資家から集めた資金を活用して稼ぎ，そしてその稼ぎを投資家に配当や利息の支払いとして還元していく。

● What Is the Value of a Company ?

The value of a company in a financial context is its market value. We will define the value of the firm as:

the present value of the cash flows the company will generate in the future.

The cash flow generated by operations is, in effect, the result of various corporate activities. Generating cash flows to maximize value should not be taken to mean that the company should make excessive profits at the expense of others. Customer satisfaction and loyalty, the leadership of top management, capable employees and branding, among many other factors, all have an impact on the value of a company. And more recently, many companies are placing greater emphasis on corporate social responsibility (CSR) activities as part of their corporate strategy. These corporate activities constitute a source of a value since they contribute to the company's future cash flows and lead to an increase in the value of the company.

Value as determined by cash flows is not limited to the company. The economic value of any good or service, including a business project or a capital investment, is determined by the present value of the cash flow it generates. (The notion of present value is introduced in detail in chapter 3.)

● 企業価値とは

ファイナンスにおける企業価値は企業の市場価値であるとされ，企業価値は以下のように定義される。

「企業が将来にわたって生み出すキャッシュフローの現在価値」

企業が生み出す現金（キャッシュフロー）は，さまざまな企業活動の最終的な結果である。価値を最大化するためにキャッシュフローを生み出すことは，企業が暴利をむさぼればいいということを意味するものではない。顧客満足度やロイヤリティー，経営者のリーダーシップ，従業員の能力，ブランドなどは企業の価値に大きな影響を及ぼす。あるいは最近多くの企業が注力しはじめているCSR（企業の社会的責任）活動は，企業が持続的であるためには避けて通れないものとなっている。これらの要素や活動はそれぞれ重要であり，価値の源泉であるといえる。なぜならば，これらの要素や活動は将来的には企業のキャッシュフローに貢献し，最終的には企業価値の増大をもたらすからである。

将来のキャッシュフローがモノの価値を決めるという関係は企業の価値にとどまらない。事業の価値，投資資産の価値など，あらゆるものの経済的価値は，そのものが生み出すキャッシュフローの現在価値によって決まるのである（なお，現在価値については第3章で詳述する）。

Value of Debt and Equity

The value of the company can be thought of as comprising two components: the value of debt and the value of equity. As we mentioned earlier, the value of the company is determined by cash flows generated by the company in the future and the stream of cash flows can be divided to those attributed to debt holders and those attributed to equity shareholders. Cash flows attributed to debt holders are in the form of interest and principal payments. These cash outflows to the creditors are considered relatively stable as they are paid at predetermined rates. It follows that the value of corporate debt is usually stable unless there is financial distress. On the other hand, cash outflows attributed to equity shareholders are the residual cash flows after subtracting the cash outflows to the creditors from the total cash flows of the company. Therefore, cash flows attributed to equity shareholders are often more volatile, and thus we can expect to see larger movements in equity values due to changes in the expectations of a company's cash flows.

Figure 1.3 | Value of Company = Value of Debt + Value of Equity

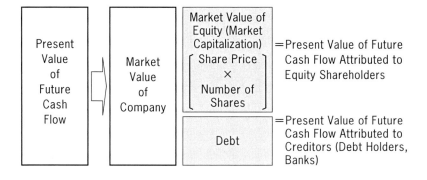

◉ 負債価値と株主価値

　企業価値は大きく負債の価値と，株式つまり株主資本の価値に分けられる。企業価値は企業が将来にわたって生み出すキャッシュフローによって決まるが，そのキャッシュフローが債権者や銀行に帰属するものと，株主に帰属するものとに分けられるということである。債権者・銀行に帰属するキャッシュフローは企業にとってみると利息の支払いと元本の返済である。このキャッシュフローは契約によって前もって決まっているから安定しており，負債の価値というのはよほどでない限り（企業が倒産の危機に瀕しない限り）変動しないと考えられる。一方，株主に帰属するキャッシュフローは，企業が生み出したキャッシュフローから，負債に帰属するキャッシュフローを差し引いた残りである。そのため，株主に帰属するキャッシュフローは安定せず，株主資本の価値は企業の将来のキャッシュフローの見通しにより大きく変動する。

図表 1.3 ｜ 企業価値＝負債価値＋株主価値

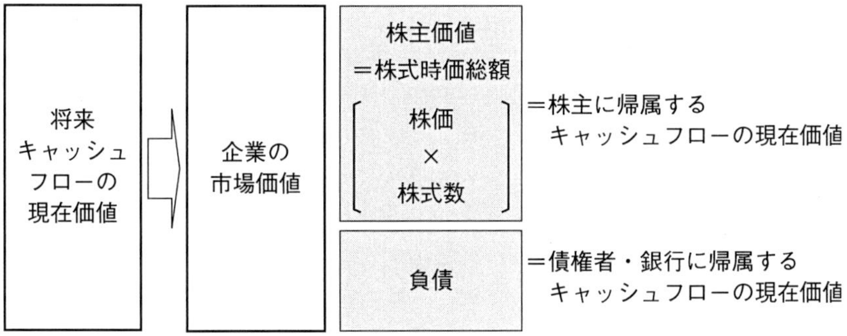

```
┌─────────┐    ┌─────────┐    ┌─────────────────┐
│ 将来     │    │         │    │ 株主価値         │ ＝株主に帰属する
│ キャッシュ│ ⇒ │ 企業の   │    │ ＝株式時価総額   │  キャッシュフローの現在価値
│ フローの │    │ 市場価値 │    │ ［株価×株式数］ │
│ 現在価値 │    │         │    ├─────────────────┤
│         │    │         │    │ 負債             │ ＝債権者・銀行に帰属する
└─────────┘    └─────────┘    └─────────────────┘  キャッシュフローの現在価値
```

If a company is publicly traded on a stock exchange, the market value of equity is equal to its market capitalization and is observable. Market capitalization is defined as the product of the number of shares and the price per share. The market value of equity can be volatile since individual share prices tend to be volatile.

The fact that the price of shares traded on the exchange change frequently does not mean that the future cash flows of a company change frequently. Most companies generally revise their earnings forecasts only on a quarterly basis. Therefore, what is changing is investors' expectations of a company's future cash flows.

We need to understand that there are a large number of investors who trade shares of listed companies. As each investor revises his or her own expectations of the performance of a company, the shares will trade accordingly, resulting in frequent changes in stock prices even though the publicly available (analyst or company management) earnings forecasts have not been revised. Even a company has difficulty in precisely forecasting its future performance, so shareholders might revise their expectations of corporate performance depending on whether they perceive the publicly available forecasted earnings to be accurate. The day-to-day movements in share prices simply reflect the day-to-day adjustment in performance forecasts made by all investors.

Based on strategic decision making and execution, along with many other factors, collectively determine the value of a company. It is the investors' assessment of these corporate decisions coupled with other factors that are reflected in the share price of the company.

企業の株主価値は，企業が株式市場に上場していれば，株式時価総額という形で明らかになっている。株式時価総額は企業の株式数と株の値段である株価を掛け合わせたものである。株主価値の変動が大きいことは，日々の株価の変動が大きいことと整合している。

　株価は毎秒のように変動しているが，だからといって，毎秒企業の将来のキャッシュフローが変動しているということではない。多くの企業は，四半期に一度利益予想を修正する程度である。変化しているのは，企業の将来のキャッシュフローに対する投資家の期待のほうなのである。

　上場している企業の株式には，数多くの投資家（株主）が投資している。証券アナリストや経営トップによる企業の業績予想が変化しないにもかかわらず，株価が変動するのは，これらの株主が企業の業績に対する予想を変えているためである。たとえ企業であったとしても，将来を正確に予測することは不可能である。株主は企業の予想する業績を信じたり，信じなかったり，また独自に修正したりする。そうした業績予想を日々調節した結果が，株価の変動となって表われていると考えることができる。

　企業の中での戦略的な意思決定とそれに伴う活動は，企業の将来のキャッシュフローに影響を与える。意思決定の結果やその他のさまざまな要因が組み合わさって企業の価値は決まる。そして，それらのさまざまな要素をさまざまな投資家がさまざまな見方をしつつ評価した結果が，株価に反映されていくのである。

Role of Financial Markets and Financial Institutions

Company's cash raising can be through financial markets or financial institutions. Figure 1.4 presents detailed components on the left side of Figure 1.1. Investors can purchase financial securities issued by a company in a financial market and provide their money to the company directly, and/or save their money in a bank which can provide a loan to a company.

A financial market is where securities are issued and traded. In addition to a stock exchange market, there are fixed income markets where bonds are traded, and a derivatives market.

A financial institution collects money from various investors and provides capital to organizations such as companies and individuals. Commercial banks mainly take deposits and make loans to companies and individuals. Investment banks underwrite shares issued by companies and resell them to investors and provide professional advice when a company considers mergers and acquisitions. Insurance companies are gigantic investors in financial securities.

Mutual funds pool investors' money and invests in diversified securities. They prepare various types of funds (focusing on particular industries or regions, pursuing high return, and so on), and offer investors opportunities for portfolio diversification and professional skills to manage investments.

◉ 金融市場と金融機関の役割

　企業の資金調達は，金融市場，金融機関のいずれかを通じて行われる。図表1.4は図表1.1の投資家と市場について細かく示したものである。投資家は金融市場において，株式や債券など，企業の発行する証券を購入することにより直接的に資金を提供することもできるし，銀行に預金をし，銀行が集めた預金を企業に貸し出すことにより間接的に資金を提供することもできる。

　金融市場とは有価証券が発行され取引される場所であり，株式市場のほか，債券市場，オプションなどのデリバティブ（金融派生商品）市場などがある。

　金融機関は投資家からの資金を集め，個人・企業などに資金を提供する組織である。主に預金を集めて個人や企業に貸し出す通常の銀行のほかにも，企業が発行する株式を引き受けて投資家に売り出したり，企業に買収や合併のアドバイスを行ったりする投資銀行・証券会社などが存在する。また，保険会社は株式や債券の巨大な投資家である。

　投資信託運用会社は投資家からの資金を集めて数多くの証券に分散投資する。リスクの度合いや産業，地域などさまざまな特徴をもつ投資信託を設定し，投資家に対して分散投資の機会と専門的な運用を提供している。

Figure 1.4 | Financial Markets and Financial Institutions

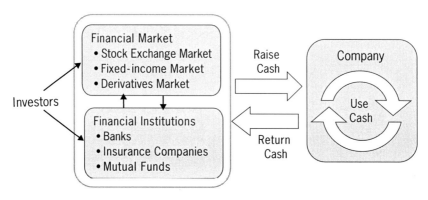

Financial markets and institutions play a significant role in the economy. They supply the place where cash is needed with unused excess cash. You can put your money in the saving account for your future expenditure, and you can borrow money from a bank and repay it in the future. Financial markets and institutions enable a transportation of cash forward and backward in time.

You can enjoy other advantages offered by financial markets and institutions. For example, the cashless payment mechanism realizes a more convenient and safer social life. Insurance companies reduce the risk of unexpected loss by issuing lots of insurance policies and averaging out the losses. Mutual funds holding thousands of stocks diversify away the company-specific risks of each company, and offer low-cost portfolio investment.

図表 1.4 金融市場と金融機関

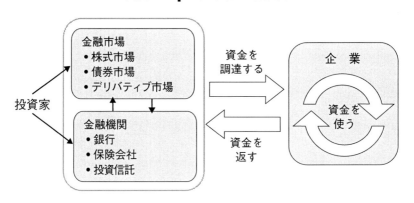

　金融市場と金融機関は，余剰となっている資金を必要な場所に供給するという経済において大きな役割を担っている。現時点において不要な資金は後の活用のために預けておくことができるし，現時点において資金が不足していても借り入れをすれば入手することができる。金融市場と金融機関は，このように時間を越えた資金の移動を可能にしている。

　そのほかにも金融市場と金融機関は多くのメリットを提供している。現金を伴わない決済機能の存在は多くの人の生活を便利にかつ安全にしている。保険会社は保険者を集めることにより起こりうる損失のリスクを分散させている。何百何千の株式に同時に投資を行う投資信託は，特定の企業が被るリスクを分散させ，低コストでの分散投資を実現している。

○ The Market Is Efficient

Financial markets also provide information about prices of securities, commodities, currencies traded in the market and interest rates. As we previously discussed, the share price in the market reflects the result of a collective assessment by investors, regarding the company's current and future performance.

The efficient market theory or hypothesis states the price of a security fully reflects all information available regarding the security, therefore the price shows the fair value. The stock market is generally referred to as an efficient market where investors will intensely compete to take advantage of new information when it emerges. That causes the impact of the new information will be immediately incorporated in the share price, and that all profit opportunities will disappear. In the meantime, the fair price denies the possibility that investors spot a mispriced stock and achieve a generous return.

Although it is persuasive that investors' competition for profits makes market pricing efficient, resulting in more reliable market prices, there are exceptions. Examples include the Japanese bubble economy in the late 1980s, and the dot-com bubble in the U.S. from the late 1990s to the early 2000s. It is not easy to answer why asset prices are sometime detached from the fundamental value. Behavior economics or behavior finance are the (sub) disciplines seeking the answer through psychology.

Despite some exceptions, it is extremely difficult for investors to overperform in the market consistently in realty, and that demonstrates that the stock market is efficient.

● 株式市場は効率的

　金融市場は市場で取引されている証券，商品や為替などの価格や金利に関する情報を提供してもいる。先ほども述べたように，市場における株価は，企業の現状と将来の業績見通しに関する，投資家の集団的な評価の結果を反映している。

　効率的市場仮説は，その証券に関するすべての情報は価格に正しく反映され，したがって価格は正当な価値を表わすとする理論である。効率的な市場とみなされることが多い株式市場においては，新しい情報が発生すると，その情報を活用して利益を得ようと多くの投資家が競い合うため，その情報の効果は即座に株価に織り込まれ，利益の機会は消滅してしまう。一方で，株価が正当であるということは，割高，割安な株式を探し出して高いリターンをあげることは不可能だということでもある。

　投資家が競い合って利益を求めるために市場の価格付け機能が効率的になり，市場価格が信頼できるようになるというこの理論は説得力があるが，例外も存在する。日本における80年代後半のバブル経済や米国の90年代後半から2000年にかけてのドットコムバブルはその例である。資産の価格が，なぜ本質的な価値から乖離することがあるのかを説明するのは簡単ではなく，その理由を心理学に求めようとする行動経済学や行動ファイナンスといった分野もある。

　このような例外はあるものの，現実に投資家が持続的に市場平均を上回る利益を持続的に上げるのは極めて難しく，このことは株式市場が高度に効率的であることを示している。

Chapter 2 Accounting and Finance

Points!

- ✔ Accounting information expressed in the income statements and the balance sheet summarize various activities in a company as numbers, ROA and ROE integrates them
- ✔ Cash flow based on the fact should be focused in finance, instead of accounting profits
- ✔ Free cash flow which is the critical measure for valuation will be calculated using accounting figures

● Accounting Figures and Financial Statements

Accounting information shows the results of various business activities. The income statement shows how much profit or loss is generated during a specific period, and the balance sheet summarizes the assets and capital at one point.

Accounting figures are important and commonly a starting point for company analysis or investment evaluation. However, we rarely use accounting profits directly in the context of finance, instead we convert them into cash flow as introduced later.

第2章 会計とファイナンス

ポイント！

- ✓ 損益計算書と貸借対照表上に表われる会計情報は企業のさまざまな活動を数値で説明するものであり，ROA，ROEはそれらを統合した財務指標である
- ✓ ファイナンスでは会計利益ではなく，事実であるキャッシュフローに注目する
- ✓ 価値評価に重要なフリー・キャッシュフローは会計数値から計算できる

● 会計数値と財務諸表

　会計情報は企業のさまざまな活動の結果を数値で表わすものである。このうち，損益計算書は一定期間にどれだけの利益・損失が生み出されたのかを示し，貸借対照表は一時点における資産と資本の状態を示す財務諸表である。

　ファイナンスにおいても会計数値は重要な情報であり，多くの場合で企業・投資分析の出発点となる。しかし，会計上の利益をそのままの形で活用することはあまりなく，後に述べるようにキャッシュフローに変換して使用する。

◉ The Income Statement

The income statement (profit and loss statement, or P/L) is a financial statement that shows the revenues, expenses and income of a company over a period of time and reveals whether a company will record a profit or a loss. Thus, an income statement provides a financial picture of the company over a specific period of time, such as one quarter or a fiscal year. We begin with the sales revenue generated from business operations. Sales revenues less the cost of goods sold (COGS) and selling, general and administrative expenses (SG&A) result in operating profits. Another profit measure is net income, which is calculated by taking operating profits and adding (subtracting) non-operating profits such as interest income (non-operating losses such as interest expense), adding (subtracting) unusual gains (losses), and subtracting corporate tax payments.

Figure 2.1 | Income Statement

	Sales Revenues
−	COGS
−	Selling, G&A expenses
=	Operating Profit
±	Non-Operating profit
±	Unusual Profit/Loss
−	Tax
=	Net Income

◯ 損益計算書

　損益計算書（P/L）は一定期間における売上高，費用，利益を示し，企業が利益を生んだのか，損失を出したのかを明らかにする財務諸表である。四半期や会計年度における財務的な業績を表わす。損益計算書は売上高からスタートし，そこから原価と販売費・一般管理費といった営業活動に伴う費用を差し引いたものが営業利益である。営業利益に利息の受け取りといった営業外利益を加え，利息の支払いといった営業外費用を差し引き，一時的に発生する非経常的な特別利益および特別損失を加味し，税金を差し引くと当期純利益が計算される。

図表2.1 ｜ 損益計算書

```
    売上高
 ー  売上原価
 ー  販売費・一般管理費
 ――――――――――――――――
 =  営業利益
 ±  営業外損益
 ±  特別損益
 ー  法人税等
 ――――――――――――――――
 =  当期純利益
```

The Balance Sheet

The balance sheet (B/S) provides us with a snapshot of the company's financial health at a point in time. The cash raised from creditors and shareholders is recorded on the right-hand side of the balance sheet. The portion attributed to creditors, including banks, is categorized as a liability. The portion attributed to shareholders is categorized under shareholders' equity or net worth. The profits retained from business operations are also recorded under shareholders' equity. The cash (capital) raised and recorded on the right-hand side is used to purchase assets to run its business operations. These assets are recorded on the left-hand side of the balance sheet. Assets include current assets (such as accounts receivable and inventories), tangible assets (such as property or equipment), intangible assets and long-term investments. Those assets that can be converted to cash within a short period of time (less than one year) are classified as current assets. Fixed assets are longer-term assets.

The balance sheet reflects the book value or recorded value of an asset, which is often different from its market value. Note that the market value of a company is determined by the cash flow it is expected to generate in the future but that the figure recorded on the balance sheet is based on the historical purchase price or original value of the asset.

Figure 2.2 | Balance Sheet

Total Assets				
	Current Assets	Cash & Securities	Payables	Current Liabilities
		Receivables	Short-term Debt	
		Inventories	Long-term Debt	Fixed Liabilities
	Fixed Assets	Tangible Assets	Shareholders' Equity	Net Worth
		Intangible Assets		

● 貸借対照表

　貸借対照表（B/S）は，ある一時点における企業の財政状態を表わす財務諸表である。企業が債権者と株主から調達した金額がB/Sの右側（貸方）に記録される。銀行のような債権者に帰属する分は負債と分類され，その残りの株主に帰属する部分は純資産（株主資本）に分類される。企業が上げた利益が内部留保されたものも株主資本となる。調達した資金は事業活動を行うための資産購入にあてられるが，どれだけの資産をどのように所有しているのかがB/Sの左側（借方）に記録される。企業の資産には売掛金や在庫（棚卸資産）に代表される流動資産や，土地・設備などの有形固定資産，無形固定資産や長期の投資が含まれる。流動・固定の分類は資産が現金に換わるまでの期間の長さによって決まる（1年以内が流動，それ以外が固定）。

　B/Sは，取得した資産の帳簿上の価値を表わすものであり，多くの場合時価とは異なる。企業の価値は生み出すキャッシュフローによって決まると説明したが，そうした時価とは異なり，B/Sには取得した価格，もともとの価格で記録される。なお，取得した資産の帳簿上の価値のことを簿価と呼ぶ。

図表2.2 ｜ 貸借対照表

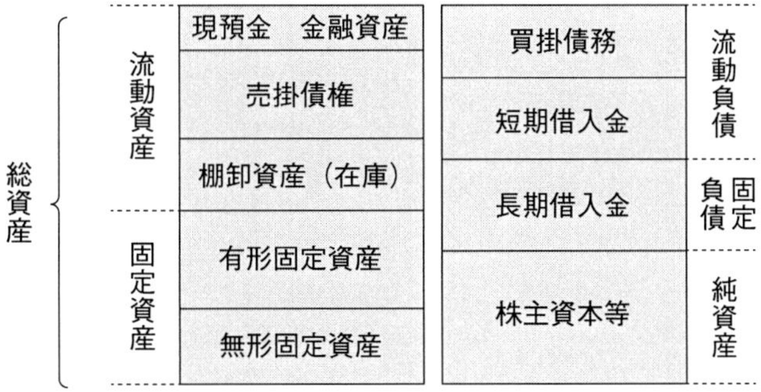

総資産	流動資産	現預金　金融資産	買掛債務	流動負債	負債
		売掛債権	短期借入金		
		棚卸資産（在庫）	長期借入金	固定負債	
	固定資産	有形固定資産	株主資本等	純資産	
		無形固定資産			

第2章　会計とファイナンス

ROA and ROE

Financial ratios make use of information from the balance sheet and income statement to help us assess the financial health of a company. ROA (Return on Assets) and ROE (Return on Equity) are commonly used profitability ratios. ROA is calculated as profits divided by total assets, and ROE is calculated as profits divided by shareholders' equity. Both are usually expressed as percentages:

$$ROA = \frac{Profit}{Assets} \qquad ROE = \frac{Profit}{Equity}$$

The profit measure used in ROA calculation often varies depending on the objective. Commonly used profit measures include operating profit and net income. Net income is most commonly used for ROE calculations.

ROA uses total assets as the denominator and thus measures how efficiently the total amount of assets are used to generate returns for the company. On the other hand, ROE tells us how much return is created from the capital provided by shareholders. ROA focuses on the left-hand side of the balance sheet and ROE focuses on the right-hand side of the balance sheet. They are measures that reveal the efficiency of business operations in generating profits relative to the amount of capital employed in the business.

Figure 2.3 | ROA and ROE

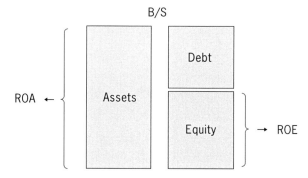

◉ ROA と ROE

企業の財務状態を評価するために P/L と B/S を統合した数値が ROA（総資産利益率・総資本利益率）や，ROE（株主資本利益率）といった利益率指標である。ROA は利益を総資産で割ることで求められ，ROE は利益を株主資本で割ることによって求められる。ともに何パーセントという率で表わされる。

$$\text{ROA} = \frac{\text{利益}}{\text{総資産}} \qquad \text{ROE} = \frac{\text{利益}}{\text{株主資本}}$$

ROA の分子にどの利益を使用するのかは，その目的によって異なり，画一的ではない。場合に応じて，営業利益，当期純利益，あるいはその他の指標が使われる。ROE の分子には当期純利益が使用されることがほとんどである。

ROA は分母に総資産をとるため，企業の使用しているすべての資産がどれだけのリターンを生み出しているのかを示している。一方で ROE は，株主から調達した資本がどれだけのリターンを生み出しているのかを示す。ROA は B/S の左側，ROE は B/S の右側に注目しているともいえる。これらの指標はどれだけの資本（お金）を使って，どれだけの利益を上げたのかという事業活動の効率性を表わす指標である。

図表 2.3 ┃ ROA，ROE

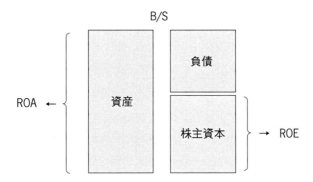

○ PER and PBR

PER and PBR are financial ratios that relate the income statement and balance sheet information with the value of the company or its share price.

The PER (Price Earning Ratio) shows how much investors are prepared to pay for a share of stock per unit of earnings.

$$PER = \frac{\text{Share Price}}{\text{Earnings per Share}}$$

Earnings per Share (EPS) is equal to net income divided by the number of shares outstanding. Earnings are measured per share to be consistent with a share price that is usually quoted on a per share basis. If we refer to total company value as opposed to per share value, then PER is equal to:

$$PER = \frac{\text{Market Capitalization}}{\text{Net Income}}$$

A high PER implies that investors expect the company to maintain its current level of profits and to improve on its performance in the future. If the average PER of companies in the same industry is 10, then we can assume the appropriate PER for the industry is also around 10. We can rearrange the equation PER = Share Price / EPS to get PER × EPS = Share Price. Now we can obtain an estimate of the fair share price by multiplying EPS of the company in question by the industry average PER of 10.

Comparing the industry average PER with the PER of the target company provides insight on investor expectations regarding profitability. For example, if the target company's PER is 12 while the average PER of the industry is 10, then the share price may be overvalued. On the other hand, if the target PER is 8 while the average PER of the industry is 10, then the share price could be undervalued.

PBR (Price to book value ratio) shows how much investors are prepared to pay for a share of stock per unit of shareholders' equity.

● PER と PBR

PER と PBR は，P/L，B/S と企業の価値，株価との関係を表わす指標である。

PER（株価収益率）は1株あたり利益（EPS）に対し，株価が何倍まで買われているのかを表わす。

$$PER = \frac{株価}{1株あたり利益}$$

ここで，EPS は当期純利益を株式数で割った数値である。株価は1株あたりの株主価値なので，PER は，1株あたりの利益に対してどれだけの価値がつけられているのかを表わす。もし，1株あたりではなく，企業全体の利益と株主価値全体を考えれば PER は以下のようにも定義できる。

$$PER = \frac{株式時価総額}{当期純利益}$$

PER が高いということは，現在の利益が将来にわたって持続していき，さらに高い利益成長が期待されていると考えることができる。もし，同じような事業を営む会社が上場しており，それらの会社の平均 PER が10倍であったとするなら，その業界での適正な PER は10倍程度だと考えることができる。

PER ＝ 株価 ÷ EPS　を変形すると　PER × EPS ＝ 株価　となるので，EPS がわかれば，その数値を10倍することによって同業界の会社の株価を簡単に推定することができる。

また，株価を推定したい会社が上場している場合はその会社の PER も把握できるので，同業他社と比較することにより，利益に対する投資家の期待を推察することができる。業界の平均 PER が10倍であったのに対し，その会社の PER が12倍であれば，株式は割高であり，逆に PER が8倍であったならば株式は割安であるというような判断することも可能である。

PBR（株価純資産倍率）は1株あたり純資産（株主資本）に対し，株価が何倍まで買われているのかを表わす。

$$\text{PBR} = \frac{\text{Share Price}}{\text{Equity per Share}}$$

Equity per share is calculated as total shareholders' equity divided by the number of shares outstanding. Recall that shareholders' equity is the book value of equity on the balance sheet. Therefore, PBR is the ratio of the market value or share price to the book value of the firm.

PBR is 1 when the share price is equal to the book value per share. A PBR of less than 1 indicates that the market value price is less valuable than the book value per share. A share with PBR less than 1 is often perceived as undervalued. Note, however, that shareholders' equity is simply a book value on the balance sheet and does not ensure that actual cash is distributed to the investors if the company liquidates.

Both PER and PBR are simple formulae providing a shortcut to evaluate a share price of a company, often referred to as value multiples.

● Cash Flow

Although we have discussed accounting figures, the value of a company is determined with cash flows. A company requires cash when it purchases machinery and builds a factory. Cash is paid when a company pays interests to the bank and dividend to shareholders. Therefore, the value of a company depends on how much cash is generated and left after making necessary investments.

Figures on income statements and balance sheets may change according to accounting standards, for example, there is some latitude given to record depreciation expenses. Alternatively, you can say that you have cash only when you have the cash on hand.

$$PBR = \frac{株価}{1株あたり純資産}$$

1株あたり純資産は，純資産を株式数で割った数値である。純資産はB/S上の株主資本の帳簿上の価値（簿価）である。したがってPBRは，時価である株価と1株あたりの簿価を比較した指標ということになる。

もし，1株あたりの簿価と株価が一致している場合にはPBRはちょうど1倍になる。そして，1株あたりの簿価よりも株価が低い場合にはPBRは1倍以下となり，株価は割安であるとの判断がなされることが多い。ただし，純資産はあくまで帳簿上の価値なので，実際に企業が解散・清算されるときに分配される額を保証するものではないことには注意が必要である。

PER, PBRは簡易的な数式で企業の株価を評価する指標であり，価値倍率とも呼ばれる。

● キャッシュフロー

これまで，会計上の数値に関して紹介してきたが，第1章でも触れたように，企業価値はキャッシュフローによって決まる。企業が設備を購入したり工場を建設する場合に必要となるのは現金である。また銀行に利息を支払う際や株主に配当を支払う際にも必要となるのは現金である。そのため，企業の価値は，企業が必要な投資を行ったうえでどれだけ現金を生み出したのかによって決まるのである。

P/LやB/Sの数値が会計基準によって変化することも忘れてはならない。たとえば，減価償却費の計上においては計上ルールにある程度の裁量が認められている。これに対し，キャッシュは現金があればある，なければない，という事実に基づいている。

⬤ Free Cash Flow

When you estimate the value of an investment or a company, free cash flows (FCF) are often used to gauge the cash flows generated by a project or company. FCF is the cash flow that remains after taking into account the cash required for investment and is defined as follows:

FCF = Profit After Tax + Depreciation − Capital Investment
       − Increase in Working Capital

Profit after tax is calculated as operating profit multiplied by (1 − the effective tax rate). Notice that the tax payment here differs from the accrued tax in financial accounting. When a company issues debt and makes interest payments, the company benefits from tax savings, or a tax shield, as interest expense is tax deductible in many countries. Therefore, we see that the accrued tax is not equivalent to operating profit×the effective tax rate. However, FCF is usually not adjusted for such tax shield effects. As we will see in chapter 10, it is the discount rate that is adjusted to take into account this tax shield effect. Profit after tax is often called NOPAT, which is an abbreviation of the net operating profit after tax.

Depreciation expense is the fraction of the cost of fixed assets, such as property or plant, distributed over the life of the asset. Although depreciation expense is allocated across the life of the asset, cash outflows do not actually occur at each point in time; rather, a lump sum cash payment is assumed when the asset is purchased. Thus depreciation is an artifact of an accounting practice that deducts the expense of the fixed asset from operating profit over time. Therefore, it should be added back to profit to obtain free cash flows.

After-tax profit also needs to be adjusted for working capital. Working capital, which is also sometimes referred to as net working capital, is defined as accounts receivables and inventories less accounts payables. An increase in working capital means more capital tied up in the business operation thus requiring additional cash. In short, an increase in working capital has a negative impact on cash flows, and vice versa.

● フリー・キャッシュフロー（FCF）

　投資や企業価値を評価する際には，その投資案件や企業が生み出すキャッシュフローとしてフリー・キャッシュフロー（FCF）が用いられる。FCF は一期間において生み出された，企業が必要な投資を行った後の残余的なキャッシュであり，以下のように定義される。

$$FCF = 税引後利益 + 減価償却費 - 設備投資額 - 運転資本増額$$

　税引後利益は，営業利益に（1 − 実効税率）を掛けて計算する。これは営業利益に対応する税金分を営業利益から差し引くためだが，この計算上の税金は，企業の会計上の税金とは異なる。企業が負債を使用すると，支払利息の分だけ課税される利益が減るという節税効果が発生し，会計上の税金は営業利益×実効税率とはならない。しかし，この節税効果は第 10 章で紹介するように割引率の計算において加味するため，FCF の計算上は織り込まない。営業利益から税金を差し引いた税引後の営業利益のことは NOPAT（ノーパット，Net Operating Profit After Tax）と呼ばれる。

　減価償却費は，工場や設備などの有形固定資産に関する費用を，それが使用できる各期間に配分したものである。減価償却費は会計上の費用であるが，その期において現金の支出があるわけではない。現金支出はすでに設備の購入時点（設備投資時点）で発生しているからである。営業利益算出の際には，減価償却費は費用の一部として差し引かれているため，キャッシュフローを計算する際には，利益に減価償却費を足し戻す必要がある。

　キャッシュフローを計算するためには，運転資本の増加額も差し引く必要がある。運転資本は，設備などの固定資産と異なり，常に中身が入れ替わっている資本である。運転資本は売掛金などの売掛債権と棚卸資産（在庫）の合計と，買掛金に代表される買掛債務の差として表わされ，買掛債務を差し引いていることから正味運転資本とも呼ばれる。運転資本は営業活動に必要な資金であり，運転資本の増加は追加的な資金の投入を意味する。したがって，運転資本の増加はキャッシュフローにマイナスの影響を，減少はキャッシュフローにプラスの影響を与える。

Net investment is defined as capital investment plus the increase in working capital less depreciation therefore,

$$FCF = \text{Profit After Tax (NOPAT)} - \text{Net Investment}$$

Profit after tax less the increase in working capital and depreciation is classified as cash flow from operating activities, or operating cash flow (OCF). FCF can be shown as follows:

$$FCF = \text{Operating Cash Flow} - \text{Capital Investment}$$

The present value of future FCF determines the value of an investment or of a company.

● Calculation of FCF

Figure 2.4 demonstrates how to derive FCF starting from operating profit.

Figure 2.4 | Profit and Free Cash Flow

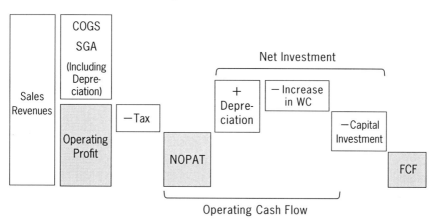

なお，設備投資額と運転資本増額から減価償却費を差し引いたものを，純投資額と呼ぶこともある。

$$FCF = 税引後利益（NOPAT）- 純投資額$$

また，運転資本の増減と減価償却費は税引後利益とあわせ，営業活動からのキャッシュフロー（営業CF）とも整理されることから，FCFは以下のように表わすこともできる。

$$FCF = 営業活動からのキャッシュフロー - 設備投資額$$

将来のFCFの現時点における価値が，投資や企業の価値を決定する。

◎ FCFの計算

図表2.4は，営業利益を出発点とし，FCFがどのように求められるのかを示す。

図表 2.4 ▎NOPAT とフリー・キャッシュフロー

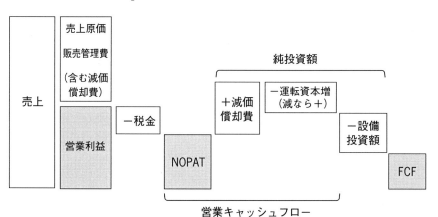

Confirm FCF calculation with numerical examples in Figure 2.5.

Figure 2.5 | Accounting Figures and FCF

	Sales	120		Operating Profit	30	
−	COGS (excluding Depr.)	50	−	Tax	12	①
−	COGS (Depreciation)	20	=	NOPAT	18	
−	SGA	20				
=	Operating Profit	30	+	Depreciation	20	②
	Tax Rate	40%	−	Inc. in WC	5	③
			=	Oprating CF	33	

		Beginning	Ending			
				−	Capital Investment	10 ④
	Accounts Receivables	100	120	=	FCF	23
+	Inventories	70	65			
−	Accounts Payables	80	90			
=	Net Working Capital	90	95			
	Increase in WC		5			
	Capital Investment		10			

① NOPAT is 18 after subtracting 40% of the 30 in operating profit. ② Adding back depreciation of 20 to NOPAT, ③ deducting the amount of increase in working capital of 5, resulting operating CF of 33. ④ Subtracting investment of 10, FCF will be 23. Figure 2.6 shows the procedure of the FCF calculation graphically.

FCF がどのように算出されるのか図表 2.5 の数値例で確認しよう。

図表 2.5 ｜ P/L，B/S データと FCF の計算

	売上高	120		営業利益	30	
－	売上原価（除く減価償却費）	50	－	税金	12	①
－	売上原価（減価償却費）	20	＝	NOPAT	18	
－	販管費	20				
＝	営業利益	30	＋	減価償却費	20	②
	税率	40%	－	運転資本増	5	③
			＝	営業 CF	33	

		期首	期末			
				－	投資額	10	④
	売掛金	100	120	＝	FCF	23	
＋	在庫	70	65				
－	買掛金	80	90				
＝	運転資本計	90	95				
	運転資本増		5				
	投資額		10				

①営業利益 30 に税率 40% を掛けた 12 を税金として差し引くと，NOPAT は 18 である。②NOPAT に減価償却費 20 を足し戻し，③運転資本の増分 5 を差し引くと，営業キャッシュフローが 33 と計算される。④営業キャッシュフローから投資額 10 を差し引くと，FCF は 23 となる。これらの算出の過程を示しているのが図表 2.6 である。

Figure 2.6 | **FCF Calculation and Components**

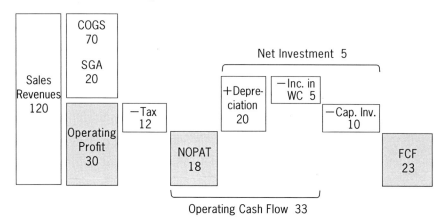

Chapter 2 Accounting and Finance

図表 2.6 ｜ FCF算出のプロセスと構成要素

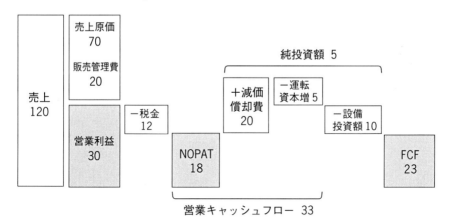

Part 2
Measuring Value

- This part begins with understanding the value today is different from the value in the future, and we study how the value in the future will be converted into the value today.

- Next, we confirm that the present value calculation and concepts will be applied to the bond and equity valuation.

- A company uses net present value (NPV) for decision-making of an investment.

- After understanding NPV, we cover another investment criteria such as the internal rate of return (IRR) and the payback period, and tricks and traps for investment evaluation.

Chapter 3   Time Value of Money

Chapter 4   Valuing Bonds

Chapter 5   Valuing Equity

Chapter 6   NPV and Other Investment Criteria

第 2 部
価値の測定

★★

- 第 2 部は，時点が異なれば同じ金額であっても価値が異なることを理解し，将来のキャッシュフローをどのように現在の価値に変換するのかを学ぶことからスタートする。

- 次に，現在価値の考え方と計算は債券や株式の価値評価に適用できることを確認する。

- 企業が投資案件を評価する際には，この考え方に基づいた正味現在価値（NPV）が用いられる。

- NPV を理解したうえで，IRR や回収期間といったそれ以外の手法との比と，投資判断を行う際の注意点を学ぶ。

第 3 章　時間価値

第 4 章　債券の価値評価

第 5 章　株式の価値評価

第 6 章　投資評価の手法

Chapter 3 Time Value of Money

> **Points!**
> - ✔ The value varies depending on the time
> - ✔ The future value will be discounted with an expected return to be present value

● Value Depends on the Time

If you were given the choice of receiving one million yen today or one year in the future, which would you prefer? If you were to choose the one million yen today, you could deposit the money in the bank and earn interest. Thus, most people would elect to receive the cash today. If the current interest rate is 5%, you would earn 50,000 yen in interest in your savings account, so you would have 1.05 million yen in total after 1 year.

The value of 1 million yen today is different from the value of that 1 million yen in 1 year time. From our example, the 1 million yen today is worth 1.05 million yen 1 year later. The reverse holds as well. The value of 1 million yen to be received 1 year in the future would be less than the value of 1 million yen when adjusted to today's value.

Figure 3.1 | Time Value of Money

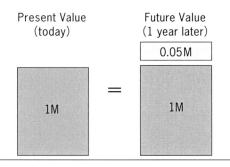

第3章 時間価値

> **ポイント！**
> ✓ 同じ金額であってもその価値は時点によって異なる
> ✓ 現在価値は，将来価値を期待リターンを用いて割り引いて算出する

◉ 時間によって異なる価値

　もし100万円を手に入れることができたとして，この100万円を今日手に入れるのか，1年後に手に入れるのかを選択することができたとしたら，どちらを選ぶであろうか。今日100万円を手に入れたとすれば，1年間利子を稼ぐことができるのだから，特殊な理由がない限り，ほとんどの人は100万円を今日手に入れることを選ぶだろう。たとえば，利子率が5％だとすれば，100万円を預金することによって1年間で5万円の利子が付く。そして元手の100万円と合わせて合計105万円の金額を1年後には手にすることになるからだ。

　このことは，今日の100万円の価値と1年後の100万円の価値は異なる，ということと，今日の100万円と1年後の105万円の価値が同じである，ということを示している。1年後の100万円の価値は今日の価値に直すと100万円以下となるともいえる。価値には時点が関係するのである。

図表3.1 ┃ 時間価値

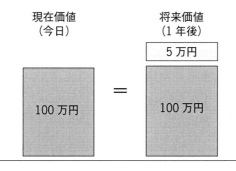

The value today is called Present Value (PV). In the example above, the present value of 1.05 million yen next year is 1 million yen. On the other hand, the value of cash at some later date in the future is called the Future Value (FV).

When valuing an asset that generates cash flows over multiple years, such as a long-term financial asset or tangible fixed investment, the value of the cash flow for each period must be adjusted to a common reference point in time, such as today. By converting cash flows into today's value, the cash flow for each time period is standardized, allowing one to compare their value to the price of any existing good in the world, including food, books, gasoline, and so on.

◯ Discounting to Present Value

Present value is calculated by taking the cash flow t periods in the future and dividing it by (1 + expected return) raised to the power t.

$$\text{PV of Future Cash Flow} = \frac{\text{Future Cash Flow}}{(1+r)^t}$$

r : expected return (discount rate)
t : time period (in the future)

The expected return is the rate of return that investors require (expect) on their investment. (This will be discussed in greater detail in part 3). Let us assume a 5% interest rate as in the previous example. This is the expected return. 1 million yen today grows to 1.05 million yen due to the 5% interest rate. Or simply put:

$$1 \text{ million} \times (1+5\%) = 1.05 \text{ million}$$

Note that the present value of 1.05 million yen is 1 million yen and can be obtained as:

$$1.05 \text{ million} / (1+5\%) = 1 \text{ million}$$

今日の価値のことは現在価値（PV）と呼ぶ。先ほどの例では，1年後の105万円の「現在価値」が100万円である。一方，1年後のように将来のある時点での価値のことは将来価値（FV）と呼ばれる。

長期的な金融資産や設備投資のように，複数年にわたってキャッシュフローが生み出される資産の価値を評価する際には，時点の違うキャッシュフローの価値をすべて同じ時点（通常は現在）にあわせる必要がある。すべてのキャッシュフローを現在価値に変換することにより，すべての基準がそろい，世の中に存在する他のものの値段，たとえば食料や本やガソリンの値段などとの比較も可能になる。

● 現在価値への割引

将来に発生するキャッシュフローを今日の価値である現在価値に変換するためには，そのキャッシュフローを（1＋期待リターン）の期間乗で割る。

$$将来のキャッシュフローの現在価値(PV) = \frac{将来のキャッシュフロー}{(1+r)^t}$$

r：期待リターン（割引率）
t：（将来の）時点

期待リターンとは，投資家がその投資を行う際に求める（期待する）リターンの率である（第3部で詳述する）。先ほどの例だと，預金に期待する5％の利子率が期待リターンである。現在の100万円に5％の利子が付いて1年後に105万円になり，この関係は以下のように表わせる。

$$100万円 \times (1+5\%) = 105万円$$

1年後の105万円の現在価値は100万円であり，以下のように計算できる。

$$105万円 \div (1+5\%) = 100万円$$

If you put 1 million yen in your savings account, in 2 years it will grow to:

1 million × (1+5%) × (1+5%) = 1.1025 million

Therefore, when you convert the cash flow in 2 years to the present, you divide by $(1+5\%)^2$.

Figure 3.2 | Calculate Present Value and Future Value

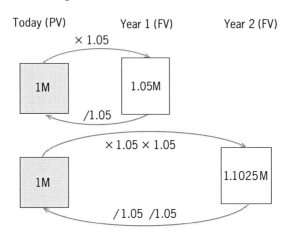

Notice that the present value of cash flows in the future becomes smaller as the number of periods into the future, t, increases. As illustrated, 1 million yen received 1 year in the future is lower in value than 1 million yen received today; and 1 million yen in 2 years is worth even less, and thus it should follow that 1 million yen in 3 years should be far less in value than 1 million yen today.

This process of converting future cash flows to a present value is called "discounting," and expected return, r, is called a "discount rate."

The reciprocal of $(1+r)^t$ is referred to as the "discount factor" or "present value factor."

$$\text{Present Value Factor} = \frac{1}{(1+r)^t}$$

Therefore,

もし100万円を2年間預金しておけば、この価値は2年後に以下になる。

$$100万円 \times (1+5\%) \times (1+5\%) = 110.25万円$$

したがって2年後の将来価値を現在価値に変換するためには$(1+5\%)^2$で割ればよい。

図表3.2 ┃ 現在価値と将来価値の計算

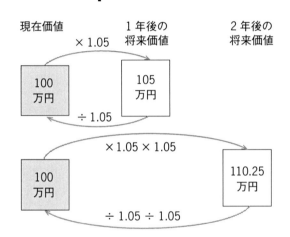

期間が増えていくに従って乗数（t）は大きくなっていくから、現在価値は小さくなる。すでに1年後の100万円は今日の100万円より価値が小さいことを確認したが、同様に2年後の100万円の価値はさらに小さく、3年後の100万円の価値はまたさらに小さくなる。

将来価値を現在価値に変換することを「割り引く」といい、ここでの期待リターン（r）は「割引率」とも言われる。

また、1＋割引率を期間乗した逆数のことを「割引係数」または「現在価値係数」という。

$$現在価値係数 = \frac{1}{(1+r)^t}$$

つまり、現在価値は次の式でも表わせる。

第3章 時間価値　65

$$\text{PV of Future Cash Flow} = \text{Future Cash Flow} \times \frac{1}{(1+r)^t}$$

The present value factor in 1 year with a discount rate of 5% is $1/(1+5\%) = 0.952$. The present value factor for 2 years is $1/(1+5\%)^2 = 0.907$. Notice that the present value factor decreases in size as the number of periods, t, increases.

◉ Funds Necessary for the Future

Suppose you plan to purchase a car with the price of 1.2 million yen in 1 year and the interest rate on the bank deposit is 3% per year. How much money must you put in your saving account now so as to pay in one year?

You need 1.165 million yen ($=1.2/1.03$). 1.165 million yen today will grow to 1.2 million in 1 year.

Suppose you postpone buying the car until the end of 3 years. You need 1.098 million yen ($=1.2/(1.03)^3$) today, assuming the same 3% interest rate.

If the interest rate is 6%, you need only 1.0075 million yen ($=1.2/(1.06)^3$) today to pay for the purchase in 3 years.

◉ Present Value of Multiple Cash Flows

To find the present value of a stream of cash flows, calculate the present value of each cash flow and then add up these values, as shown in the following formula.

$$PV = \frac{CF_1}{(1+r)^1} + \frac{CF_2}{(1+r)^2} + \cdots$$

CF_t : cash flow at time t
r   : expected return (discount rate)

$$将来のキャッシュフローの現在価値 = 将来のキャッシュフロー \times \frac{1}{(1+r)^t}$$

割引率が5%の場合の1年後の現在価値係数は $1 \div (1+5\%) = 0.952$，2年後の現在価値係数は $1 \div (1+5\%)^2 = 0.907$ であり，遠くの将来ほど現在価値係数は小さくなる。

● 将来のために現在必要な資金

時間価値の考え方を応用して以下のような例を考えてみよう。1年後に120万円の車を買おうとしているとする。金利が3%だとすると，現時点でいくら用意しておけばよいだろうか。

答えは116.5万円（= 120万円 ÷ 1.03）である。現時点での116.5万円は1年後に120万円になるからである。

では3年後に車を買うと計画している場合はどうだろうか。金利3%を前提とすると 120万円 ÷ $(1.03)^3$ = 109.8万円を現時点で保持しておけばいいことになる。

もし金利が6%であるならば，3年後の120万円は，120万円 ÷ $(1.06)^3$ = 100.75万円でまかなえることになる。

● 複数のキャッシュフローの現在価値

複数のキャッシュフローの現在価値は以下の数式のように，それぞれのキャッシュフローの現在価値を計算し合計すればよい。

$$PV = \frac{CF_1}{(1+r)^1} + \frac{CF_2}{(1+r)^2} + \cdots$$

CF_t：t時点におけるキャッシュフロー
r ：期待リターン（割引率）

Recall the car you hope to purchase, if the car dealer offers the installment payment plan with an initial payment of 0.5 million and 0.25 million each at the end of the next three years. Assuming 3% interest rate, the present value of the installments can be calculated as follows:

$$.50 + \frac{.25}{1.03} + \frac{.25}{1.03^2} + \frac{.25}{1.03^3} = 1.2071 \text{ million}$$

The installment plan will be slightly more expensive.

● Inflation and Present Value Calculation

A general rise of prices of goods and services is known as inflation, and the rate at which prices as a whole are increasing is called the inflation rate. Whenever we refer an interest rate, it is usually a nominal interest rate. When you take out the effect of inflation from nominal interest rate, you get a real interest rate, calculated by:

$$1 + \text{Real interest rate} = \frac{1 + \text{Nominal interest rate}}{1 + \text{Inflation rate}}$$

Suppose you deposit $1,000 in the bank at a nominal interest rate of 4%, you will have $1,040 in one year. But if the inflation rate during the year is 4%, prices of goods and services also rise at 4%, and your nominal 4% return is offset. Your gain is nothing in real terms.

For present value calculation, you must use nominal rates to discount nominal cash flows, and use real rates to discount real cash flows. You will get the identical results if you make quantities in numerators and denominators consistent. Usually it is easiest to use all nominal quantities because you forecast future cash flows in nominal terms unconsciously.

However, it is advisable to use real term quantities if you are in hyperinflation where the inflation rate is extremely and uncontrollably high.

先ほどの車を買う例に戻り、もし、カーディーラーが、50万円の頭金と1年後、2年後、3年後それぞれ25万円を支払う分割払いを提案したとする。金利が3%だとするとこの分割払いの現在価値は以下のように計算できる。

$$50+\frac{25}{1.03}+\frac{25}{1.03^2}+\frac{25}{1.03^3}=120.71\text{万円}$$

分割払いのほうがわずかに車を買うコストが高くなることがわかる。

● インフレーションと現在価値の計算

インフレーションとは物価の上昇のことであり、この率のことをインフレ率という。また通常目にする金利といえば名目金利であり、ここからインフレの影響を取り除いた金利が実質金利である。

$$1+\text{実質金利}=\frac{1+\text{名目金利}}{1+\text{インフレ率}}$$

もし、1,000ドルを名目金利4%で銀行に預金したとすると、1年後には1,040ドルを有していることになる。しかし、その1年間のインフレ率が4%であったならば、物価全体が4%上昇しているので、実質的な利益はゼロということになる。

現在価値を計算する際には、名目ベースのキャッシュフローは名目ベースでの金利・割引率を、実質ベースのキャッシュフローは実質ベースでの金利・割引率を使用しなければならない。割引計算の分子であるキャッシュフローと分母である割引率を一貫させれば、いずれの計算であっても同じ結果が得られる。通常は将来のキャッシュフローの予測は無意識のうちに名目ベースで行うので、すべて名目ベースでの数値を使用するのが最も簡単である。

ただし、インフレ率が極めて高いハイパーインフレーションのような状況の場合には実質ベースで計算を行うことが望ましい。

Chapter 4 Valuing Bonds

Points!

- ✓ The present value calculation will be applied to bond valuation
- ✓ The value of the bond with certain patterns of cash flow schedules can be calculated with simple formula
- ✓ Credit ratings are measurements of the creditworthiness of a specific bond and a company

● Bond Value

Let us apply "discounting" to bond valuation. A bond is a fixed income security that obligates the issuer to make specified payments to the bondholder over a pre-defined time horizon.

Bond cash flows are in the form of a coupon payment based on a promised coupon rate on the principal (par) value and repayment of the principal at the bond's maturity. A coupon is simply the payment based on a percentage or coupon rate of the principal and made to the bond investor, which is different from the return expected by investors.

The price of a bond is the present value of all cash flows generated by the bond (i.e., coupons and principal) discounted at the expected rate of return.

$$PV = \frac{cpn}{(1+r)^1} + \frac{cpn}{(1+r)^2} + \cdots + \frac{cpn+par}{(1+r)^t}$$

cpn : coupon
par : principal
r   : expected return (discount rate)
t   : time period

第4章 債券の価値評価

> **ポイント!**
> ✓ 現在価値の計算は債券の価値評価に応用できる
> ✓ 特殊なキャッシュフローパターンをもつ債券の価値は簡易的な数式で計算できる
> ✓ 債券格付は債券や企業の信用リスクを表わす

● 債券の価値

キャッシュフローを割り引くというアプローチを,債券の価値評価に適用してみよう。債券は,発行体が決められた額の支払いを約束する証券である。

債券の生み出すキャッシュフローは,額面に対して約束した利率(表面利率)に応じて定期的に支払われる利息(クーポン)と,償還期限における元本(額面)の返済である。なお,表面利率(クーポンレート)は単に額面に対して支払われる利息の率であり,投資家の期待リターンとは異なる。

債券の価値は利息と元本からなるキャッシュフローを期待リターンで割り引いた額である。

$$PV = \frac{cpn}{(1+r)^1} + \frac{cpn}{(1+r)^2} + \cdots + \frac{cpn+par}{(1+r)^t}$$

cpn:利息
par:元本
r :期待リターン(割引率)
t :時点

What is the price of a 5% annual coupon bond with a $100 face value (principal) that matures in 3 years? Let us assume an expected return of 4%:

$$\text{Bond Value} = \frac{5}{1.04} + \frac{5}{1.04^2} + \frac{(5+100)}{1.04^3} = 102.78$$

When the expected return is lower than the bond's coupon rate, the bond is worth more than its face value. Notice that when the coupon rate is equal to the expected return, the bond sells for its face value. This is known as a par bond.

On the other hand, when the expected return is higher than the bond's coupon rate, the bond is worth less than its face value. Suppose that interest rates rise and the expected return reaches 6%, then

$$\text{Bond Value} = \frac{5}{1.06} + \frac{5}{1.06^2} + \frac{(5+100)}{1.06^3} = 97.33$$

When the expected return rises, the present value of the payments to be received by the bondholders falls and the bond price falls. Conversely, declines in the expected return increase the present value of those payments and result in higher prices. The bond price and expected return move in opposite directions.

If we assume that the bond is currently traded with a price of $95, we can calculate the expected return:

$$\frac{5}{(1+r)} + \frac{5}{(1+r)^2} + \frac{(5+100)}{(1+r)^3} = 95$$

r can be calculated to be 6.9%, the rate of return if you purchase this bond now and hold it to maturity. The expected return for bonds is also called "yield to maturity."

たとえば，表面利率が 5% で満期まで 3 年の額面 100 ドルの債券の価値を計算しよう。期待リターンは 4% とする。

$$債券の価値 = \frac{5}{1.04} + \frac{5}{1.04^2} + \frac{(5+100)}{1.04^3} = 102.78$$

この場合は，表面利率が期待リターンを上回っているため，債券の価値は額面よりも高くなる。もし，期待リターンが表面利率と同じ 5% であったとすると，債券の価値は額面と同一になることがわかる。

また，表面利率よりも期待リターンが高い場合には，債券価値は額面よりも低くなる。たとえば，金利が上昇して期待リターンが 6% になった場合には以下となる。

$$債券の価値 = \frac{5}{1.06} + \frac{5}{1.06^2} + \frac{(5+100)}{1.06^3} = 97.33$$

このように，期待リターンが上がるとキャッシュフローの現在価値が目減りするため，債券の価値は下落する。逆に期待リターンが下がると，キャッシュフローの現在価値が上昇するため，債券の価値は高くなる。すなわち，期待リターンと資産価値は逆方向に動くのである。

同じ債券が 95 ドルで取引されているなら，期待リターンを計算することもできる。

$$\frac{5}{(1+r)} + \frac{5}{(1+r)^2} + \frac{(5+100)}{(1+r)^3} = 95$$

r は 6.9% と計算される。この率は，この債券を現在購入して満期までもち続けた場合の「最終利回り」である。

Value of Perpetuity

Under certain conditions the bond valuation can be simpler. The British government issued a unique bond referred to as a consol bond. The consol bond did not have a maturity date. The government was not obligated to repay the principal but only to make the coupon payments (forever). If the coupon payment is the same each year, such bonds are perpetuities. The price of the consol bond was calculated simply as the coupon payment divided by an expected return:

$$PV = \frac{cpn}{r}$$

cpn : coupon
r : expected return (discount rate)

The perpetuity valuation formula can be applied to assets that generate cash flows indefinitely and is not limited to the pricing of consol bonds.

$$PV = \frac{CF}{r}$$

CF : cash flow (starting one period from now)
r : expected return (discount rate)

Suppose that an annual cash flow of 100 starting at the end of the first year is expected to continue forever; with the expected return of 5 percent, the present value of this infinite stream of cash flows would be $100/5\% = 2,000$. The perpetuity formula is frequently used in finance.

● 永久年金の価値

債券価値の評価は，一定の条件のもとでさらに簡略化して行うこともできる。イギリス政府が発行していたコンソル債（Consols）は償還期限がないという特殊な債券である。政府はその債券を返済する必要はないが，その代わりに，永遠に約束した利息を支払う。このような債券を永久年金と呼び，永久年金の価値は利息を期待リターンで割ることによって算出される。

$$PV = \frac{cpn}{r}$$

cpn：利息
r　：期待リターン（割引率）

この式は債券だけではなく，同じ金額が永久に続く場合には広く適用できる。すなわち以下である。

$$PV = \frac{CF}{r}$$

CF：翌期から発生するキャッシュフロー
r　：期待リターン（割引率）

たとえば，1年後から100というキャッシュフローが永久に続く場合の現在価値は，期待リターンが5％の場合，100 ÷ 5% = 2,000と求められる。この式は「永久年金式」と呼ばれ，ファイナンスの分野で頻繁に使われる。

● Value of an Annuity

The valuation of an annuity can be understood as an application of the perpetuity formula. An annuity makes level cash payments for a limited time period. The installment payments for a home mortgage is frequently arranged in the form of annuity.

The value of an annuity can be expressed as a combination of two perpetuities with different time periods. For example, a 5-year annuity is equivalent to the value of taking a perpetuity today and subtracting the value of a perpetuity in year 5.

Figure 4.1 | Perpetuity and Annuity

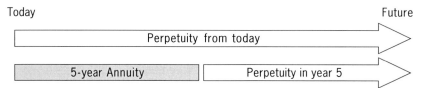

The annuity for t years is given as:

$$PV = CF \left[\frac{1}{r} - \frac{1}{r(1+r)^t} \right]$$

r : expected return (discount rate)
t : time period

The first term in brackets is the value of the perpetuity today, and the second term is the value of the perpetuity at time t discounted back to today's value.

● 有期年金の価値

永久年金式を応用すると，有期年金の価値評価も簡便にできる。有期年金とは同じ金額が一定の期間受け取れるものであり，住宅ローンの支払額の計算などに頻繁に適用される。

有期年金の価値は，時点の異なる永久年金を組み合わせることで表わされる。たとえば，5年間の有期年金の価値は，現在の永久年金の価値から，5年後の永久年金の価値を差し引いたものである。

図表4.1 ┃ 永久年金と有期年金

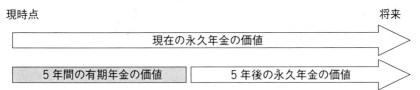

永久年金式を組み合わせて，有期年金の価値は以下のように表わされる。

$$PV = CF\left[\frac{1}{r} - \frac{1}{r(1+r)^t}\right]$$

r：期待リターン（割引率）
t：時点

[ ]内の最初の項は現在の永久年金の価値を，後半の項はt年後の永久年金の現在価値を表わしていることがわかるだろう。

● Value of a Perpetuity with Growth

Let us assume that the cash flows are no longer level but continue to grow into the future at a constant rate. The following formula with a constant growth rate for the cash flows, g, in the denominator is referred to as a "perpetuity with growth formula":

$$PV = \frac{CF_1}{r-g}$$

CF_1 : cash flow in year 1
r   : expected return (discount rate)
g   : growth rate

For example, to obtain the present value of a perpetual stream of cash flows where the initial cash flow in year one is 100, the constant growth rate is 2% forever, and the expected return is 5%, the formula would look like this:

$$\frac{100}{5\%-2\%=3\%} = 3{,}333$$

As can be seen from the above examples, when the future cash flow exhibits a certain pattern, the present value calculations are straightforward. (Note that the formula requires that r > g.) These formulas will be referred to later in this book.

● 永久成長年金の価値

支払額が永久に一定の率で増えていく場合でも，その価値は簡単に計算できる。一定の成長率（g）を分母に含んだ以下の式を「定率成長の永久年金式」という。

$$PV = \frac{CF_1}{r-g}$$

CF_1：1年後のキャッシュフロー
r　：期待リターン（割引率）
g　：成長率

たとえば，1年後における最初のキャッシュフローが100であり，これがそれ以後2%の成長で永久に続いていく場合の現在価値は，期待リターンを5%とすると，以下のように計算される。

$$\frac{100}{5\%-2\%=3\%} = 3,333$$

このように，将来のキャッシュフローが一定のパターンをとる場合には，現在価値は簡単に計算できる（ただし，この式は r＞g となることが必要である）。これらの計算式は，後の章でも触れる。

第4章　債券の価値評価

○ Default Risk and Credit Risk Premium

The expected return or yield on corporate bonds depends on the creditworthiness of the company (issuer). The required yield on bonds issued by the highly reliable company is low, and that by the less reliable company is high. It is less probable that a credit-worthy company will have difficulties in paying interest and principal. Lending money to such a company carries a low risk. Therefore, the expected return would be low. Providing money to less credit-worthy companies carries a higher risk and the expected return would be higher.

As we will discuss in chapter 10, the expected return on debt consists of the expected return on a riskless asset, or the risk free rate, and a credit risk premium that is the extra return required according to the risk of default, or credit risk.

○ Credit Rating

Debt ratings issued by credit rating agencies reflect the credit risk of a company. Credit ratings are measurements of the creditworthiness of a specific bond and its issuer and are depicted as letter grades. Figure 4.2 summarizes the various grades issued by the major credit rating agencies in and outside of Japan.

The most credit-worthy companies would be rated AAA (triple-A, Aaa in Moody's). The second from the safest is AA (double-A), followed by A (single-A) and then BBB (triple-B). The credit risk premiums of higher grades are relatively low, with a AAA company's being the lowest. The companies with higher grades can be regarded as less risky, resulting in a lower expected return; consequently, they are able to finance debt at low interest rates.

● 社債の債務不履行リスクと信用リスク・プレミアム

企業が発行する社債の利回りは，その企業の信用力によって変わる。信用力の高い企業に求められる利回りは低く，信用力の低い企業に求められる利回りは高い。信用力が高いということは，借りたお金の利子を払ったり，返済したりすることに問題が生じる可能性が低いので，貸し手から見た場合リスクが低く，期待リターンが低くなるためである。一方で信用力が低いということはリスクが高いので，期待リターンは高くなる。

第10章で詳しく見ていくが，負債の期待リターンはリスクがゼロの投資資産に求められるリターンであるリスクフリー・レートと，信用リスクに応じたリターンの上乗せ分である信用リスク・プレミアムからなる。

● 債券格付

企業の信用リスクを表わしているのが，国内外の格付機関によって付与された格付である。格付は債券，あるいはその債券の発行体である企業の信用力に対する評価の指標であり，債券の元本と利息支払いの確実性がアルファベットで表示されている。図表4.2は，国内外の代表的な格付機関の格付の符号を表わしている。

最も信用力が高く，債券が投資資産として安全だという企業の符号がAAA（トリプルA，Moody'sではAaa）である。その次に安全なのがAA（ダブルA）で，A（シングルA），BBB（トリプルB）と続く。上位の格付となる企業の信用リスク・プレミアムは低く，AAA格の企業の信用リスク・プレミアムは最も小さいということになる。このような企業はリスクが小さいため，期待されるリターンが低くて済み，結果として非常に低金利の資金調達が可能になる。

Figure 4.2 | Credit Rating Agencies and Credit Grades

		Rating and Investment Information (R&I)	Standard & Poor's (S&P)	Moody's
(high) ↑ Degree of Safety ↓ (low)	Investment Grade	AAA AA A BBB	AAA AA A BBB	Aaa Aa A Baa
	Speculative Grade	BB B CCC CC C	BB B CCC CC C	Ba B Caa Ca C

There is a significant difference between BBB and BB. The grades of BBB and higher are referred to as investment grade and are regarded as appropriate financial assets for investment, whereas the grades of BB and lower, by contrast, are called speculative grades, which are regarded as risky for investment.

The expected return for bonds with BB or lower grades would be considerably high due to the higher credit risk premium. Bonds with speculative grades are called "High Yield Bonds." High yield sounds attractive but it actually corresponds to higher risk.

The same bonds are also called "Junk Bonds" because they have a relatively high probability of default.

図表 4.2 格付機関と格付

		格付投資情報 センター (R&I)	Standard & Poor's (S&P)	Moody's
（高い）↑ 安全度 ↓（低い）	投資適格 格付	AAA AA A BBB	AAA AA A BBB	Aaa Aa A Baa
	投機的 格付	BB B CCC CC C	BB B CCC CC C	Ba B Caa Ca C

BBB と BB との間で格付の意味は大きく変わる。BBB 以上の格付が投資資産として適当だという投資適格格付であるのに対して，BB 以下は投資と呼ぶにはリスクが高く，もはや投機的な債券であるということを示す投機的格付だからである。

BB 以下の債券の期待リターンは，高い信用リスク・プレミアムにより高くなる。このため，投機的格付の債券のことは高利回り債とも呼ばれる。高利回りというと非常に魅力的に聞こえるが，これは高いリスクに対応したものだということを忘れてはならない。

同様の債券は，企業が倒産して紙くずになってしまう可能性も比較的高いことから，ジャンク債とも呼ばれる。

Appendix

(1) Deriving the Perpetuity Formula

$$PV = \frac{CF}{1+r} + \frac{CF}{(1+r)^2} + \frac{CF}{(1+r)^3} + \cdots \quad \cdots A$$

Multiply by $1/(1+r)$,

$$\frac{1}{1+r}PV = \frac{CF}{(1+r)^2} + \frac{CF}{(1+r)^3} + \frac{CF}{(1+r)^4} + \cdots \quad \cdots B$$

A−B, then,

$$\left(1 - \frac{1}{1+r}\right)PV = \frac{CF}{1+r}$$

Rearrange, and get the following equation:

$$PV = \frac{CF}{r}$$

(2) Deriving Perpetuity with Growth Formula

$$PV = \frac{CF_1}{(1+r)} + \frac{CF_1(1+g)}{(1+r)^2} + \frac{CF_1(1+g)^2}{(1+r)^3} + \cdots \quad \cdots A$$

Multiply $(1+g)/(1+r)$,

$$\frac{1+g}{1+r}PV = \frac{CF_1(1+g)}{(1+r)^2} + \frac{CF_1(1+g)^2}{(1+r)^3} + \frac{CF_1(1+g)^3}{(1+r)^4} + \cdots \quad \cdots B$$

A−B, then,

$$\left(1 - \frac{1+g}{1+r}\right)PV = \frac{CF_1}{1+r}$$

Rearrange, and get the following equation:

$$PV = \frac{CF_1}{r-g}$$

● 参　考

（1）　永久年金式の導出

$$PV = \frac{CF}{1+r} + \frac{CF}{(1+r)^2} + \frac{CF}{(1+r)^3} + \ldots \quad \cdots 式A$$

$1/(1+r)$ を掛け，

$$\frac{1}{1+r}PV = \frac{CF}{(1+r)^2} + \frac{CF}{(1+r)^3} + \frac{CF}{(1+r)^4} + \ldots \quad \cdots 式B を得る。$$

式Aから式Bを引いて得られた

$$\left(1 - \frac{1}{1+r}\right)PV = \frac{CF}{1+r}$$

を変形すると以下になる。

$$PV = \frac{CF}{r}$$

（2）　定率成長の永久年金式の導出

$$PV = \frac{CF_1}{(1+r)} + \frac{CF_1(1+g)}{(1+r)^2} + \frac{CF_1(1+g)^2}{(1+r)^3} + \ldots \quad \cdots 式A$$

$(1+g)/(1+r)$ を掛け，

$$\frac{1+g}{1+r}PV = \frac{CF_1(1+g)}{(1+r)^2} + \frac{CF_1(1+g)^2}{(1+r)^3} + \frac{CF_1(1+g)^3}{(1+r)^4} + \ldots \quad \cdots 式B を得る。$$

式Aから式Bを引いて得られた

$$\left(1 - \frac{1+g}{1+r}\right)PV = \frac{CF_1}{1+r}$$

を変形すると以下になる。

$$PV = \frac{CF_1}{r-g}$$

Chapter 5 Valuing Equity

Points!

✓ The dividend discount model (DDM) estimates the value of a share assuming the share price is determined with future dividends
✓ The perpetuity concept, coupled with the DDM, provides insight on the expected growth of a firm

● Dividend Discount Model

Recall that the bondholder receives cash flows in the form of periodic coupon payments as well as principal repayment at the time of maturity. An equity shareholder receives cash flows in the form of dividends and in the form of proceeds from selling stock. Therefore, the value of equity, or the share price today can be expressed as follows:

$$P_0 = \frac{Div_1}{(1+r)^1} + \frac{Div_2}{(1+r)^2} + \cdots + \frac{Div_H + P_H}{(1+r)^H}$$

P_t : share price at time t
Div_t : dividend payment at time t
r : expected return (discount rate)
H : investment horizon

Assume that a company will pay dividends of $10, $12 and $15 over the next 3 years, respectively. At the end of 3 years, you anticipate selling your one share of the company at the price of $300. The share price of the company, given a 7% expected return, is:

$$\text{Share Price} = \frac{10}{1.07} + \frac{12}{1.07^2} + \frac{(15+300)}{1.07^3} = 277$$

The share price of the stock sold in period H in the future (P_H) is based on the expected dividend payments from that date forward. Thus, the current share price (P_0) can be thought of as the present value of all future dividends per share. This model is

第5章 株式の価値評価

> **ポイント！**
> - ✓ 株価は将来の配当によって決まるという前提に基づき，株式を価値評価するのが配当割引モデルである
> - ✓ 定率成長の永久年金式と配当割引モデルを組み合わせることで，企業の成長期待が把握できる

● 配当割引モデル

債券の生み出すキャッシュフローが，利息（クーポン）と償還期限における元本（額面）の返済であるのに対し，株式の生み出すキャッシュフローは，株式の配当と売却価格である。したがって株式の価値，つまり株価は以下のように表わせる。

$$P_0 = \frac{Div_1}{(1+r)^1} + \frac{Div_2}{(1+r)^2} + \cdots + \frac{Div_H + P_H}{(1+r)^H}$$

P_t：t時点における株価　　r：期待リターン（割引率）
Div_t：t時点における配当　　H：投資期間

ある会社が今後3年間にわたり，1株あたり10ドル，12ドル，15ドルの配当を支払うと予想されており，この株式は3年後に300ドルで売却できると考えられているとする。期待リターンが7%だとすると，この企業の現在の株価は以下のように計算できる。

$$株価 = \frac{10}{1.07} + \frac{12}{1.07^2} + \frac{(15+300)}{1.07^3} = 277$$

株式の売却価格（P_H）はその後の配当期待によって決まるため，現時点での株価（P_0）は将来のすべての配当の現在価値となる。この株価の推定式を配当割引モデル（DDM）という。

referred to as the dividend discount model (DDM).

If dividends going forward are forecasted to be constant forever, then the share price can be calculated as a perpetuity where the expected dividend payment is divided by the expected return:

$$P_0 = \frac{Div_1}{r}$$

The assumption that dividends will remain constant forever is appropriate for companies that do not have growth opportunities, have no need to retain earnings and that pay out all earnings as dividends. If such a company reinvests a fraction of its earnings, its dividends will change in the future. Therefore, when future dividends are forecasted to be constant, profits should be equal to dividends, as follows:

$$P_0 = \frac{Div}{r} = \frac{EPS}{r}$$

If the company forecasts paying a $20 dividend next year, which represents 100% of its earnings per share, the share price of the company, assuming an 8% expected return, will be:

$$\$20 / 8\% = \$250.$$

When a company has future growth opportunities and is expected to reinvest part of its earnings to fund future growth, the share price can be estimated using the perpetuity with growth formula

$$P_0 = \frac{Div_1}{r-g}$$

The growth rate (g) can be derived by multiplying the return on equity by the percentage of earnings reinvested or plowed back into operations (plowback ratio):

$$g = ROE \times Plowback\ Ratio$$

If the company in our example were to consistently retain 40% of its earnings while generating a 10% return on the reinvested equity, the growth rate would be:

$$g = 10\% \times 40\% = 4\%$$

もし配当が翌期以降将来にわたり一定であると期待される場合には，株価は永久年金式を使用して，配当を期待リターンで割ることによって計算できる。

$$P_0 = \frac{Div_1}{r}$$

ところで，配当が将来にわたって一定であるということは，企業に成長機会が存在せず，そのため利益を内部留保する必要がなく，利益のすべてを配当する場合である。利益が内部留保され投資されていけば，将来の配当は変化していくはずだからである。したがって将来の配当が一定である場合には配当と利益の額は同額になる。

$$P_0 = \frac{Div}{r} = \frac{EPS}{r}$$

たとえば，来期のEPSが20ドルであり，これをすべて配当する場合，期待リターンが8%だとすると，株価は以下のようになる。

$$20 ドル \div 8\% = 250 ドル$$

次に，企業に成長機会があり，利益のうち一部を内部留保して投資することによって，企業が一定の成長率を実現するのであれば，「定率成長の永久年金式」により，株価は以下のように表わされる。

$$P_0 = \frac{Div_1}{r-g}$$

成長率（g）は内部留保される利益の割合とそのリターンを掛け合わせて計算する。

成長率（g）＝内部留保される投資のリターン（ROE）×内部留保率

先の例で，EPSの40%を内部留保することで，10%のリターンを生み出す投資を継続していくとすると，成長率は以下となる。

$$g = 10\% \times 40\% = 4\%$$

Because 40% of earnings are retained, the remaining $20 \times (1-40\%) = \$12$ is paid out in the form of dividends. Applying the perpetuity with growth version of the DDM, the share price is then

$$\$12 / (8\% - 4\%) = \$300$$

If the company did not retain any earnings, the stock price would remain flat at $250, whereas at a 40% retention rate, the price would rise to $300 (because, in this case, return on equity retained is 10%, higher than the expected return).

● Growth Rate and PER

Figure 5.1 summarizes the numerical examples outlined above. Notice that the higher PER corresponds with the higher growth rates.

Figure 5.1 | Growth Rates and PER

EPS	20	20
Plowback Ratio	0 %	40 %
Dividend	20	12
ROE	10 %	10 %
Expected Return	8 %	8 %
Growth Rate	0 %	4 %
Share Price	250	300
PER	12.5	15

Let's show that the growth rate depends on the fraction of earnings retained and the return on equity (ROE).

When 40% of EPS is retained, the equity position of the company in the following year increases by 8 ($= 20 \times 40\%$). Since the return on equity is 10%, the EPS for the following year should increase by 0.8 ($= 8 \times 10\%$) to 20.8. EPS thus grows by 4% from 20 to 20.8. Note that the dividend per share also grows at 4% as it is derived from EPS.

来期の利益のうち40%が内部留保されるので，配当は 20 ×(1 − 40%)＝ 12ドルとなる。「定率成長の永久年金式」により，株価は以下のように推定される。

$$12ドル ÷ (8\% − 4\%) = 300ドル$$

利益を内部留保せずすべて配当した場合は，株価は 250 ドルであったのに対し，利益の 40% を内部留保して再投資する場合には，（再投資される分の利益率が 10% と期待リターン以上であるため）株価は 300 ドルに上昇する。

成長率と PER

図表 5.1 は，これまでのケースでの株価と PER をまとめている。高い PER は成長率の高さを表わすことがわかる。

図表 5.1 成長率と PER

EPS	20	20
内部留保率	0%	40%
配当	20	12
ROE	10%	10%
期待リターン	8%	8%
成長率	0%	4%
株価	250	300
PER	12.5	15

成長率は事業に再投資される金額の割合とその利益率（ROE）によって決まることをこの例で確認してみよう。

EPS20 の内，40% が内部留保されると，翌年は資本が 20 × 40% ＝ 8 増加する。これに対するリターンは 10% であるため，翌年の EPS は 0.8（＝ 8 × 10%）増加して 20.8 となる。EPS は 20 から 20.8 へと 4% 増加している。配当は EPS の一定比率としているから，配当の成長率も同様に 4% となる。

The company attains this growth with capital generated from within the company independent of funds raised from external sources; therefore this is known as the "sustainable growth rate."

Suppose that the shares of this company trade at a price of $400 but neither the dividend forecasts nor the earnings forecasts have changed. You can derive the dividend growth rate assumed by investors using the perpetuity with growth formula:

$$\$400 = 12 / (8\% - g)$$
$$g = 5\%$$

This implies that investors who sell and buy the shares for $400 expect a 5% growth in dividends. This growth rate is called an "implied growth rate" since it is implied from the current share price.

● The Relation Between ROE, Expected Return and PBR

The price-to-book ratio (PBR) can also be understood using the perpetuity framework. Given constant dividends and earnings, the share price is given as:

$$P_0 = \frac{EPS}{r}$$

If you divide both sides by equity per share, you get:

$$\frac{\text{Share Price}}{\text{Equity Per Share}} = \frac{\frac{EPS}{\text{Equity Per Share}}}{\text{Expected Return}}$$

Notice that the PBR emerges on the left-hand side of the formula and ROE appears on the right-hand side, or

$$PBR = \frac{ROE}{\text{Expected Return}}$$

If the long-run ROE forecast by investors exceeds the investors' expected return, then the estimated PBR will be greater than 1.

この成長は,外部からの資金調達に頼っておらず,内部で創出する利益によって可能な成長であるため,「サステイナブル成長率」とも呼ばれる。

では,この会社の株式が 400 ドルの値段で売買されていると考えてみよう。翌年の配当予想と期待リターンは変わらないとする。この場合,同じ式より株式市場が想定する配当成長率を割り出すことができる。

$$400 ドル = 12 \div (8\% - g)$$
$$g = 5\%$$

400 ドルでこの株を取引する投資家は 5% の配当成長率を期待していることになる。この成長率は,株価に織り込まれた成長率という意味で,「インプライド成長率」と呼ばれる。

● ROE,期待リターンと PBR の関係

次に永久年金式を活用して PBR を別の角度から見てみよう。配当,利益が一定であるとした場合の株価は以下のように表わせた。

$$P_0 = \frac{EPS}{r}$$

この式の両辺を 1 株あたり株主資本で割ると,

$$\frac{株価}{1 株あたり株主資本} = \frac{\frac{EPS}{1 株あたり株主資本}}{期待リターン}$$

と,左辺に PBR が現れる。一方,右辺には ROE が現れており,以下のようになる。

$$PBR = \frac{ROE}{期待リターン}$$

この式は,投資家が長期的に予想する ROE が期待リターンよりも高ければ PBR は 1 倍を超え,その逆の場合には 1 倍よりも小さくなることを示している。

Chapter 6 NPV and Other Investment Criteria

> **Points!**
> - ✓ Net present value (NPV) is the commonly used and recommended criterion for a capital budgeting decision
> - ✓ Two related criteria such as the internal rate of return (IRR) and the payback period are often used in practice, but have drawbacks
> - ✓ It becomes more complicated when selecting a project from multiple alternatives

● Net Present Value

A company invests in a wide array of projects in order to grow its business operations. When making a decision of whether to invest in a project, a company should consider the present value of cash flows generated by the project. Net Present Value (NPV) is a decision-making tool comparing the present value of projected cash flows (cash inflow) with the initial cash expenditure (cash outflow). A company should undertake the investment when the sum of the PV of cash flows generated in the future is greater than the initial cash expenditure. In short, if the NPV is positive, then a company should invest in the project; and if it is negative, the company should think carefully about the investment.

$$NPV = PV \text{ of Cash Flow} - \text{Initial Cash Expenditure}$$

$$NPV = CF_0 + \frac{CF_1}{1+r} + \frac{CF_2}{(1+r)^2} + \frac{CF_3}{(1+r)^3} + \cdots$$

CF_t : cash flow at time t, CF_0 is the initial cash expenditure and is usually negative
r : expected return (discount rate)

Cash flows used for investment decisions (also called capital budgeting) are usually referred to as free cash flows (FCF) discussed in chapter 2.

第6章 投資評価の手法

> **ポイント！**
> - ✓ 正味現在価値（NPV）は投資評価の際に広く使われている，望ましい手法である
> - ✓ 投資評価の際にはIRRや回収期間法も同時に用いられることが多いが，留意すべき点がある
> - ✓ 複数の投資案件から選択が必要な場合には投資評価はさらに複雑になるので注意が必要である

● 正味現在価値（NPV）

　企業は，事業活動を行うために，さまざまな投資を行う。投資の意思決定の際には，債券や株式の価値評価と同様に，その投資が生み出すキャッシュフローの現在価値に注目する。正味現在価値（NPV）法は，投資が生み出す将来キャッシュフローの現在価値と初期投資額を比較するという意思決定手法である。企業は，投資から生み出されるキャッシュフローの現在価値が初期投資額（支出額）よりも大きい場合には投資すべきである。すなわちNPVがプラスであれば投資を行い，マイナスであれば基本的に投資を行わない，これがNPV法である。

$$\text{NPV} = \text{キャッシュフローの現在価値} - \text{初期投資額}$$

$$\text{NPV} = CF_0 + \frac{CF_1}{1+r} + \frac{CF_2}{(1+r)^2} + \frac{CF_3}{(1+r)^3} + \cdots$$

CF_t：t時点におけるキャッシュフロー，CF_0は初期投資額であり通常マイナス
r　：期待リターン（割引率）

　なお，投資評価の際のキャッシュフローは，通常は第2章で紹介したフリー・キャッシュフロー（FCF）が使用される。

Calculation of NPV

Suppose that you undertake a project that is expected to generate a cash flow of 350 for each of the next 3 years. The project requires an initial investment of 1,000 today. Assuming a 5% expected return, should you invest in this project?

At first glance, this appears to be an attractive investment opportunity since total expected benefits generated by the project, 1,050 = 350 × 3 years, outweighs the cost of the initial expenditure of 1,000. Note however, that the cash flows are produced at three different points in time, and as we have learned the values cannot be compared because of the time value of money. The present value of the initial expenditure of 1,000 is simply 1,000 since the investment is made today. On the other hand, the cash flows of 350 generated over the next 3 years are projected into the future and should be discounted.

$$\text{PV of cash flows} = \frac{350}{1.05} + \frac{350}{1.05^2} + \frac{350}{1.05^3} = 953$$

The sum of the PV of the cash flows generated by this investment is 953, which is less than the initial expenditure of 1,000. It follows that the NPV of this project is negative 47, which implies that the project would destroy value and should be avoided if possible.

$$NPV = 953 - 1,000 = -47$$

Figure 6.1 | **NPV**

PV of Future Cash Flow 953	−	Initial Investment 1,000	=	NPV −47

● NPV の計算

　1,000 の投資を行うと，1 年後，2 年後，3 年後の 3 年間にわたって毎年 350 ずつのキャッシュフローが得られる機会があるとする。期待リターンが 5% である場合に，この投資を行うべきか考えてみよう。

　一見すると，1,000 という投資を行う対価として 350 × 3 回 = 1,050 のキャッシュフローが得られるので，この投資は行うべきであるという判断になるかもしれない。しかし，これらのキャッシュフローは発生する時点が異なるため，単純に金額を比較してはならない。1,000 という投資は今行うため，この投資額の現在価値は 1,000 である。一方，1 年後からの 3 年間において得られる 350 は将来の価値なので，現在価値に割り引くと以下のようになる。

$$将来のキャッシュフローの現在価値 = \frac{350}{1.05} + \frac{350}{1.05^2} + \frac{350}{1.05^3} = 953$$

　投資から得られるキャッシュフローの現在価値の合計は 953 である。初期投資額の 1,000 よりも小さく，この投資は 1,000 を 953 と交換するものだといえる。NPV はマイナス 47 であり，価値を棄損するものだから行うべきではない。

$$NPV = 953 - 1,000 = -47$$

図表 6.1 ┃ NPV

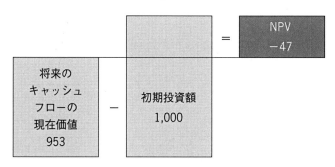

The NPV measures the value created by the investment. Therefore, when you choose one project from multiple investment opportunities with a positive NPV, you should simply adopt the maximum NPV project in order to maximize the value of the company.

The NPV approach is also referred to as the discounted cash flow (DCF) approach, stemming from its process.

● Internal Rate of Return

The internal rate of return (IRR) is the expected return, which makes the NPV equal to zero. Thus, IRR is the return level where the investment project breaks even:

$$NPV = CF_0 + \frac{CF_1}{1+IRR} + \frac{CF_2}{(1+IRR)^2} + \frac{CF_3}{(1+IRR)^3} + \cdots = 0$$

$$-CF_0 = \frac{CF_1}{1+IRR} + \frac{CF_2}{(1+IRR)^2} + \frac{CF_3}{(1+IRR)^3} + \cdots$$

CF_t: cash flow at time t, CF_0 is the initial cash expenditure and is usually negative

Obtaining IRR for a multiyear project by hand is not an easy task, so we use a simple example to illustrate the basic concept of IRR. Suppose the investment opportunity is expected to generate $110 in 1 year and the initial outlay is $100.

$$100 = \frac{110}{1+IRR}$$

The IRR in this simple example is calculated to be 10%.

Let's obtain the NPV of the project assuming an expected return of 5% and an expected return of 15%.

$$NPV = -100 + \frac{110}{1.05} = 4.76$$

$$NPV = -100 + \frac{110}{1.15} = -4.35$$

NPVの額は，その投資によってどれだけの価値が創造されるのかを表わす。したがって，NPVがプラスの投資案件が複数あり，いずれかを選ばなければならない場合には，単純にNPVが最も大きいプロジェクトを優先的に選択することによって，企業価値は最大化される。

なお，NPV法は，キャッシュフローを割り引くというプロセスを経ることから，割引キャッシュフロー法（DCF, Discounted Cash Flow）とも呼ばれる。

● 内部利益率法（IRR）

内部利益率法（IRR, Internal Rate of Return）は，投資のNPVをゼロにする期待リターンのことである。NPVがゼロになる割引率とは，初期投資額とキャッシュフローの現在価値の合計とを同じにする率ということもできる。

$$NPV = CF_0 + \frac{CF_1}{1+IRR} + \frac{CF_2}{(1+IRR)^2} + \frac{CF_3}{(1+IRR)^3} + \cdots = 0$$

$$-CF_0 = \frac{CF_1}{1+IRR} + \frac{CF_2}{(1+IRR)^2} + \frac{CF_3}{(1+IRR)^3} + \cdots$$

CF_t：t時点におけるキャッシュフロー，CF_0は初期投資額であり通常マイナス

複数年にわたる投資案件のIRRを手計算で求めるのはほぼ不可能だが，理解のために今100の投資を行うと1年後に110のキャッシュフローが生み出されるシンプルな投資案件を考えてみよう。

$$100 = \frac{110}{1+IRR}$$

これを解くと，IRRは10%と計算できる。

ここで，この投資の期待リターンが5%と15%の場合のNPVを計算してみると以下のようになる。

$$NPV = -100 + \frac{110}{1.05} = 4.76$$

$$NPV = -100 + \frac{110}{1.15} = -4.35$$

As we can see, the NPV is positive when the expected return is 5% and negative when the expected return is 15%. Next, let's turn our attention to the relationship between NPV and IRR. Under a set of strict conditions,

If Expected Return = IRR, then NPV is zero.
If Expected Return < IRR, then NPV is positive.
If Expected Return > IRR, then NPV is negative.

IRR is given as a percentage and thus does not provide us with information on the magnitude of the investment. Note that the project with the highest IRR is not necessarily the highest NPV project.

For example, if you pay $1 and receive $2 in a year, the IRR is 100%. On the other hand, if you pay $10,000 and receive $15,000 in a year, then the IRR is 50%. A project that generates benefits of $5,000 (50% × 10,000) can be viewed as more attractive than a project that generates $1.

Therefore, when you need to choose one from a number of mutually exclusive alternatives, the IRR rule is not the appropriate decision-making criteria.

Another drawback of IRR is that if the sign of the future cash flows (+/−) changes more than once, then you obtains more than one IRR solution.

期待リターンが5%の場合にはNPVはプラスに，期待リターンが15%の場合にはNPVはマイナスになることがわかる。一般化すると，IRRはNPVと非常に関連しており，以下のような関係が成立する。

期待リターン＝IRRのとき，NPVはゼロ
期待リターン＜IRRのとき，NPVはプラス
期待リターン＞IRRのとき，NPVはマイナス

しかしながら，IRRは%で表わされる数値であり，必然的に投資規模が加味されない。そのため，IRRの最も高い投資案件が必ずしもNPVが最も大きい案件とは限らないことには注意が必要である。

規模の影響を示すために例をあげよう。1ドルの投資を今行い，その対価として翌年に2ドルもらえるとすると，IRRは100%である。一方，1万ドル投資し，その対価として1.5万ドルが得られたら，IRRは50%である。いかにIRRが100%だとしても，1ドルが2ドルになったところで魅力的な投資とはいえない。5,000ドル（1万ドル×50%）を生み出すほうがよほど魅力的だろう。

そのため，同時に選択できない複数の投資案件が存在し（このことを相互に排他的という），いずれかを選択する場合には，IRRは適切な手法ではないのである。

さらに，投資案件によっては複数のIRRが存在する場合があることにも注意が必要である。将来のキャッシュフローの符号が変わると，そのたびごとに算出されるIRRの数が増えていく。

Payback Period

As noted in the previous section, NPV should be used whenever possible, yet in practice we find that many businesses also make use of the payback period approach. This approach evaluates the amount of time required for cash inflows to pay back the initial investment and is usually measured in years.

Figure 6.2 illustrates the cash flow streams of two projects. Both projects require $1,000 for the initial expenditure. Project A generates cash flows of $200 in year 1 and $800 in year 2. The year 1 and year 2 cash flows of the project together sum to the initial cash expenditure. The payback period is thus two years. Project B generates zero cash flow for the first 2 years but generates $300 and $700 in years 3 and 4, respectively. The payback period is 4 years for project B as it would take 4 years to recover the initial expenditure.

Figure 6.2 | Payback Period

	Initial Expenditure	Year 1	Year 2	Year 3	Year 4	Year 5	Payback Period
Project A	1,000	200	800	200	− 100	− 400	2
Project B	1,000	0	0	300	700	1,300	4

The payback approach states that the project should be accepted if the payback period is shorter than the specified cutoff period and is rejected otherwise. When faced with the decision of choosing from a multiple number of projects, the project with the shortest payback period is given preference over the other projects. The payback period emphasizes early cash. It follows that one would most likely choose Project A over Project B (Figure 6.2) since Project A has a shorter payback period. Is this the correct decision?

Notice that the payback approach does not take into account the negative cash flows in years 4 and 5 for Project A. In other words, one of the drawbacks of this approach is that it takes into account the cash flows generated up to the payback period but misses all cash flows that are forecasted after the payback period.

● 回収期間法

前項で確認したように,投資の評価の際には基本的には NPV 法を使うべきである。しかし,回収期間法を活用する企業も多い。回収期間法は,初期投資額を回収するために要する期間を計算し,その期間の長短によって投資案件を評価する方法である。

図表 6.2 は 2 つの投資案件のキャッシュフローの例を示している。いずれの案件も,1,000 という初期投資額が必要である。A は 1 年度に 200,2 年度に 800 というキャッシュフローが生み出されるため,キャッシュフローの累計額は 2 年目で初期投資額と一致する。したがって回収期間は 2 年となる。B は 1 年度,2 年度ともにキャッシュフローが発生しない。しかし 3 年度 300,4 年度 700 となり,4 年での回収となる。

図表 6.2 | 回収期間法

	初期投資額	1 年度	2 年度	3 年度	4 年度	5 年度	回収期間
案件 A	1,000	200	800	200	-100	-400	2 年
案件 B	1,000	0	0	300	700	1,300	4 年

回収期間法では,企業が設定する基準よりもプロジェクトの回収期間が短ければ投資が行われ,長ければ投資を行わない。また,複数のプロジェクトを比較する際には回収期間が短いプロジェクトが優先される。回収期間法は,早期に資金回収ができるほど優れた案件として評価するので,資金回収の安全性に着目した方法といえる。図表 6.2 のケースを回収期間法のみによって判断すると,回収期間が短い A が採択されるが,これは正しい意思決定だろうか。

A は回収期間が過ぎた後の,4・5 年度のキャッシュフローがマイナスになっているが,回収期間法では捉えられない。回収期間法は,回収までの期間のキャッシュフローのみに基づいて投資を評価し,回収期間後のキャッシュフローを見逃してしまう。回収期間には投資案件から生み出されるすべてのキャッシュフローを考慮していないという欠点があるのである。

● More Complex Choices

When you choose among mutually exclusive projects, you should calculate the NPV of each competing project, compare them and pick the project with the highest NPV. However, you will get into a more complicated situation if your decision today affects or relates to future investments.

A typical example is the selection from alternatives whose life of operation are not identical. It may be a difficult choice of purchasing an expensive electric shaver or hair dryer, or purchasing a cheaper but less durable electric shaver or hair dryer. It may be troublesome to change electric devices to the latest model.

Figure 6.3 shows costs of two machines, A and B. Both accomplish identical functions and have the exact same capacities. Machine A initially costs 250 and will operate for 3 years. It cost 30 to maintain and operate annually. Machine B is an economical model, costing 150 initially and will operate for only 2 years. It cost 50 to maintain and operate annually. Assuming a 5% discount rate, the total present value of costs for Machine A and B are calculated as 331.7 and 243.0, respectively. Machine B looks more attractive because its total cost is cheaper.

Figure 6.3 | Compare Projects with Different Time Horizon

	Costs				PV at
	0	1Y	2Y	3Y	5%
Machine A	250	30	30	30	331.7
Machine B	150	50	50		243.0

However, Machine A and B have different life periods of operation. The total cost for Machine A covers 3 years, whereas Machine B only covers 2 years. You can not directly compare these two total costs. In order to compare the two alternatives you convert the total present value into annual costs for the life of operation. Recall annuity formula:

● より複雑な案件選択の例

相互に排他的な投資案件の中で選択を行うためには，すべての投資案件のNPVを計算し，最もNPVが大きい案件を選択すればよい。しかし，現時点での意思決定が将来の投資案件に影響を与えることもあり，その場合には案件の選択は複雑になる。

このような例の代表的なものは，稼動期間が異なる設備を比較して投資の意思決定をする場合である。電気シェーバーやヘアドライヤーを選ぶ際，高価だが何年間も使い続けられそうなものと，安価だが壊れやすく長持ちしないものとのどちらがいいのか悩んだことはないだろうか。また，まだ使える電子デバイスを最新の機種に買い換えるタイミングにも迷うことが多い。

図表6.3は，全く同じ作業を同じ能力で行える設備Aと設備Bがあるとする。設備Aの初期導入コストは250であり，3年間稼動する。年間のランニングコストは30である。一方で，安価モデルである設備Bの初期導入コストは150であるが，2年間しか稼動しない。年間のランニングコストは50である。割引率を5%としてそれぞれの設備のコストの現在価値合計を求めると，設備Aは331.7，設備Bは243.0であり，設備Bのほうが安く魅力的に見える。

図表6.3 期間が異なる投資の比較

	コスト				現在価値
	0年度	1年度	2年度	3年度	割引率5%
設備A	250	30	30	30	331.7
設備B	150	50	50		243.0

しかし，設備AとBでは稼動する期間が異なり，そのため設備Aのコストは3年分であるのに対し，設備Bのコストは2年分であることを忘れてはならない。この場合において2つの設備のコスト総額を比べて判断することは誤りである。比較のためには，現在価値の合計額を1年分に換算したコストを把握する必要がある。ここで活用できるのが以下の有期年金の計算式である。

$$PV = CF \left[\frac{1}{r} - \frac{1}{r(1+r)^t} \right]$$

r: expected return (discount rate)
t: time period

Using annuity formula, you can calculate annual costs which make equal to the total present value of costs. The annual cost is called equivalent annual annuity. For Machine A, solve:

$$331.7 = \text{Equivalent Annual Annuity For Machine A} \left[\frac{1}{5\%} + \frac{1}{5\%(1+5\%)^3} \right]$$

The annual cost of A is calculated to be 121.8. With similar calculation results the annual cost of B is 130.7. You can conclude you should choose Machine A due to its lower annual cost.

Next, suppose you use an old machine expecting to run 2 more years. The running cost per year is 100. If you replace the old machine with a new one, it costs 200 initially but running cost per year will decrease to 75. The new machine will last 5 years. Should you renew it, or wait assuming a 5% discount rate?

Figure 6.4 | Replace or Not

	Costs						PV at
	0	1Y	2Y	3Y	4Y	5Y	5%
New Machine	200	75	75	75	75	75	524.7
Equivalent Annnual Annuity		121.2	121.2	121.2	121.2	121.2	

Figure 6.4 shows the equivalent annual annuity cost for the new machine, calculated with the annuity formula. The annual cost is 121.2 which is higher than that of the old one (100). You will conclude that you should not replace it and wait for a while.

$$PV = CF\left[\frac{1}{r} - \frac{1}{r(1+r)^t}\right]$$

r：期待リターン（割引率）
t：時点

　有期年金式を用いると，コストの現在価値合計額と同額となる年間の金額が以下の通り求められる。この年間コストは年金等価コストと呼ばれる。設備Aの場合であれば，以下の式を解くことにより，年間コストは121.8と計算できる。

$$331.7 = 設備Aの年金等価コスト\left[\frac{1}{5\%} + \frac{1}{5\%(1+5\%)^3}\right]$$

　同様に設備Bのコストを計算すると130.7となる。この結果から，年間コストの低い設備Aを選ぶべきと結論付けられる。

　次に，現在あと2年は稼動すると思われる古い設備を使用しているとしよう。この設備を動かすコストは年間100とする。この設備を今後5年間稼動する新たな設備に更新するには200の初期コストがかかるが，年間のランニングコストは75に低減する。割引率が5％の場合，設備を更新すべきであろうか，それとももう少し先延ばしにするべきであろうか。

図表6.4　設備更新の意思決定

	コスト						現在価値
	0年度	1年度	2年度	3年度	4年度	5年度	割引率5％
新設備	200	75	75	75	75	75	524.7
年金等価コスト		121.2	121.2	121.2	121.2	121.2	

　図表6.4は，先ほどと同様に有期年金式を活用して，新設備の年金等価コストを計算した結果が示されている。年金等価コストは121.2であり，古い設備のランニングコスト100よりも高いため，設備の更新は当面見送るほうがいいということになる。

○ Terminal Value

In practice we rarely find projects that are short lived. A factory for example, might operate for decades, and the acquisition of a company can be thought of as an investment in an asset with an infinite life. Therefore, forecasting cash flows far into the future is an inevitable requirement when valuing investment opportunities.

It is technically feasible to forecast FCF every year over the life of the project even as far out as 100 years. However, obtaining reasonable forecasts for FCF in each year would be difficult and quite cumbersome. Thus, in practice FCF is forecasted with attention to detail over a fixed period of time (the forecast period) such as 10 years. The FCF beyond the forecast period is estimated by making simplifying assumptions. The value of the FCF beyond the forecast period is referred to as the terminal value. The value of the investment is then obtained by taking the sum of the PV of the forecast period FCF and the PV of the terminal value.

Value of an investment, company
= PV of CF of the forecast period + PV of terminal value

$$PV = \frac{CF_1}{1+r} + \frac{CF_2}{(1+r)^2} + \frac{CF_3}{(1+r)^3} + \cdots + \frac{CF_H}{(1+r)^H} + \frac{TV_H}{(1+r)^H}$$

PV : present value of investment or company
CF_t : cash flow at time t
r : expected return (discount rate)
TV : terminal value
H : forecast horizon, final period of forecast period

● ターミナル・バリュー

　これまでの例で示してきたような，数年間という短期間で終了する投資案件は，実際には多くない。工場の建設では数十年の稼動を前提とするものもあるし，企業の買収は，永続する資産への投資と考えることもできる。これらの投資評価を行う際には，必然的に長期間にわたるキャッシュフローを予想する必要がある。

　このような場合に，もちろんすべての期におけるキャッシュフローを予想してもかまわない。100年間のキャッシュフローを年度別に予想することも技術的には可能である。しかし，そのような遠い年度のキャッシュフローを精緻に予想することは非常に困難であり，また長期にわたるすべての年度のキャッシュフローを予想することは煩雑である。そのため，たとえば10年間など，ある一定の期間（予想期間）はキャッシュフローの予想を詳細に行い，残りの期間（予想期間後）については，何らかの簡単な前提をおき価値を推定することがよく行われる。この，予想期間後の価値のことを「ターミナル・バリュー」と呼ぶ。予想期間における毎年のキャッシュフローの現在価値と，ターミナル・バリューの現在価値の合計が投資の価値となる。

　　投資・企業の価値 ＝ 予想期間におけるキャッシュフローの現在価値 ＋
　　　　　　　　　　　　ターミナル・バリューの現在価値

$$PV = \frac{CF_1}{1+r} + \frac{CF_2}{(1+r)^2} + \frac{CF_3}{(1+r)^3} + \cdots + \frac{CF_H}{(1+r)^H} + \frac{TV_H}{(1+r)^H}$$

PV　：投資や企業の現在価値
CF_t　：t時点におけるキャッシュフロー
r　：期待リターン（割引率）
TV　：ターミナル・バリュー
H　：予想期間の終了時点

The terminal value of an investment project is usually estimated in one of two ways.

One is based on the assumption that the project will end at some point in the future and so the estimated liquidation value of the project at that point in time provides us with a terminal value. The liquidation value includes the estimated proceeds from the sale of inventories as well as the equipment and plant facilities that can be sold for alternative uses. The liquation-based terminal value tends to be relatively conservative.

The second approach assumes that the investment project will continue forever and can thus be valued using the perpetuity formula.

- Liquidation Value:
  - ☞ based on the assumption that the project will end at some point in the future
- Perpetuity Value:
  - ☞ based on the assumption that the project will continue beyond the forecast period in a "steady state" (using the perpetuity formula)
  - ☞ based on the assumption that the project will continue beyond the forecast period at a specified growth rate (using the perpetuity with growth formula)

Note that the terminal value as measured at the end of the forecast period must be discounted back to present value when obtaining the present value of the investment. For example, if the explicit forecast period is 5 years and the FCF from year 6 is 100, then assuming a 5% expected return, the terminal value would be calculated as $100/5\% = 2,000$. This 2,000 is the value of all future cash flows into infinity discounted back to year 5. The present value of the terminal value today is then $2,000/(1.05)^5 = 1,567$.

ターミナル・バリューを算出する際によくおかれる前提が2つある。

1つは，プロジェクト（投資案件）が将来のある時点において終了するという前提である。この場合は，清算価値がターミナル・バリューとなる。たとえば，その時点で在庫があれば在庫の売却可能金額が，設備・工場などが転用できるのであればその価値が，ターミナル・バリューに含まれる。この前提においてはターミナル・バリューは比較的保守的となる。

もう1つは予想期間後もプロジェクト（投資案件）が永遠に継続するという前提であり，永久年金式および定率成長の永久年金式を活用する。

- 清算価値：
  - ☞ プロジェクトが将来において終了するという仮定に基づく価値

- 永続価値：
  - ☞ プロジェクトの業績が一定という仮定に基づく価値（永久年金式を活用）
  - ☞ プロジェクトの業績が一定の率で成長していくという仮定に基づく価値（定率成長の永久年金式を活用）

ターミナル・バリューを投資の価値に反映させるためには，ターミナル・バリューを現在価値に割り引く必要がある。たとえば，6年度以降は「キャッシュフロー＝100」が永久に続くと仮定した場合，期待リターンが5%だとすると，ターミナル・バリューは $100 \div 5\% = 2,000$ となる。この2,000という価値は1つ前の期である5年度時点の価値である（債券の利息は1年後から支払われるため）。したがって，現在価値は，$2,000 \div (1.05)^5 = 1,567$ となる。

◉ Incremental Cash Flows

For investment evaluation, all incremental cash flows produced from the project should be considered. The investment to launch upgrade products may have a negative effect on the sales of existing product lines. On the other hand, a new product may boost the sales of existing brands or have a positive effect on other business in the company. You should take into account all possible indirect effects.

The benefits or cash flows forgone as a result of your decision should be taken into consideration too. Suppose you build a new factory. You need land for the factory but alternatively you can sell the land. If you decide to use the land, you are required to earn more money than the expected proceeds of it.

On the other hand, past and irreversible costs, so called sunk costs should be ignored for investment evaluation because they remain the same and independent of your decision.

● 追加的なキャッシュフローに注目

　投資案件の評価を行う際には，その投資案件がもたらす追加的なキャッシュフローに注目すべきである。既存の商品をバージョンアップした商品を発売すれば，既存商品の売上は減少することが考えられる。一方で，新商品は既存の商品やビジネスに貢献することもあるだろう。このような間接的な効果も考慮に入れるべきである。

　また，その意思決定を行うことによってあきらめなければならないキャッシュフローは，考慮すべきである。新しい製造拠点には新たな土地が必要だが，その土地は売却することもできる。土地を製造拠点として活用するのであれば，売却するよりも多くのもうけを生み出さなければならない，ということである。

　一方で，すでにかかってしまって，今後どのような意思決定を行っても取り返しのつかない費用（埋没コスト）は投資評価の際には無視すべきである。

Part 3
Risk and Cost of Capital

- This part begins with calculation of return and risk. Variance and standard deviation are the relevant measures of risk.

- After understanding that risk-taking investors expect higher return as a compensation, we discuss how risk can be reduced through the portfolio diversification.

- The following chapter introduces the capital asset pricing model (CAPM) which is the model to estimate the expected return of an asset, which assumes that investments are fully diversified. Finally, we examine the weighted average cost of capital (WACC) which is the overall expected return on a company.

- The detailed discussion about portfolio theory is prepared as an independent chapter 9 handling advanced topics.

Chapter 7   Risk and Return

Chapter 8   Portfolio Risk and CAPM

Chapter 9   (Advanced Topic) Detail Discussion about Portfolio Diversification

Chapter 10 Weighted Average Cost of Capital

第3部
リスクと資本コスト

★★★

- 第3部では，まずリターンとリスクの計測方法を学ぶ。リスクは，標準偏差と分散によって表わされる。

- 次に，リスクをとる投資家はその見返りとして高いリターンを期待するが，リスクは，ポートフォリオとして分散投資を行うことによって低減できることを理解する。

- その後，分散投資を前提とした期待リターンの推定モデルCAPMを学んだうえで，企業に求められる期待リターンとは加重平均資本コストであることを学ぶ。

- なお，ポートフォリオの分散効果に関する第9章は，数式を交えた説明を行う上級トピックとしている。

第7章　リスクとリターン

第8章　ポートフォリオリスクとCAPM

第9章　ポートフォリオ分散効果の詳述（上級トピック）

第10章　加重平均資本コスト

Chapter 7 Risk and Return

Points!

- ✓ The returns of investment comes in two forms; income gains and capital gains
- ✓ Variance and standard deviation are the relevant measures of risk
- ✓ Risk-taking investors require an extra return as a compensation to take risk, called a risk premium

● Calculating Return

When investors purchase a stock or a bond, their return comes in two forms. One is through dividend and interest payments, which are called income gains. The other is through capital gains or losses, which result from price appreciation or price depreciation.

$$\text{Income Gains} = \frac{\text{Dividends or interest received}}{\text{Price at the beginning of the period}}$$

$$\text{Capital Gains} = \frac{(\text{Price at the end of the period} - \text{Price at the beginning of the period})}{\text{Price at the beginning of the period}}$$

The return from dividends is called the dividend yield and, together with capital gains, it forms the basis of the total shareholder return. The total shareholder return is written as:

$$\frac{P_1 - P_0}{P_0} + \frac{Div_1}{P_0} = \frac{P_1 - P_0 + Div_1}{P_0}$$

P_t : Price at the time t
Div_t : Dividends at the time t

第7章 リスクとリターン

> **ポイント！**
> - ✔ リターンにはインカムゲインとキャピタルゲインとがある
> - ✔ リスクを表わす指標が分散と標準偏差である
> - ✔ リスクをとる投資家は，リスクに応じたリターンの上乗せ分であるリスク・プレミアムを期待する

● リターンの計算

投資家が株式や債券を購入した際のリターンは2通りの形でもたらされる。1つは配当や利息の支払いであり，これをインカムゲインという。もう1つが価格の値上がり益（値下がり損）であり，これをキャピタルゲイン（キャピタルロス）という。

$$\text{インカムゲイン} = \frac{\text{配当あるいは利子}}{\text{期初価格}}$$

$$\text{キャピタルゲイン} = \frac{\text{期末価格} - \text{期初価格}}{\text{期初価格}}$$

特に株式配当からのリターンを配当利回りと呼び，株式の総合利回りは以下のように表わせる。

$$\frac{P_1 - P_0}{P_0} + \frac{Div_1}{P_0} = \frac{P_1 - P_0 + Div_1}{P_0}$$

P_t：t時点における価格
Div_t：t時点における配当

Suppose you bought a share (stock) of Toyota Motor at the beginning of April 2017 when its price was 6,042 yen. By the end of March 2018, the price of the share had appreciated to 6,825. Additionally, Toyota paid a dividend of 220 yen per share. Total shareholders' return is calculated as:

Income gain = 220 / 6,042 = 3.64%
Capital gain = (6,825 − 6,042) / 6,042 = 12.96%
Total Return = 3.64% + 12.96% = 16.60%

○ Expected Return and Risk

The probability-weighted return of an investment in the future is called the expected return. The expected return for Figure 7.1 is calculated as:

$$\text{Stock A} \quad \frac{10+5+0}{3} = 5(\%)$$

$$\text{Stock B} \quad \frac{16+5+(-6)}{3} = 5(\%)$$

Figure 7.1 | **Expected Return**

	Probability (%)	Return (%) Stock A	Stock B
Boom	33.3	10	16
Normal	33.3	5	5
Recession	33.3	0	−6
Average		5	5

The expected returns of stock A and B are equivalent.

Chapter 7 Risk and Return

たとえば，2017年4月1日の初め（2017年3月末）のトヨタ自動車の株価は6,042円であり，2018年3月末の株価は6,825円であった。また，トヨタは年間220円の配当を支払っていた。株式の総合利回りは以下の通り計算できる。

$$\text{インカムゲイン} = 220 \div 6{,}042 = 3.64\%$$

$$\text{キャピタルゲイン} = (6{,}825 - 6{,}042) \div 6{,}042 = 12.96\%$$

$$\text{総合利回り} = 3.64\% + 12.96\% = 16.60\%$$

● 期待リターンとリスク

その投資に期待できる平均的な収益率のことを期待リターンという。図表7.1の例で考えてみよう。期待リターンは以下のように計算される。

$$\text{株式A} \quad \frac{10+5+0}{3} = 5\,(\%)$$

$$\text{株式B} \quad \frac{16+5+(-6)}{3} = 5\,(\%)$$

図表7.1 ｜ 期待リターン

		リターン（%）	
	確率（%）	株式A	株式B
好景気	33.3	10	16
普　通	33.3	5	5
不景気	33.3	0	−6
平　均		5	5

株式A，Bの期待リターンは同じである。

Next, we consider the volatility of returns on equity (stock) investments (Figure 7.2). The returns on equity investments are uncertain. The degree of uncertainty is measured by the variance and the standard deviation of the return. The variance is the expected (average) value of the squared deviations of returns from the expected (average) return. And the standard deviation is the square root of the variance. The variance and the standard deviation are statistical measures of volatility and uncertainty.

Figure 7.2 | **Variance and Standard Deviation**

Stock A	Probability (%)	Return (%)	Deviation from the Mean	Squared Deviation	Squared Deviation × Probability
Boom	33.3	10	5	25	8.33
Normal	33.3	5	0	0	0.00
Recession	33.3	0	−5	25	8.33
Average		5		Variance	16.67
				Standard Deviation	4.08

Stock B	Probability (%)	Return (%)	Deviation from the Mean	Squared Deviation	Squared Deviation × Probability
Boom	33.3	16	11	121	40.33
Normal	33.3	5	0	0	0.00
Recession	33.3	−6	−11	121	40.33
Average		5		Variance	80.67
				Standard Deviation	8.98

The returns of stock A vary from 10% to 0%, depending on the forecast scenario, while the returns of stock B vary more widely from 16% to −6% across the three different scenarios. The range of possible outcomes is reflected in the magnitude of the variance and the standard deviation of the respected shares. Even though the average return for A and B is the same, stock B is more volatile and more uncertain.

次にリターンがどれだけ変動するのかを考えよう（図表7.2）。株式のリターンは不確実であり，この不確実性を表わすのが分散および標準偏差である。分散とは，各状態におけるリターンの期待リターン（平均リターン）からの乖離（これを偏差という）の2乗の期待値（平均値）である。また，分散の平方根が標準偏差である。分散，標準偏差ともに統計的な不確実性の尺度である。

図表7.2 | 分散と標準偏差

株式A	確率(%)	リターン(%)	偏差	偏差の2乗	偏差の2乗×確率
好景気	33.3	10	5	25	8.33
普通	33.3	5	0	0	0.00
不景気	33.3	0	−5	25	8.33
平均		5		分散	16.67
				標準偏差	4.08

株式B	確率(%)	リターン(%)	偏差	偏差の2乗	偏差の2乗×確率
好景気	33.3	16	11	121	40.33
普通	33.3	5	0	0	0.00
不景気	33.3	−6	−11	121	40.33
平均		5		分散	80.67
				標準偏差	8.98

株式Aのリターンは10%から0%の間で変動するのに対して，株式Bのリターンは16%から−6%の間で変動するため，リターンの振れ幅が大きい。この差が分散や標準偏差の大きさの違いとなって現れる。平均的なリターンは同じであっても，Bのリターンのほうが変動性が大きく，不確実性が高いということである。

The uncertainty of the return is what determines the degree of risk. Investments in shares of stock are generally high-risk because it is difficult to forecast future dividend payments and share price movements with a high degree of accuracy. In contrast, government bonds issued by developed countries are low-risk investments because the interest and principal payments are assured by financially strong countries; accordingly, the return is more certain.

○ The Risk-Free Rate and the Risk Premium

An investment for which the return is completely certain is a riskless investment, and the expected return on a riskless investment is called the "risk-free rate." The return on a government bond is considered to be certain, and therefore, the yield on government bonds is used as a proxy for the risk-free rate.

The return on risky assets is uncertain, carrying the risk. Since it is preferable to avoid risk, a rational investor requires a higher return as compensation for taking more risk. This compensation is called a "risk premium."

The yield on the 10-year Japanese government bond, which is used as a proxy for the risk-free rate in Japan has remained at less than 2% since the late 1990s. The expected return on risky investments, such as equity, would be greater than the risk-free rate by the amount of the risk premium.

The expected return of A and B in Figure 7.2 are identical. However, investors would not be willing to invest in B because it is riskier than A. Company B would need to increase its expected return in order to be attractive to investors.

このリターンの不確実性がリスクである。株式は、そのリターンを決める配当の支払い額や株価の変化を予想することが難しいため、一般にリスクの高い投資資産である。一方で、先進国が発行する債券である国債は、国が元本の返済と利息の支払いを約束しているものであり、投資家にとってほぼ確実にリターンのあるリスクの低い投資資産である。

● リスクフリー・レートとリスク・プレミアム

リターンが完全に確実な資産はリスクが全くない資産であり、リスクがない資産の期待リターンのことを「リスクフリー・レート」という。国債のリターンは確実であると考えられるので、実務的には、国債の利回りがリスクフリー・レートとして使用される。

リスクのある投資資産からのリターンは不確実であり、リスクが付きまとう。通常リスクは避けたいものであるから、投資家はリスクの高い資産に対して、その代償としてより高いリターンを求めると考えるのが妥当である。これがリスク・プレミアムである。

リスクフリー・レートに使用される日本の10年物国債の利回りは、90年代後半から長きにわたって2%以下の水準となっている。株式などへの、リスクをとって投資する場合の期待リターンは、このリスクフリー・レートにリスク・プレミアムを加えた分となる。

図表7.2の例であれば、株式Aと株式Bの期待リターンは同じであった。同じ期待リターンであれば、リスクが高い株式Bに投資しようと考える人はいないだろう。株式Bに投資を呼び込むためには、期待リターンが高まることが必要となる。

第7章 リスクとリターン

○ Market Return

As we have discussed, equity investments are risky. Figure 7.3 shows the monthly returns of the TOPIX, the representative stock index of Japan, from December 1987 through December 2018.

Figure 7.3 | Return of the TOPIX

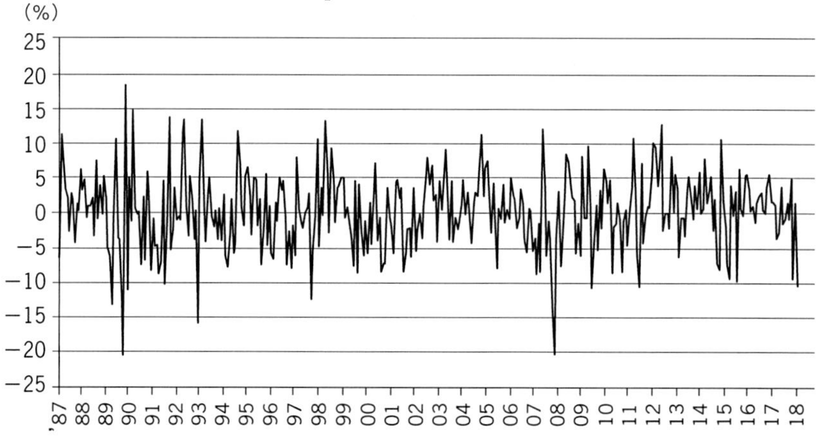

Source : Derived from Yahoo! Finance (Japan)

Returns over this period vary roughly from +20% to −20%, demonstrating the volatile nature of the stock market. We select a stock market index in order to measure the overall performance and volatility of the stock market. The TOPIX (Tokyo stock price index) and the Nikkei average (Nikkei 225) are the most popular market indexes in Japan. Between the two, the TOPIX is more frequently used in practice because it is weighted based on market capitalization, and accordingly, it is believed to more accurately reflect changes in the value of the entire market.

In the United States, the Standard & Poor's Composite Index (the S&P 500), which is calculated similarly to the TOPIX, is used as the measure to gauge the overall market return. The Dow Jones Industrial Average is calculated by a similar method to the Nikkei average.

● **市場リターン**

株式への投資はリスクがあるが，実際の株式市場のリターンの状況を見てみよう。図表7.3は日本の代表的な株式指数であるTOPIXの1987年12月から2018年12月までの月次リターンを示したものである。

図表 7.3 ▎TOPIX のリターンの推移

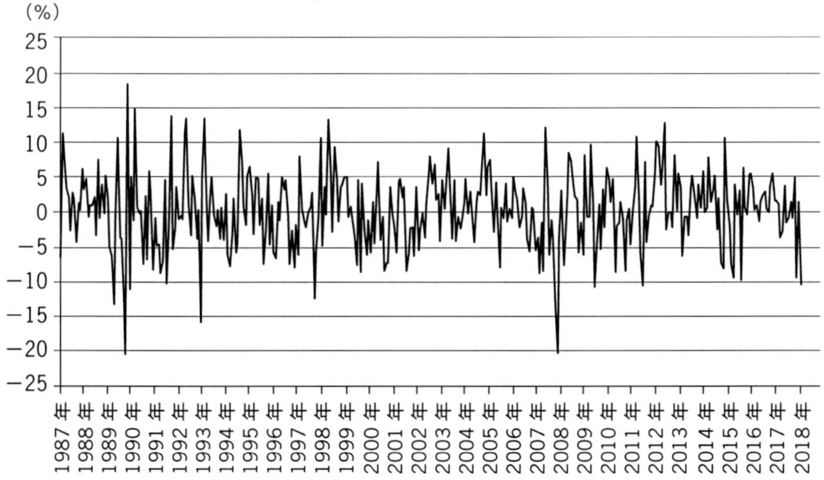

出所：Yahoo! ファイナンスのデータから著者計算

リターンはおよそ20%から－20%の間で大きく振れており，変動性が高いことがわかる。株式市場全体のリターンや変動性を測るためには株価指数（株式インデックス）を見るが，この代表的なものが日本ではTOPIX（東証株価指数，Tokyo Stock Price Index）と日経平均株価である。この2つのうち，時価総額加重型のTOPIXのほうが特定銘柄の株価の影響を受けにくく，市場全体の価値の変化をより正確に反映するため，実務において好んで使用される。

米国においてもTOPIXと同様の計算がなされるStandard & Poor's Composite Index (The S&P 500) が，株式市場全体のリターンを測る指標として使用される。なお日経平均と同じ方法で計算される米国の株価指数がダウ平均株価指数 (Dow Jones Industrial Average) である。

The required risk premium, assuming you invest in the overall market, is referred to as the "market risk premium." In the case of the Japanese market, the market risk premium is approximated to be the extra return expected on the TOPIX, above the yield on Japanese government bonds.

○ Estimate Market Risk Premium

The market risk premium is the average risk premium that investors demand for investing the overall market. It depends on the degree of risk aversion of investors at that time (more risk averse investors require higher premium). The demographic change as well as change in attitudes toward risk (as right after financial crisis) can influence it. Therefore, it is not easy to estimate the market risk premium in practice.

The market risk premium is commonly estimated based on past data, calculating the historical difference between the return of stock index and the yield of government bonds. This approach assumes the extra return in the past will be expected in the future but can have wide fluctuations depending on the time period when the data is analyzed. While the yield of government bond as a proxy for the risk-free rate is relatively stable over time, the return on stock markets are very volatile and can be negative. Sometimes the results of your estimate is found to be unreasonable, for example, you might calculate a negative risk premium (meaning your compensation for taking risk is negative) which obviously makes no sense.

Other possible approaches include calculating the risk premium based on the current share price and forecasted future performance, or simply distributing a questionnaire asking investors opinion. Many analyses for the market risk premium have been conducted by academic researchers and practitioners, but none of them are conclusive. Having said that, we share the common view of the appropriate range of the market risk premium, which is between 4% and 6% in general.

市場全体に投資した場合のリスク・プレミアムのことを「市場リスク・プレミアム」と呼ぶ。日本の場合であれば，TOPIX に投資するときに，国債の利回りに加えてどれだけのリターンを求めるのかが市場リスク・プレミアムである。

● 市場リスク・プレミアムの推定

　市場リスク・プレミアムは市場全体に投資した場合の平均的なリスク・プレミアムであるが，これはその時点における投資家のリスク回避度合い（リスクを嫌う投資家はより高いプレミアムを求める）に依存する。投資家そのもの（人口構成など）が変化したり，金融危機が発生して投資家がリスクに対して敏感になったりすることの影響を受けることも考えられる。そのため，市場リスク・プレミアムの推定は簡単ではないのが現実である。

　市場リスク・プレミアムを推定するアプローチとして，一般的なものは，過去のデータに基づくものである。過去の国債のリターンと TOPIX のような株式インデックスのリターンの差を計算し，その実績値を使用するのである。このアプローチは，過去の実際の超過リターンが今後も期待されるという前提に立っているが，過去データの期間によって大きく値が変動するという欠点がある。国債のリターン，つまりリスクフリー・レートは時系列的にも比較的安定している一方で，株式市場全体のリターンは大きく変動し，しばしばマイナスになり得る。そのため，市場リスク・プレミアムの推定値は安定せず，またリスクをとった見返りがマイナスのプレミアムというナンセンスな分析結果となる場合もある。

　現在の株価と将来の業績予想の推移から，リスク・プレミアムを逆算するというアプローチや，単純に投資家にアンケートを配付して集計するというアプローチもあり得る。学者，実務家ともに多くの実証分析が行われているが，いずれも決定的な手法はない。しかし，一般的に市場リスク・プレミアムの水準としては 4 〜 6% 程度というのが共通の認識となっている。

Chapter 8

Portfolio Risk and CAPM

Points!

- ✓ Risk can be reduced through the diversification of investments
- ✓ There are two types of risk: unique risk and market risk, and only unique risk can be reduced through diversification
- ✓ Beta is a measure for risk assuming an investment is fully diversified, and the capital asset pricing model (CAPM) is the model to estimate the expected return of an asset, which incorporates beta

● Portfolio Risk

Although the variance and the standard deviation of expected returns are the appropriate measures to gauge the degree of risk for individual stocks, investors do not have to accept them at face value. Investors can invest their portfolio in a number of assets simultaneously, not only in a single company's shares. When you think of a "portfolio", which comprises multiple investments, and consider an individual stock as a component of it, the volatility of that single stock would no longer be the measure of risk.

Let's consider an example: The combination of possible outcomes for the shares of a brand-name product company and a fast-moving consumer goods (FMCG) company, in terms of rate of return, are illustrated in Figure 8.1.

Figure 8.1 | The Risk and Return of Two Companies

		Rate of Return (%)	
Scenario	Probability (%)	Brand	FMCG
Boom	33.3	20	1
Normal	33.3	5	20
Recession	33.3	−10	−10
Expected Return		5	3.67
Variance		150.0	153.6
Standard Deviation		12.2	12.4

第8章 ポートフォリオリスクとCAPM

> **ポイント！**
> - ✓ リスクは分散投資によって減少させることができる
> - ✓ リスクには個別リスクと市場リスクの2つがあり，分散投資により低減できるのは個別リスクのみである
> - ✓ 分散投資を前提とした場合のリスクはベータによって表わされ，これに基づいて期待リターンを推定するモデルがCAPMである

● ポートフォリオのリスク

　個別株式のリターンの分散や標準偏差はリスクを測る数値だが，投資家はこれらを直接リスクとしてとらえる必要はない。投資家は1つの株式だけにではなく，複数の資産に分散して投資することができるからである。複数の証券の組み合わせからなる「ポートフォリオ」を考え，個別の株式をポートフォリオを構成する資産と考えると，個別株式の変動性はリスクを表わす指標ではなくなるのである。

　このことを例で考えてみよう。図表8.1はブランド品を扱う企業と，より大衆的な日用品を扱う企業の株式のリターンを表わしている。

図表8.1 ｜ 2業種の株式のリターンとリスク

	確率（%）	リターン（%） ブランド品	リターン（%） 日用品
好景気	33.3	20	1
普通	33.3	5	20
不景気	33.3	−10	−10
期待リターン		5	3.67
分散		150.0	153.6
標準偏差		12.2	12.4

Three economic scenarios—boom, normal and recession—are projected to occur with the same probabilities. In the economic boom scenario, the return of the brand shares would be 20% and the return of the FMCG shares would be 1%; in the normal scenario, 5% and 20%, respectively; and in the recession scenario, the return of either share would be −10%. Figure 8.1 also shows the expected returns as well as the variances and the standard deviations for the returns of both companies' shares. The expected return of the FMCG shares is lower, whereas the variance and the standard deviation are higher in comparison to the brand stock.

When you consider these companies as unique investment opportunities, few would want to invest in the FMCG shares that offer a lower expected return with more volatility. However, if the FMCG stock is held as part of a portfolio, the conclusion may be different.

Suppose that an investor who has put money in brand stocks shifts some money to FMCG stocks. Figure 8.2 illustrates the expected return, the variance and the standard deviation of the portfolio when 50% of the funds are invested in brand shares and 50% are invested in FMCG shares. FMCG have a greater variance and standard deviation than brand, but they have the effect of narrowing the range of possible outcomes and decreasing the overall portfolio variability. The FMCG offsets the swing in performance of the brand, reducing the best-case return but improving the normal-case return, and accordingly stabilizing returns. The incremental risk of the FMCG shares is negative despite the fact that FMCG's returns are highly volatile.

Figure 8.2 | **The Risk and Return of the Two-Company Portfolio**

Scenario	Probability (%)	Rate of Return (%)		Portfolio Return (%)
		Brand	FMCG	Brand 50%, FMCG 50%
Boom	33.3	20	1	10.5
Normal	33.3	5	20	12.5
Recession	33.3	−10	−10	−10
Expected Return		5	3.67	4.33
Variance		150.0	153.6	103.4
Standard Deviation		12.2	12.4	10.2

好景気，通常の景気，不景気が同じ確率で訪れるとし，好景気時にはブランド品のリターンは20%なのに対して，日用品は1%，通常時は5%に対して20%，不景気時にはいずれにも－10%のリターンが予想されるとする。期待リターンと分散および標準偏差の計算結果も表わしているが，日用品の期待リターンはブランド品よりも低く，分散および標準偏差はブランド品よりも高いことがわかる。

　これらの株式を単独の投資対象と考えた場合，リターンが低くリスクの大きい日用品の株式に投資をしたいと考える人はいないであろう。しかし，日用品の株式をポートフォリオの一部とした場合はどうであろうか。

　いま，ブランド品の株式に投資する人が，資産の一部を日用品の株式に移したとする。図表8.2は，投資資産の50%をブランド品の株式に，残りの50%を日用品の株式に投資したポートフォリオの期待リターンと分散および標準偏差を示している。日用品の株式はブランド品の株式よりも分散および標準偏差が大きいが，ポートフォリオのリターンの振れ幅をせばめ，ポートフォリオの分散および標準偏差は小さくなっている。日用品の株式は，ブランド品の好景気時のリターンを小さくするが，普通時のリターンを改善させ，ポートフォリオ全体のリターンを安定させているのである。つまり，日用品の株式のリターンは変動性が高いものの，ポートフォリオに与える追加的なリスクはマイナスなのである。

図表8.2　2業種からなるポートフォリオのリターンとリスク

	確率(%)	リターン(%) ブランド品	リターン(%) 日用品	ポートフォリオのリターン(%) ブランド品50%，日用品50%
好景気	33.3	20	1	10.5
普通	33.3	5	20	12.5
不景気	33.3	－10	－10	－10
期待リターン		5	3.67	4.33
分散		150.0	153.6	103.4
標準偏差		12.2	12.4	10.2

◉ Effect of Diversification

An investor can reduce the risk of an investment by diversifying his/her portfolio across different investments. This is known as the diversification effect. Portfolio diversification works because the returns of individual investments are not the same. The fact that prices of different shares do not move together results in a reduction in the risk of the portfolio. The degree of this diversification effect depends on the degree to which the return of one investment varies relative to the other investments in the portfolio.

◉ Two Types of Risk

Investors can reduce risk by diversifying their portfolios across a number of assets; however, they cannot eliminate risk completely. Risk as reflected by the variance and the standard deviation consists of two types of risk: market risk, and unique risk.

$$\text{Total Risk} = \text{Market Risk} + \text{Unique Risk}$$

Market risk is economy or system-wide risk that affects the overall market. The returns of individual stocks are related to overall market fluctuations. The fluctuation that is related to the overall market is called "market risk." Market risk is derived from the entire system of the market; therefore, it is also called "systematic risk."

On the other hand, unique risk is that which affects only that particular stock (company) and is not related to overall market fluctuations. Unique risk is also called "unsystematic risk."

It is important to divide risk into these two components. Diversification can offset the unique swings of an individual stock's return and reduce risk as a whole, but it is only unique risk that can be reduced. Diversifying with other stocks can offset the unique risk that affects only an individual stock, but market risk affects all stocks and cannot be offset.

● 分散投資の効果

投資家は多くの資産に分散して投資することにより，リスクを下げることができる。これが分散投資効果である。分散投資効果は，個別の投資資産のリターンが異なることから生じる。個別の株価がすべて同様に変化しないことがポートフォリオとしてのリスクを下げる原因となるのである。分散効果の大きさは，それぞれの投資資産のリターンが，ポートフォリオの別の資産のリターンと同様に変化するのか，異なる動きをするのかによって決まる。

● 2種類のリスク

投資家は分散投資を行うことによってリスクを低減できることを確認した。しかしすべてのリスクが低減できるわけではない。分散や標準偏差によって表わされる株式投資のリスクは「市場リスク」と「個別リスク」の2つから成り立っている。

$$総リスク＝ 市場リスク ＋ 個別リスク$$

市場リスクとは，市場全体に影響を与える経済要因がもたらすリスクである。個別の証券のリターンは市場全体の変動と関係して変動している。この変動分が市場リスクである。市場リスクは市場というシステム全体がもたらすリスクであるから「システマティック・リスク」とも呼ばれる。

一方，個別リスクは市場全体の変動とは無関係な，その証券（その企業）に固有のリスクである。「アンシステマティック・リスク」とも呼ばれる。

リスクをこのように2つに分類するのには理由がある。分散投資を行うと，各証券のリターンの変動が部分的に相殺され，全体としてのリスクは低減されるが，ここで低減できるのは個別リスクのみだからである。その証券のみに影響を与える要因は他の証券と組み合わせることによって相殺することが可能だが，どの証券にも影響を同時に与える市場リスクは相殺することができない。

As Figure 8.3 illustrates, unique risks of individual stocks will be eliminated as the number of stocks contained in the portfolio increases. Since market risk would not be reduced, no matter how much the portfolio is diversified, total risk would only approach the level of market risk. Therefore, the level of total risk would be the same as the level of market risk, assuming that the market is comprised of well-diversified investors.

Figure 8.3 | Reducing Risk through Diversification

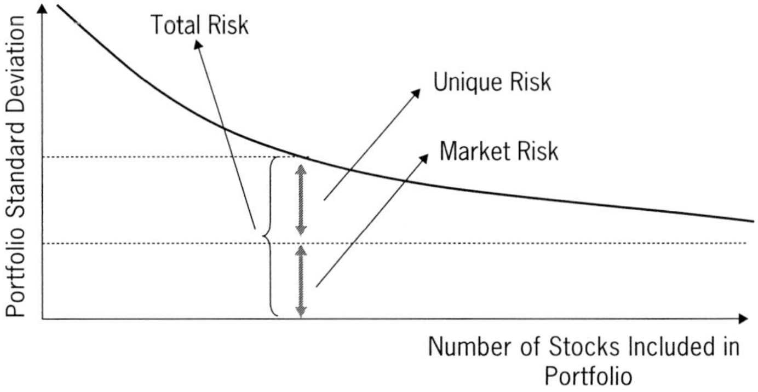

Diversification reduces unique risk rapidly at first and then more slowly as the number of stocks in the portfolio increases. When the number of stocks in the portfolio is limited, unique risk dominates overall risk and there is considerable room for risk to be reduced. However, a portfolio containing a number of stocks has minimal unique risk that could be subject to diversification benefits.

In order to estimate the expected return of an individual stock, only undiversified market risk is taken into account because investors can reduce unique risk on their own through portfolio diversification. Since unique risk would be eliminated, the risk premium or extra return on unique risk can be ignored.

図表8.3が示す通り，証券の個別リスクは投資する証券の数を増やすことによって（ポートフォリオ内の証券数を増やすことによって），取り除くことができる。しかしながら，市場リスクは低減できないため，いくら投資を分散させようとも，総リスクは市場リスクの水準に近づくだけで，それ以上にリスクを低減することはできない。したがって，分散投資を前提とすると総リスクは市場リスクと同レベルになる。

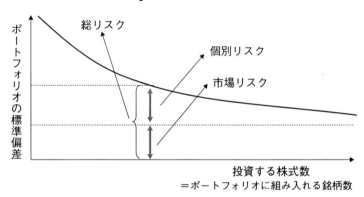

図表8.3 ｜ 分散投資によるリスクの低減

　また，個別リスクを低減する分散効果はポートフォリオ内の証券数が少ないうちは大きいが，証券数が増えるに従って逓減していく。ポートフォリオ内の証券数が少ない場合には，総リスクに含まれる個別リスクの割合が大きいため，リスク低減の余地が大きいが，多くの証券が組み入れられたポートフォリオは低減される個別リスクが少なくなっているためである。

　証券の期待リターンを推定する際には，投資家が分散投資することができることを加味し，分散投資によっても除去できない市場リスクのみを考慮する。分散投資によって消去できる個別リスクには追加的なリターンであるリスク・プレミアムは求められないと考えるのである。

◯ The Risk Measure for a Diversified Portfolio: Beta

Only market risk matters for measuring the risk of an equity (stock) investment in an investment portfolio where unique risk is diversified away. The risk measure to be focused on here is β (beta).

Beta reflects the sensitivity of the return of an individual stock to the return of the overall market. In comparison to the overall market, the relative volatility, or the relative degree of risk, for the individual stock is depicted as beta.

Figure 8.4 illustrates how to estimate the degree of relative risk for Toyota Motor when using the TOPIX index as a proxy for the overall market. The horizontal and the vertical axes plot the return of the TOPIX and Toyota, respectively, using actual monthly return data for 60 months ending March 2018. When a line is fixed to the scatter plot, the slope of this line shows the sensitivity of the return of Toyota's stock to the return of the TOPIX. The formula of this line reflects a slope of 1.13. Setting the risk of the TOPIX at 1, the relative degree of risk for Toyota is 1.13.

The slope coefficient of 1.13 shows that when the return of the TOPIX is 1%, the return of Toyota will tend to be 1.13%, and that if the return of TOPIX is −1%, the return of Toyota will tend to be −1.13%. Hence, the volatility of the return of Toyota's stock is greater than the return of the TOPIX, which means that Toyota's stock is riskier than the overall market average.

● 分散投資におけるリスク指標　ベータ

　すでに示したように，ポートフォリオ投資を前提とした場合，個別リスクは分散されるため，株式投資のリスクを測る際には市場リスクのみを考慮すればいい。このために注目されるリスク指標が β（ベータ）値である。

　ベータは，市場全体のリターンに対する個別株式のリターンの感応度を表わす。市場全体と比較して，個別の株式リターンの相対的な変動性の大きさ，すなわち相対的なリスク量を示すのである。

　図表8.4は，市場全体を表わすポートフォリオを TOPIX で代替し，トヨタ自動車の相対的なリスクを推定する模様を示している。横軸は TOPIX のリターンを，縦軸はトヨタ自動車の株価リターンをとっており，60カ月分の月次リターンの結果をプロットしている（図の中には60個の点がある）。60個の点の関係を近似する線を引くと，右上がりの直線が得られる。この線の傾きは TOPIX のリターンに対するトヨタ自動車の株式リターンの感応度を表わしている。表示されている近似線の式からは直線の傾きが1.13であることがわかる。この1.13が，TOPIX のリスクを1としたときのトヨタ自動車の株式の相対的なリスク量である。

　1.13という数式の係数は，TOPIX が1％のリターンだった場合にトヨタの株式リターンが1.13％になり，TOPIX のリターンがマイナス1％だった場合にトヨタの株式リターンがマイナス1.13％になる傾向があるということを示す。つまり，TOPIX のリターンの振れ幅よりもトヨタの株式リターンの振れ幅は大きい，ということであり，トヨタの株式は市場全体よりもリスクが大きいことを表わしている。

Figure 8.4 | **Returns of Toyota Motor and the TOPIX**

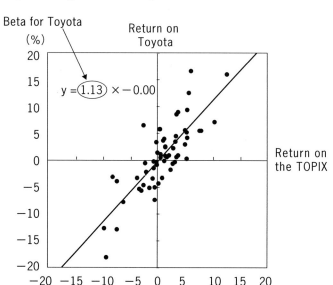

Source: 60 months data (to March 2018),
Calculated based on data provided on Yahoo! Finance (Japan)

The coefficient is called beta because the mathematical formula is generally written as $y = \alpha + \beta x$. Statistical analysis called "linear regression" is undertaken to compute beta. When beta is calculated using actual stock price data, the determinant coefficient of the regression line (which reflects the explanatory power of the line, and is called R-square) is commonly between 0.1-0.5. This value may seem low, especially if one is familiar with statistics, but it is actually quite normal. Beta, the slope of the regression line, shows the sensitivity to the market return, which means market risk. On the other hand, the vertical distances between each plot and the line are not explained by beta and reflect the movement in stock returns to news or events that affected the company but did not affect the overall market. They are referred to as unique risk, which can be eliminated through investment diversification and can be ignored accordingly.

図表8.4 ｜ TOPIXとトヨタ自動車の株価リターン

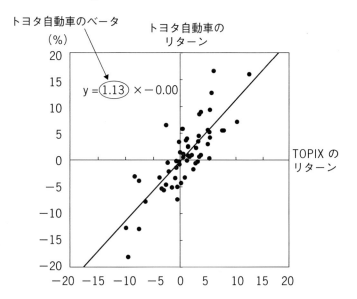

出所：2018年3月末までの60カ月のデータ。
Yahoo!ファイナンスのデータを加工し著者計算

　一般的に数式は$y = α + βx$と表わされるため，この係数はベータと呼ばれる。ベータの推定においては，統計分析の一手法である回帰分析を行っている。株式市場の実際のデータを使用してベータを推定する場合，回帰分析における直線がどれだけ説明力があるのかを示す決定係数（R2乗，アール・スクエアと呼ばれる）は，おおよそ0.1～0.5程度になるケースがほとんどである。エンジニアリングの常識や統計に詳しい方からすると，この値はとても低いと感じるかもしれないが，実際には問題ない。なぜなら，この直線の傾きであるベータが説明しているのは市場リターンとの感応度，つまり市場リスクだからである。一方，各データと直線との上下の乖離は統計的にベータが説明できない部分だが，これはこの企業だけに影響を与えたが，市場全体には影響を及ぼさなかったイベント，要素に対する株式リターンの反応度を表わしている。つまり，分散投資によって取り除かれる個別リスクにあたるため，無視してよいのである。

○ Beta for a Japanese Company

The average beta of all stocks is 1.0 by definition. Some stocks are less affected than others by market fluctuations; such stocks would have a beta of less than 1.0 and are sometimes called "defensive" stocks. On the other hand, beta for companies that are significantly influenced by market movements would be greater than 1.0. Beta varies by industry. Figure 8.5 shows the average beta for each industry in Japan. You can see that betas for industries that are vulnerable to the economic environment are generally high, and the betas for industries that are relatively insulated from the economic climate tend to be low.

Figure 8.5 | **Industry Beta for Japanese Companies**

Industry	Beta
Public Utility	0.2
Foods	0.4
Pharmaceutical	0.5
Beverage, Clothing, Home Products	0.6
Telecom, Paper, Hotel, Restaurant, Travel	0.7
Media (broadcasting, advertisement)	0.8
Transportation, Railway, Automobile, Auto Components, Oil	0.9
Leisure Items, Electronics, Non-life Insurance, Retail, Construction	1.0
Chemical	1.1
Services	1.2
Technologies (internet, software, computer), Real Estate, Banks, Industrial Machineries	1.3
Industrial Materials (steel, metal)	1.4

Source : Calculated based on data provided by Thomson Reuters Datastream

Beta estimates are provided by financial data companies, but you can calculate beta using the "=slope" function in Microsoft Excel as long as you has the data for the market return (such as the TOPIX) and the company return.

日本企業のベータ

すべての株式のベータの平均値は定義上 1.0 になる。企業によって，市場の変動を受けにくい企業の株式のベータは 1 以下になり，これらの株式はディフェンシブ株と呼ばれる。一方で，市場の変動を大きく受ける企業のベータは 1 以上となる。ベータは産業によっても異なる。図表 8.5 は日本での各産業の平均ベータを算出した例である。景気の影響を受けやすい業界は概してベータが高く，景気の影響を受けにくい業界のベータは低い傾向にあることがわかる。

図表 8.5 ┃ 日本企業の産業別ベータ

産　業	ベータ
電力・ガス	0.2
食品	0.4
医薬品	0.5
飲料，衣料，生活製品	0.6
電話通信，紙，ホテル，飲食，旅行	0.7
メディア（放送，広告）	0.8
運輸，鉄道，自動車，自動車部品，石油	0.9
レジャー商品，エレクトロニクス，損害保険，小売，建設	1.0
化学	1.1
サービス	1.2
テクノロジー（インターネット, ソフトウエア, コンピューター），不動産，銀行，産業機械	1.3
産業素材（鉄，金属）	1.4

出所：Thomson Reuters Datastream のデータから著者計算

なお，ベータは株式市場の情報を提供するデータベース会社も提供しているが，市場全体（たとえば TOPIX）のリターンと株式リターンのデータさえあれば，マイクロソフトの表計算ソフト Excel で「slope」関数を用いることで簡単に計算することができる。

It is common to calculate beta using 5 years of monthly return data. However, sometimes weekly returns or a period of less than 5 years of returns are used. Since beta can vary considerably depending on the time period used, data for peer companies in the same sector may also be referred to in practice. In addition, peer data would be used to estimate beta for unlisted companies, which do not have available stock price data.

◉ CAPM

The Capital Asset Pricing Model, or CAPM, reflects the underlying theory of the relationship between risk and return, which states that the expected risk premium on any security equals its beta times the market risk premium. The expected return would be the risk premium plus the risk-free rate.

$$\text{Expected Return} = \text{Risk-Free Rate (rf)} + \text{Risk Premium}$$
$$= rf + \text{Beta} \times \text{Market Risk Premium}$$

The CAPM assumes that the stock market is dominated by well-diversified investors who are concerned only with market risk. The CAPM expressed in a simple formula, which earned its creators' the Nobel Prize in Economics, is the most popular model in use for estimating the expected return on securities.

ベータの算出にあたっては60カ月の月次リターンが使用されることが多いが，場合によっては週次リターンが使用されたり，あるいは期間を36カ月にしたりということも行われる。算出されるベータは使用するデータの期間によって大きく異なることも多いため，実際には同業他社のデータなども参考にする。未公開企業の場合は，そもそも株価データがないので，競合他社・同業種企業のデータを参考にしつつ推定することが必要になる。

● CAPM

　CAPM（Capital Asset Pricing Model，キャップエム）は，リスク・プレミアムは，ベータと市場リスク・プレミアムを掛け合わせたものだとする理論である。期待リターンはこのリスク・プレミアムにリスクフリー・レートを加えたものとなる。

期待リターン ＝ リスクフリー・レート ＋ リスク・プレミアム
　　　　　　＝ リスクフリー・レート ＋ ベータ × 市場リスク・プレミアム

　CAPMでは，市場にかかわるリスクしか考慮しないので，株式市場に参加する投資家はすべて分散投資を行っているという前提をおいていることになる。CAPMはノーベル経済学賞を受賞したほどの理論的な精緻さを誇るうえに，リスクを決める要因が市場リスクのみであるというシンプルさから，実務において最も一般的に用いられている期待リターンの推定モデルである。

Figure 8.6 represents the CAPM graphically by taking the risk measure of beta on the horizontal axis and the expected return on the vertical axis. It shows that when beta is zero, the risk premium is zero, and that the larger the beta gets, the larger the expected return becomes. In the case of Toyota Motor, beta was 1.13, which is to the right of the market average. As a result, the expected return on Toyota's stock is higher than the expected return of the overall market on average.

Figure 8.6 | Expected Return of Toyota Motor Based on CAPM

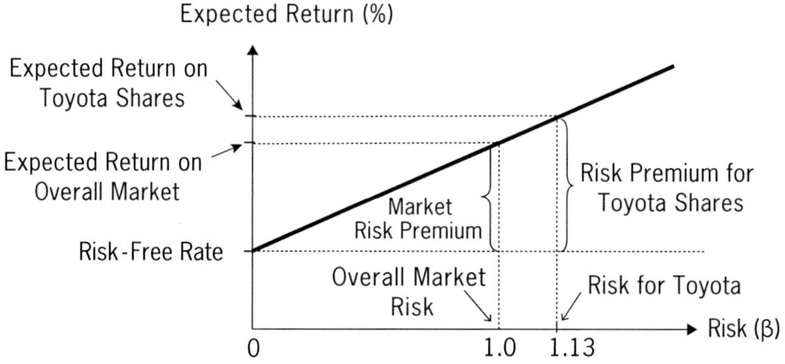

Expected Return (%)

- Expected Return on Toyota Shares
- Expected Return on Overall Market
- Risk-Free Rate
- Market Risk Premium
- Overall Market Risk
- Risk Premium for Toyota Shares
- Risk for Toyota
- Risk (β)
- 0, 1.0, 1.13

Here we estimate the expected return for Toyota assuming that the market risk premium is 5% and the risk free rate is 0.1%. The equity risk premium of Toyota is calculated as the beta of 1.13 multiplied by the 5% market risk premium, resulting in 5.65%. Adding the 0.1% risk free rate, the expected return on Toyota's stock would be 5.75%.

図表8.6は横軸にリスク指標のベータをとり，縦軸に期待リターンをとって，CAPMを図示したものである。ベータがゼロの時はリスク・プレミアムはゼロだが，ベータが大きくなるに従い期待リターンが大きくなるというリスク・リターンの関係性が示されている。先ほど示したトヨタ自動車のベータは1.13であったから，市場全体のリスクよりも右に位置し，その結果としてトヨタの株式に求められるリターンは株式市場全体に求められるリターンよりも高くなる。

図表8.6 ｜ CAPMによるトヨタ自動車の期待リターン

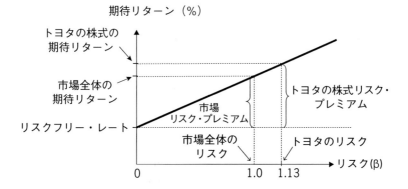

　市場リスク・プレミアムが5％，リスクフリー・レートが0.1％であるとして，トヨタの期待リターンを計算してみよう。トヨタの株式リスク・プレミアムはベータの1.13と市場リスク・プレミアム5％を掛け合わせた5.65％。これにリスクフリー・レート0.1％を足し合わせた5.75％がトヨタの株式に対する期待リターンとなる。

第8章　ポートフォリオリスクとCAPM　　145

● Security Market Line

The line of the CAPM is called the Security Market Line, or SML. The SML shows how the expected rate of return depends on beta, and explains theoretically the risk-return relationships for all investment assets. According to the CAPM, the expected rates of return for all securities and all portfolios lie on the SML.

Figure 8.7 | Security Market Line

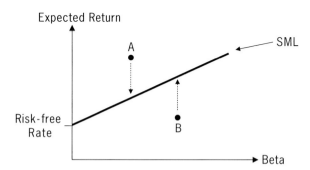

If a stock is located above the SML (such as stock A in Figure 8.7), the expected return would be higher with respect to its risk, and therefore it is an attractive investment asset. A number of investors would likely rush to purchase this stock, and the price of the stock would climb upward. As the price and the return move in the opposite direction, the expected return of the stock would slide toward the SML. Conversely, a stock located below the SML (such as stock B in Figure 8.7) reflects low return expectations with respect to its risk; the price of this stock would fall and the expected return of the stock would move upward to the SML.

Any point on the SML can be attained with a combination of the overall market portfolio, such as the TOPIX and a risk free asset like government bonds. If you wanted a beta of 0.5, you would allocate one-half of your funds to the TOPIX and the other half to government bonds. If you wanted a beta lager than one, you would borrow money and invest it in the TOPIX. The SML is straight because any point on the SML can be realized as a weighted average of the TOPIX and government bonds.

● 証券市場線

CAPMにおける斜めの直線のことを，証券市場線（SML）と呼ぶ。SMLはベータと期待リターンの関係を示しており，理論上すべての投資資産のリスク・リターンの関係はこの直線によって説明される。つまり，CAPMによれば，すべての投資資産がSML上にあるということである。

図表8.7 | 証券市場線

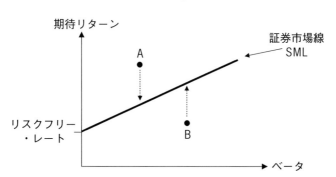

もし，この線より上に位置する株があったとする（図A点）。この株式はリスクの割に期待リターンが大きいため，魅力的な投資資産である。すると多くの人がこの株式を購入したいと思い，買い注文が増えるから株価は上昇する。価格とリターンは逆方向に動くためリターンは下がり，いずれはSML上に移動する。逆に，この線より下に位置する株式（図B点）の場合には，リスクの割に期待できるリターンが小さいため，株価は下落し，リターンが上がってやはりSML上に移動する。

また，TOPIXと国債を組み合わせることによってSML上のすべての点は達成できる。ベータを0.5にしたければ，TOPIXと国債に半分ずつ資金を配分すればいいし，ベータを1以上にしたければ，借金をしてその分でTOPIXに投資すればよい。SML上のどの点もTOPIXと国債の加重平均として実現できるので，SMLは曲線ではなく，直線なのである。

Chapter 9 (Advanced Topic) Detail Discussion about Portfolio Diversification

Points!

- ✓ The degree of diversification effect depends on the covariance and the correlation
- ✓ The efficient frontier can be attained by spreading a portfolio across many investments
- ✓ All investors will select the market portfolio

● Covariance and Correlation

The degree of diversification effect depends on how the return of an individual asset moves similarly or differently with the return of other assets in the portfolio. The covariance and the correlation coefficient (ρ) provide a measure of the returns on each asset to vary either in tandem or in opposition to each other.

The covariance is the expected (average) value of the product of the deviations from the expected (average) return of each asset. The product of the deviation of each asset is positive (covariance is positive) if the returns of each asset move together, while it is negative (covariance is negative) if they move inversely. The absolute value of covariance will be bigger when the returns of assets in the portfolio are more volatile.

The correlation is the measure in which the covariance is divided by the product of the standard deviations of the return on each asset. This standardizes the directional relationship from values of -1 to $+1$.

$$\text{Correlation Coefficient }(\rho) = \frac{\text{Covariance}}{\text{Product of standard deviations}}$$

$$-1.0 \leq \rho \leq +1.0$$

第9章 ポートフォリオ分散効果の詳述（上級トピック）

> **ポイント！**
> - ✓ 分散投資の効果は共分散や相関によって異なる
> - ✓ 複数の資産に分散して投資することにより，投資の効率的フロンティアは実現される
> - ✓ すべての投資家が選択する唯一のポートフォリオは市場ポートフォリオである

● 共分散と相関

　第8章では，分散投資効果の度合いは，個別の投資資産のリターンが，ポートフォリオの別の資産のリターンと同様に変化するのか，異なる動きをするのかによって決まると述べた。これを表わすものが共分散や，相関関係を表わす相関係数（ρ）である。

　共分散は，それぞれの証券の各状態におけるリターンの期待リターン（平均リターン）からの乖離（偏差）を掛け合わせた数値の期待値（平均値）である。各証券の偏差の積は，それぞれの証券が同方向に動けば正の値となり，逆方向に動けば負の値となる。また，各証券の動く幅が大きければ共分散の絶対値は大きくなる。

　相関（係数）は，共分散をポートフォリオの各証券の標準偏差で割ることにより，－1から＋1の間に標準化したものである。

$$相関係数(\rho) = \frac{共分散}{各証券の標準偏差の積}$$

$$-1.0 \leq \rho \leq +1.0$$

If ρ = 1.0, then the returns of two securities are perfectly positively correlated (move exactly in the same direction). If ρ = −1.0, then the returns of the securities are perfectly negatively correlated (move in the exact opposite direction). If ρ = 0, then the returns on the assets are completely unrelated to each other (move independently).

Figure 9.1 calculates the covariance and the correlation for the previous case of a brand-name product company and a FMCG company. The correlation of 0.36 indicates two companies' stock tend to move similar to the some extent, but not completely together.

Figure 9.1 | **Covariance and Correlation of the Two-Company Portfolio**

Scenario	Probability (%)	Rate of Return (%)		Deviation From Averrage Return		Product of Deviation	Product of Deviation × Probability
		Brand	FMCG	Brand	FMCG		
Boom	33.3	20	1	15	−2.67	−40.00	−13.33
Normal	33.3	5	20	0	16.33	0.00	0.00
Recession	33.3	−10	−10	−15	−13.67	205.00	68.33
Expected Return		5	3.67	Covariance			55.00
Variance		150.0	153.6	Correlation			0.36
Standard Deviation		12.2	12.4				

ρが1.0であれば，複数資産のリターンが完全に正の相関関係がある（全く同じ方向に動く）ことを示し，ρが−1.0であれば，複数資産のリターンが完全に負の相関関係がある（全く反対方向に動く）ことを示す。また，ρが0であるということは，複数資産のリターンが全く相関していない（全く関係なく動く）ということである。

ブランド品と日用品の株式の例での，共分散と相関係数を示したのが図表9.1である。相関係数は0.36であり，この2つの株式の価格はある程度同方向に動くが完全ではないことが示されている。

図表9.1　2業種からなるポートフォリオの共分散と相関

	確率(%)	リターン(%) ブランド品	リターン(%) 日用品	平均リターンからの乖離（偏差） ブランド品	平均リターンからの乖離（偏差） 日用品	偏差の積	偏差の積 ×確率
好景気	33.3	20	1	15	−2.67	−40.00	−13.33
普通	33.3	5	20	0	16.33	0.00	0.00
不景気	33.3	−10	−10	−15	−13.67	205.00	68.33
期待リターン		5	3.67	共分散			55.00
分散		150.0	153.6	相関関係			0.36
標準偏差		12.2	12.4				

Return, Variance and Standard Deviation of a Two-Asset Portfolio

To understand the effect of diversification, let's consider a portfolio that is comprised of two risky investment assets. The expected return of a portfolio comprised of stocks A and B is:

$$r_P = w_A r_A + w_B r_B$$

r_P : expected return of portfolio
r_A : expected return of stock A
r_B : expected return of stock B
w_A : weight of stock A in portfolio
w_B : weight of stock B in portfolio
$w_A + w_B = 100\%$

The expected return of the portfolio is simply a weighted average of the expected return of each individual stock.

On the other hand, the variance of the portfolio (σ_P^2) can be measured as:

$$\sigma_P^2 = w_A^2 \sigma_A^2 + w_B^2 \sigma_B^2 + 2 w_A w_B \sigma_A \sigma_B \rho_{AB}$$

σ_P : standard deviation of return of the portfolio
σ_A : standard deviation of return of stock A
σ_B : standard deviation of return of stock B
ρ_{AB} : correlation coefficient of return of stock A and stock B
w_A : weight of stock A in portfolio
w_B : weight of stock B in portfolio
$w_A + w_B = 100\%$

The formula indicates that the standard deviation of the portfolio is influenced by the correlation of the returns, and not simply by taking a weighted average standard deviation of the returns for each stock.

● 2資産のポートフォリオのリターン，分散，標準偏差

ポートフォリオの分散効果を理解するために，2つのリスクのある投資資産の組み合わせによるポートフォリオを考える。証券Aと証券Bの2つの投資資産からなるポートフォリオの期待リターン（r_P）は以下のようになる。

$$r_P = w_A r_A + w_B r_B$$

r_P：ポートフォリオの期待リターン
r_A：証券Aのリターン
r_B：証券Bのリターン
w_A：証券Aの比率
w_B：証券Bの比率
w_A と w_B の合計は100%

ポートフォリオの期待リターンは，各証券のリターンの加重平均ということである。
一方で，ポートフォリオの分散（σ_P^2）は以下のように表わされる。

$$\sigma_P^2 = w_A^2 \sigma_A^2 + w_B^2 \sigma_B^2 + 2 w_A w_B \sigma_A \sigma_B \rho_{AB}$$

σ_P：ポートフォリオのリターンの標準偏差
σ_A：証券Aのリターンの標準偏差
σ_B：証券Bのリターンの標準偏差
ρ_{AB}：証券Aと証券Bのリターンの相関係数
w_A：証券Aの比率
w_B：証券Bの比率
w_A と w_B の合計は100%

この式から，ポートフォリオのリスクを表わすリターンの標準偏差は，各証券のリターンの標準偏差の加重平均ではなく，相関が影響していることがわかる。

Investment Opportunity Set of a Two-Asset Portfolio

The expected return and the standard deviation of a two-asset portfolio change according to the proportion of their combination. Figure 9.2, which shows the expected return on the vertical axis and the standard deviation on the horizontal axis, demonstrates changes in the portfolio that follow along with the change in the relative proportion of stocks A and B. The set of available portfolio risk-return combinations is called the investment opportunity set. Compared to stock B, both the expected return and the standard deviation of stock A are low. Notice that the line connecting stocks A and B is not straight. The combination of stocks A and B could result in a portfolio whose standard deviation is lower than that of either individual stock (diamond in Figure), which is caused by correlation.

Investors desire investments located in the upper left region as much as possible since they would prefer higher returns as well as lower risk. The position in the upper left corner can be achieved through diversification.

Figure 9.2 | **Investment Opportunity Set of a Portfolio of Two Risky Assets**

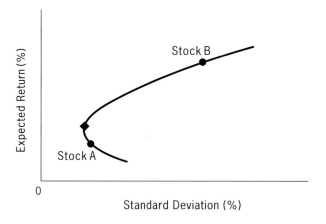

● 2資産のポートフォリオの投資機会集合

2つの資産の組み合わせによるポートフォリオは，その組み合わせ比率により，ポートフォリオの期待リターンと標準偏差が変化する。図表9.2は縦軸に期待リターン，横軸に標準偏差をとり，証券Aと証券Bの組み合わせを変化させたときのポートフォリオの状態の例を示している。この実現可能なリターンとリスクの組み合わせ一式を投資機会集合と呼ぶ。証券Aと証券Bを比べると，証券Aは期待リターン，標準偏差ともに小さい。このとき，証券Aと証券Bをつなぐ線が直線ではないことに注目してほしい。2つの証券を組み合わせることによって，どちらの証券の標準偏差よりも小さい状態（図表中のひし形の点）を作り出せる。この線の「たわみ」が相関の影響である。

投資家はより高いリターンを期待し，より低いリスクを求めるから，できるだけ左上の状態を好む。そして，左上の状態は分散効果によって実現される。

図表9.2 | **2つのリスク資産からなるポートフォリオの投資機会集合**

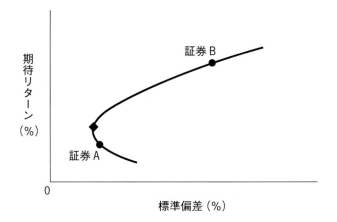

Remember that the formula for portfolio variance is:

$$\sigma_P^2 = W_A^2 \sigma_A^2 + W_B^2 \sigma_B^2 + 2W_A W_B \sigma_A \sigma_B \rho_{AB}$$

When the correlation of returns for stocks A and B is 1.0, they are perfectly positively correlated, and the standard deviation of the portfolio would be:

$$\sigma_P^2 = W_A^2 \sigma_A^2 + W_B^2 \sigma_B^2 + 2W_A W_B \sigma_A \sigma_B$$

Then,

$$\sigma_P^2 = (W_A \sigma_A + W_B \sigma_B)^2$$
$$\sigma_P = W_A \sigma_A + W_B \sigma_B$$

The standard deviation of the portfolio is the weighted average of the standard deviation of stocks A and B. Accordingly, the line between stocks A and B is straight. There is no diversification effect to reduce the risk of the portfolio.

But if the correlation is zero, then the variance of the portfolio would be:

$$\sigma_P^2 = W_A^2 \sigma_A^2 + W_B^2 \sigma_B^2$$

The last term in the formula disappears, and the standard deviation of the portfolio would be smaller. If the correlation is negative, then the standard deviation would become even smaller. Figure 9.3 demonstrates that a low correlation increases the deflection of the curve between stocks A and B.

ポートフォリオの分散を表わす式を振り返ってみよう。

$$\sigma_P^2 = w_A^2 \sigma_A^2 + w_B^2 \sigma_B^2 + 2w_A w_B \sigma_A \sigma_B \rho_{AB}$$

ここで，もし，証券Aと証券Bのリターンの相関が1.0，つまり完全に正の相関があるとしたら，ポートフォリオの標準偏差は

$$\sigma_P^2 = w_A^2 \sigma_A^2 + w_B^2 \sigma_B^2 + 2w_A w_B \sigma_A \sigma_B$$

となり，

$$\sigma_P^2 = (w_A \sigma_A + w_B \sigma_B)^2$$
$$\sigma_P = w_A \sigma_A + w_B \sigma_B$$

であるから，ポートフォリオの標準偏差は証券Aと証券Bの加重平均となり，証券Aと証券Bをつなぐ線は直線となる。この場合，リスクを低減させる分散効果は生じない。

では，相関が0の場合はどうであろうか。ポートフォリオの分散は

$$\sigma_P^2 = w_A^2 \sigma_A^2 + w_B^2 \sigma_B^2$$

となり，最後の項がなくなるため，標準偏差は小さくなる。相関がマイナスの場合はさらにポートフォリオの標準偏差は小さくなり，証券Aと証券Bをつなぐ線のたわみはさらに大きくなる。これを示したのが図表9.3である。

Figure 9.3 | Investment Opportunity Set with Various Correlation Coefficient

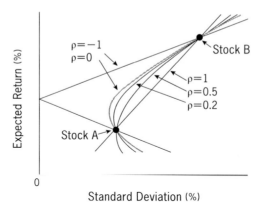

The correlation between the brand stock and the FMCG stock is 0.36. Figure 9.4 illustrates a feasible combination of expected returns and standard deviations. The portfolio mixing the brand and the commodity stock reduces the standard deviation, minimizing the standard deviation of the portfolio when investing almost equally in two stocks.

Figure 9.4 | Investment Opportunity Set of the Two-Company Portfolio

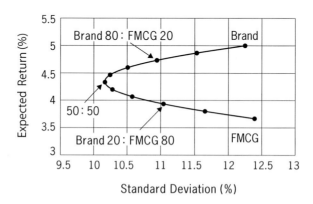

図表 9.3 さまざまな相関係数によるポートフォリオの投資機会集合

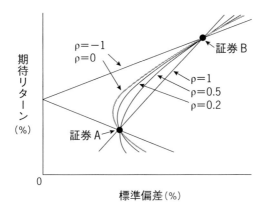

ブランド品と日用品の株式の相関係数は 0.36 であった。図表 9.4 は 2 つの株式を組み合わせることによって到達できる期待リターンと標準偏差を表わしている。2 つの株式に投資することにより、ポートフォリオの標準偏差は小さくでき、均等に投資するあたりで標準偏差は最小になることがわかる。

図表 9.4 ブランド品と日用品のポートフォリオの投資機会集合

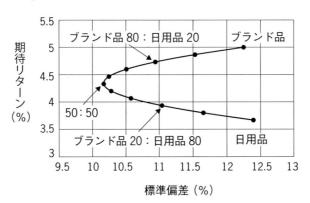

Diversification in order to reduce risk works whenever returns are less than perfectly correlated. An investor can also enjoy a significant degree of benefit with diversification when correlations are negative; however, it is difficult to find assets with negative correlations.

● The Efficient Frontier

Investors typically include more than two assets in their portfolio. Figure 9.5 illustrates that the efficiency of the portfolio could be improved by adding another stock.

By combining stocks A and B, investors can reach point E, which neither stock A nor stock B could realize individually. In addition, investors can shift the investment opportunity set up to the left to reach the more preferable point F by incorporating stock C.

Figure 9.5 | **Investment Opportunity Set of a Portfolio Comprising Three Risky Stocks**

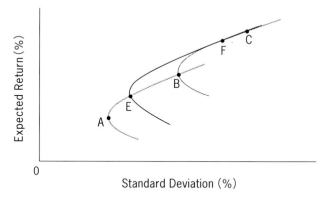

By increasing the number of assets in a portfolio, the points that maximize the expected return at each level of the standard deviation, or that minimize the standard deviation at each level of the expected return, can be obtained. The curved line of the graph representing the set of the most preferable points is called the "efficient frontier of risky assets" (Figure 9.6).

分散効果はポートフォリオに組み入れる投資資産のリターンの相関関係が1.0未満であれば生じる。相関がマイナスであれば大きな分散効果を得ることができるが，実際にはそのような投資資産を見つけることは難しい。

● 効率的フロンティア

　投資家がポートフォリオに組み込む資産は2つに限らない。図表9.5はさらに別の証券を組み込むことで，ポートフォリオの状態をもう一段望ましいものにできることを表わしている。

　証券Aと証券Bの組み合わせによって，投資家は最も左上の位置にある点Eの状態を得ることができた。しかし，証券Cを組み入れることによって，投資家は投資機会集合をさらに左上にシフトさせ，点Fというさらに望ましい状態に到達することができる。

図表9.5 ┃ 3つのリスク資産からなるポートフォリオの投資機会集合

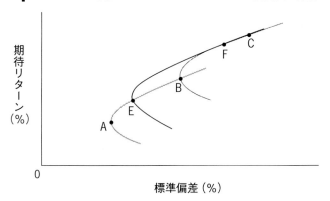

　このようにポートフォリオに組み入れるリスク資産を増やしていくことにより，それぞれの標準偏差において期待リターンを最大化する点，それぞれの期待リターンにおいて標準偏差を最小化する点を得ることができる。これらをつないだものが「リスク資産の効率的フロンティア」である（図表9.6）。

Figure 9.6 | The Efficient Frontier of Risky Assets

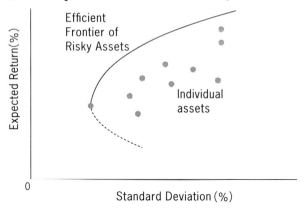

◉ The Efficient Frontier with Risk-Free Assets

Next, we introduce risk-free assets. The expected return of the riskless asset is the risk-free rate (meaning the standard deviation is zero), corresponding to the intercept of the straight line in Figure 9.7. Investors can combine riskless assets with risky assets in a portfolio. Therefore, they can attain a position on any straight lines connecting the risk-free rate with risky portfolios. Among the possible slopes, the line which is tangent to the efficient frontier of risky assets becomes the "efficient frontier with risk-free assets".

Figure 9.7 | The Efficient Frontier with Risk-Free Assets

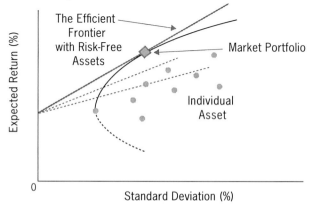

図表 9.6 リスク資産の効率的フロンティア

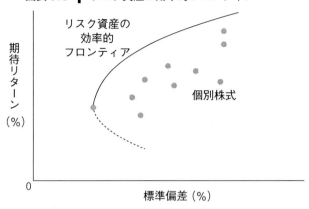

無リスク資産がある場合の効率的フロンティア

次に無リスク資産を想定してみよう。無リスク資産の期待リターンはリスクフリー・レートであり，標準偏差はゼロということだから，図表9.7の直線の切片にあたる。投資家はリスク資産と無リスク資産を組み合わせて投資を行うことが可能である。そのため，リスクフリー・レートと，リスク資産のポートフォリオをつなぐ直線上の状態を実現できる。その中でも，リスク資産の効率的フロンティアと接する直線が，「無リスク資産がある場合の効率的フロンティア」となる。

図表 9.7 無リスク資産がある場合の効率的フロンティア

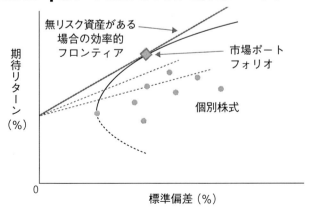

Considering risk-free assets, only one risky portfolio on the steepest line from the risk-free rate is effective (diamond in Figure 9.7). This is the risky portfolio solely selected by investors regardless of their risk preferences. The risk averse investors include risk-free assets in their portfolio and try to attain the position on the line left to the diamond. The risk tolerant investors borrow money and invest more in risky assets, attaining the position on the line right of the diamond.

Since any investor can choose the sole risky portfolio, the risky portfolio includes any existing assets traded, called the market portfolio. The assets not included in the market portfolio will neither be traded nor held by rational investors, therefore, the market portfolio is referred to as including all assets available.

In theory, the market portfolio includes all assets in the world, not only stocks but also other financial assets such as bonds, real estate, and so on. However, broad market indices such as TOPIX and S&P 500 are used as a proxy for the market portfolio in practice.

The slope of the lines in Figure 9.7 is known as the Sharpe ratio, measuring the return of a portfolio corresponding to the risk taken, calculated as:

$$\text{Sharpe ratio} = \frac{\text{Portfolio return} - \text{Risk-free rate}}{\text{Standard deviation of portfolio return}}$$

The greater the Sharpe ratio, the more efficiently the portfolio generates the return. The market portfolio maximizes the Sharpe ratio.

無リスク資産を考えると，リスク資産の効率的フロンティアの中でも，リスクフリー・レートからの直線が接するポートフォリオ（図表9.7上のひし形）のみが有効となる。投資家のリスク許容度が異なり，どれだけリスクをとろうが，選択されるリスク資産のポートフォリオは唯一である。リスクを回避したい投資家は無リスク資産を投資に組み入れてひし形よりも左の直線上の位置を実現しようとし，よりリスクを許容する投資家は借り入れを行ってリスク資産に投資することによりひし形よりも右の直線上の位置を実現しようとする。

　すべての投資家が唯一のポートフォリオ選択するのであるから，このポートフォリオは，存在し取引されている資産のすべてを含んでいる市場ポートフォリオとなる。市場ポートフォリオに含まれていない資産は取引されず，合理的な投資家に保有されないはずであるため，市場ポートフォリオはすべての資産を含むと考えることができる。

　理論的には市場ポートフォリオは株式だけではなく，債券などほかの金融資産や，不動産なども含むすべての投資資産を含むものである。しかし，実務においてはTOPIXやS&P 500といった株式インデックスが市場ポートフォリオとみなされる。

　なお，図表9.7の直線の傾きはポートフォリオのリスクに応じたリターンの高さを測るシャープ・レシオとしても知られており，以下のように求められる。

$$シャープ・レシオ = \frac{ポートフォリオのリターン - リスクフリー・レート}{ポートフォリオの標準偏差}$$

シャープ・レシオが高いほどとったリスクに応じて効率よくリターンを上げているということであり，市場ポートフォリオでシャープ・レシオは最大となる。

Contents of Beta

Statistically, the beta of company i is defined as:

$$\beta_i = \frac{\sigma_{im}}{\sigma_m^2}$$

σ_{im} : the covariance of the stock return of company i and the market return
σ_m^2 : the variance of the return on the market

We have seen the relationship between the covariance and the correlation.

$$\text{Correlation Coefficient}(\rho) = \frac{\text{Covariance}}{\text{Product of standard deviations}}$$

So, the covariance can be expressed as the product of the correlation coefficient (ρ) of stock i return and market return, and the two standard deviations:

$$\sigma_{im} = \rho_{im}\, \sigma_i\, \sigma_m$$

σ_{im} : the covariance of the stock return of company i and the market return
ρ_{im} : correlation coefficient of the stock return of company i and the market
σ_i : standard deviation of stock return of company i
σ_m : standard deviation of market return

Hence, the beta can be expressed as:

$$\beta_i = \frac{\rho_{im}\, \sigma_i\, \sigma_m}{\sigma_m^2} = \frac{\rho_{im}\, \sigma_i}{\sigma_m}$$

This indicates the beta is determined with both the volatility of stock returns and the correlation with market return.

ベータの中身

統計的には企業 i の株式のベータは以下のように定義される。

$$\beta_i = \frac{\sigma_{im}}{\sigma_m^2}$$

σ_{im}：企業 i の株式リターンと市場リターンの共分散
σ_m^2：市場リターンの分散

すでに確認したように，相関係数と共分散には以下の関係にある。

$$相関係数(\rho) = \frac{共分散}{各証券の標準偏差の積}$$

そのため，共分散は株式リターンと市場リターンの相関（ρ）とそれぞれのリターンの標準偏差を掛け合わせて求められる。

$$\sigma_{im} = \rho_{im}\,\sigma_i\,\sigma_m$$

σ_{im}：企業 i の株式リターンと市場リターンの共分散
ρ_{im}：企業 i の株式リターンと市場リターンの相関係数
σ_i：企業 i の株式リターンの標準偏差
σ_m：市場リターンの標準偏差

すなわち，ベータは以下のように表わせる。

$$\beta_i = \frac{\rho_{im}\,\sigma_i\,\sigma_m}{\sigma_m^2} = \frac{\rho_{im}\,\sigma_i}{\sigma_m}$$

この数式は，企業のベータは，その企業の株式リターンの変動性の大きさ，市場リターンとの相関の強さ，の双方によって決まることを示している。

Chapter 10 Weighted Average Cost of Capital

Points!

- ✔ The expected return of an investor is equal to the cost of capital for a company
- ✔ The overall cost of capital of company or weighted average cost of capital (WACC) is calculated as the average of the cost of debt and equity according to its financing mix
- ✔ The cost of capital of each business can be different from WACC of the company

○ Expected Return = Cost of Capital

Companies raise money from investors and use it as capital for their operations. The capital provided by an investor is not free; rather, some level of return is required. Without receiving any type of return for taking on risk, no investor would be willing to provide capital.

An investor's expected return can be viewed as a usage fee for capital from a company's perspective. This is the cost associated with capital, or the "cost of capital." It might seem counterintuitive that the expected return is the same as the cost of capital, but it is in fact the same thing seen from different perspectives. An investor would require a return on the capital provided, and a company would bear this cost.

The rate of the expected return depends on the form of capital provided. Capital is broadly separated into two categories: debt and equity. Debt capital consists of bank borrowing and bonds issued. Equity capital arises from the issuance of company shares. Equity investors are exposed to a different degree of risk than banks and bondholders and, accordingly, would expect different rates of return. Therefore, the cost of capital corresponds to the form of the capital provided: debt or equity. The

第10章 加重平均資本コスト

> **ポイント！**
> - ✓ 投資家の期待するリターンは企業においては調達した資本にかかわるコストである
> - ✓ 企業の資本コストは負債コストと株主資本コストを加重平均することによって算出する
> - ✓ 事業の資本コストと会社全体の資本コストは異なることがある

● 期待リターン ＝ 資本コスト

　企業は投資家から資金を得て，事業活動への資本として使用する。投資家から提供される資金には当然リターンが求められており，決してその資金はただで使えるものではない。もしリターンが得られないのであれば，誰も資金を提供してくれないはずだからである。

　投資家からの期待リターンは，資金を資本として使用する企業にとっては，資本を使用することにかかわるコストということになる。ゆえに，これを「資本コスト」と呼ぶ。期待リターンと資本コストが同じであることには違和感があるかもしれないが，単に同じものを異なる立場から見ているだけのことである。資金の出し手である投資家から見ればそこからのリターンであり，資金の受け手である企業から見ればそこにかかるコストということである。

　資金提供者の期待リターンは，資本の形態，つまり資金の提供方法によって異なる。資本の形態は大きく負債と株主資本に分けられる。負債は銀行からの借入や社債の発行による資金調達であり，株主資本は株式発行，増資による資金調達である。銀行や債券投資家と株式投資家では負うリスクが異なるから，企業に求めるリターンは異なる。それに対応して，異なる資本の形態によりコストも違ってくる。債権者（銀行・債券投資家）の期待するリターンは負債コ

return on debt expected by creditors (banks and bondholders) is referred to as the cost of debt, and the return on equity expected by equity shareholders is known as the cost of equity.

Weighted Average Cost of Capital

The overall cost of capital for a company is determined by the cost of debt, the cost of equity, and the company's capital structure or the mix of debt and equity financing. The capital structure varies with the company's mix of debt and equity financing. Note, that non-interest bearing liabilities such as accounts payables and reserves are not considered part of debt capital.

The overall cost of capital is calculated as the average of the cost of debt and the cost of equity based on their relative proportion and is therefore called the Weighted Average Cost of Capital, or WACC.

$$WACC = \frac{D}{V} \times (1-T) r_d + \frac{E}{V} \times r_e$$

D : market value of debt
E : market value of equity, market capitalization
V : market value of company = D + E

T : effective corporate tax rate
r_d : cost of debt
r_e : cost of equity

Figure 10.1 | Weighted Average Cost of Capital

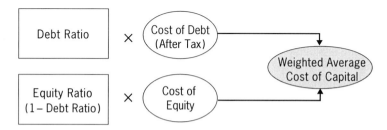

Chapter 10 Weighted Average Cost of Capital

スト，株主が期待するリターンは株主資本コストである。

加重平均資本コスト

企業の資本全体にかかるコストは，負債コスト，株主資本コストと企業の資本構成によって決まる。資本構成とは企業の資本全体における負債，株主資本それぞれの割合のことである。なお，ここでの負債には買掛債務や引当金のような無利子の負債は含まない。

企業全体の資本コストは負債コストと株主資本コストを資本構成によって加重平均して算出されるため，加重平均資本コスト（WACC）と呼ばれる。

$$WACC = \frac{D}{V} \times (1-T) r_d + \frac{E}{V} \times r_e$$

D：負債の時価　　　　　T：法人実効税率
E：株式時価総額　　　　r_d：負債コスト
V：企業の市場価値＝D+E　r_e：株主資本コスト

図表 10.1 ｜ 加重平均資本コスト

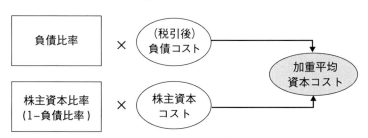

The capital structure for the WACC calculation should be based on the market value rather than the book value (value on the balance sheet) because investors expect a return on the current value of their investment. The market value of equity is equal to the market capitalization, which is generally calculated as the share price multiplied by the number of shares. The market value of debt can be considered the same as the book value unless the company faces financial difficulty. It is common in practice that a company's target capital structure is used for the WACC calculation.

WACC is the overall expected return on capital employed in the company and is used as the discount rate in present value calculations.

○ Cost of Equity and Cost of Debt

The cost of equity is calculated as the risk-free rate + beta × the market risk premium, based on CAPM introduced in chapter 8.

The cost of debt is the cost of interest-bearing liabilities such as bank borrowing and bonds. This corresponds to bank interest whenever a company borrows money from a bank. The more credit worthy a company is, the lower the interest rate, and vice versa. The cost of debt consists of the risk free rate and a "credit risk premium" that is the extra return required according to the risk of default, or credit risk.

You can see the cost of debt is estimated based on the interest rate of existing debt in practice. But, in principle you should use the marginal cost of debt which is the interest rate on marginal debt finance because you use the cost of capital for the marginal investment decision.

WACCの算出においては，資本構成は簿価（B/S上の価格）ではなく時価ベースを使用する。投資家が期待するリターンは現時点の価値に対するリターンだからである。株主資本の時価は，一般的に株価と株式数を掛け合わせた時価総額である。負債の時価は企業が倒産の危機に瀕しない限り簿価と同じと考えてよい。資本構成の算出にあたっては，企業が目標とする資本構成を使用する場合も実務的には多くみられる。

WACCは企業の資本全体にとっての利率であり期待リターンであるから，現在価値を算出する際の割引率として使用される。

◉ 株主資本コストと負債コスト

株主資本コストは，第8章で説明したCAPMに基づき，リスクフリー・レート＋ベータ×市場リスク・プレミアムで計算される。

負債コストは借入金・社債などの有利子負債にかかるコストである。通常お金を借りれば銀行金利のように利子が発生するが，それに相当するものである。負債コストは企業の信用力が高いほど低く，信用力が低いほど高くなる。負債コストはリスクがゼロの投資資産に求められるリターンである「リスクフリー・レート」と，信用リスクに応じたリターンの上乗せ分である「信用リスク・プレミアム」からなる。

負債コストの推定にあたっては，既存の負債の利子率を使用することも一般的には行われるが，投資の意思決定は今後に向けた意思決定であるため，本来的には，その時点で借り入れたら利子率はいくらになるのかという「限界的な」負債コストを使用すべきである。

Tax Savings Effect of Debt

In order to estimate the WACC, one more adjustment is required to the cost of debt. Debt has a tax benefit because the associated interest expense is tax deductible.

The left-hand side of Figure 10.2 illustrates earnings for a company without debt. Net income is 60 after subtracting 40% of the 100 in earnings before tax. The right-hand side illustrates a situation in which the company records identical performance but also has debt of 100. When the interest expense of 5 is subtracted, earnings before tax is 95, which is subject to a 40% tax rate. Tax is then 38 and net income becomes 57 instead of 60.

Figure 10.2 | Tax Savings Effect of Debt

Debt		0	Debt		100
Earnings before Interest and Tax		100	Earnings before Interest and Tax		100
Interest Expense	5%	0	Interest Expense	5%	5
Earnings before Tax		100	Earnings before Tax		95
Tax	40%	40	Tax	40%	38
Net Income		60	Net Income		57

Despite the fact that interest expense is 5, the ultimate impact on financial performance is limited to 3, from 60 to 57. Interest expense lowers taxable income and results in reducing the tax payment. The tax benefit is calculated as interest expense multiplied by $(1-$ tax rate$)$: $5 \times (1-40\%) = 3$ in this case. The cost of debt is expressed as a percent rather than as an absolute value, and the tax savings effect can be measured in the same manner as $5\% \times (1-40\%) = 3\%$. The cost of debt after incorporating a tax benefit (cost of debt before tax $\times (1-$ tax rate$))$ is used to estimate the cost of capital.

◯ 負債の節税効果

　企業の加重平均資本コストを算出する際には、負債コストにもう一段の調整が必要である。負債コストに該当する支払利息が、税金の計算上差し引かれるという「節税効果」があるためである。

　図表10.2の左は、企業の負債がゼロの場合の利益を表わしている。税前利益の40%が税金として引かれ、税引後の純利益は60である。一方、右は全く同じ業績だが負債を100もっている場合を示している。支払利息の5を引くと税前利益は95になり、そこに40%の税金が課される。税金は38となり税引後の純利益は57となる。

図表10.2　負債の節税効果

負債		0	負債		100
税前金利前利益		100	税前金利前利益		100
支払利息	5%	0	支払利息	5%	5
税前利益		100	税前利益		95
税金	40%	40	税金	40%	38
税引後利益（純利益）		60	税引後利益（純利益）		57

　支払利息は5であるのに、最終的な業績へのインパクトは60から57の3にとどまっている。支払利息が課税対象となる税前利益を小さくするため、支払う税金の額が少なくなったためである。この効果は支払利息に（1−税率）を掛けることで加味でき、この例では5×（1−40%）=3となる。負債コストは絶対額ではなく%だが、同様に利率であったとしても節税効果は5%×（1−40%）=3%と計算できる。このように、税前の負債コストに（1−税率）を掛け合わせ、節税効果も反映させた税引後の負債コストを、資本コストの計算では用いる。

● Calculation of WACC

Figure 10.3 illustrates the calculation of the WACC for Toyota Motor at the end of March 2018. The risk-free rate is assumed to be 0.1%. Toyota has a credit rating of AA and the credit risk premium is estimated to be 0.4%. Adding the 0.4% to the risk-free rate brings the cost of debt to 0.5%. Multiplying this rate by 0.7, which is 1 minus the effective corporate tax rate in Japan, the after-tax cost of debt is calculated to be 0.35%.

The beta of Toyota Motor is estimated to be 1.13 as we have seen in Figure 8.4. Assuming a market risk premium of 5%, the equity risk premium is 1.13×5% = 5.65%. The cost of equity is 5.75% after adding the risk-free rate.

The capital structure is calculated based on the book value of interest-bearing debt and the market capitalization at the end of the latest fiscal year (March 2018). Taking into account the debt and equity ratio of 48.1% and 51.9% respectively, the WACC is estimated to be 3.15%.

Figure 10.3 | WACC for Toyota Motor

	Risk-Free Rate	0.1%
	Credit Rating AA+	
+	Credit Risk Premium	0.4%
=	Cost of Debt	0.5%
	Tax Rate (T)	30.0%
	After Tax Cost of Debt	0.35%

	Beta	1.13
×	Market Risk Premium	5.0%
=	Equity Risk Premium	5.65%
+	Risk-Free Rate	0.10%
=	Cost of Equity	5.75%
	Debt / (Debt + Equity)	48.1%
	Equity / (Debt + Equity)	51.9%
	WACC	3.15%

● 加重平均資本コストの計算

それでは，2018年3月末時点におけるトヨタ自動車のWACCを計算してみる（図表10.3）。リスクフリー・レートは0.1%とする。まず負債コストだが，トヨタの格付はAA格であり，それに対応した信用リスク・プレミアムは0.4%と推定された。これをリスクフリー・レートに上乗せし，負債コストは0.5%となる。ここに日本の実効税率を1から引いた0.7を掛けると税引後負債コストは0.35%と算出される。

次に株主資本コストだが，図表8.4で示されたようにトヨタ自動車のベータは1.13であった。市場リスク・プレミアムが5%とすると，株式リスク・プレミアムは1.13 × 5% = 5.65%となる。ここにリスクフリー・レートを加えると株主資本コストは5.75%である。

資本構成は直前決算期末時点（2018年3月末）の有利子負債の簿価と株式時価総額に基づいて計算した。負債比率48.1%，株主資本比率51.9%をそれぞれ加味すると加重平均資本コストは3.15%と推定される。

図表10.3 トヨタ自動車の加重平均資本コスト

	リスクフリー・レート	0.1%
	格付　AA+	
+	信用リスク・プレミアム	0.4%
=	負債コスト（税引前）	0.5%
	税率	30.0%
	税引後負債コスト	0.35%

	ベータ値	1.13
×	市場リスク・プレミアム	5.0%
=	株式リスク・プレミアム	5.65%
+	リスク・フリーレート	0.10%
=	株主資本コスト	5.75%
	負債比率	48.1%
	株主資本比率	51.9%
	加重平均資本コスト（WACC）	3.15%

● Business Cost of Capital and WACC of the company

In the case that the risk of the overall company is different from the risk of businesses or projects in the company, you should apply the cost of capital corresponding to the risk of each business or project. Suppose a company running an electronic business tries to expand to the riskier entertainment business, the company will be exposed to a different level of risk. If the company utilizes WACC based on the current electronic business for the entertainment business, it can make inappropriate investment decisions (please note that if you apply an unfairly low cost of capital, the present value of future cash flows will be wrongly overestimated).

● Cost of Debt < Cost of Equity

As a final note to this chapter, we recall the principle that the cost of equity is always greater than the cost of debt because of its higher risk. The return to debt holders is paid in the form of interest expense and principal repayments, which are agreed to in advance. Therefore, the return for debt holders is unchanged unless the company faces financial distress. On the other hand, the share price, which impacts the return to equity holders, changes constantly. Changing returns increase volatility and represent risk, so equity investment is considered to be "high risk and high return."

Companies might try to lower WACC by changing their capital structure, by shifting from equity to debt because the cost of debt is lower. However, when the company increases its debt ratio, both debt and equity will become riskier. As a result, debt holders and equity holders require higher returns to compensate for the increased risk, and the WACC will not come down. We will discuss this further in the next chapter where we cover capital structure in more detail.

● 事業の資本コストと加重平均資本コスト

　企業全体のリスクと，企業が所有するそれぞれの事業や投資プロジェクトのリスクが異なる場合には，それぞれのリスクに応じた資本コストを使用すべきである。エレクトロニクス業を営んでいる企業がエンターテイメント事業への進出を検討する際には，これまでとは異なるリスクにさらされることになるだろう。もしエンターテイメント事業のリスクがエレクトロニクス事業のリスクよりも高いにもかかわらず，既存事業であるエレクトロニクス事業に対応した加重平均資本コストを使用してエンターテイメント事業の投資を判断してしまうと，本来投資すべきではない案件に投資をするといったことが発生してしまう可能性がある（本来よりも低い資本コストを使用することによって，投資案件からのキャッシュフローの現在価値が本来よりも高く見積もられる）。

● 負債コスト ＜ 株主資本コスト

　本章の最後に大原則をおさえておこう。株主資本コストは，リスクの高さを反映して負債コストよりも常に高い，ということである。債権者にとってのリターンは利息収入と元本の返済であり，これらの額はあらかじめ合意されている。つまり債権者のリターンは企業が危機的な状況に陥らない限り変動しない。一方で，株主にとってのリターンを決める株価は日々変動する。リターンが変動するということはリスクが大きいということであり，株式への投資は「ハイリスク・ハイリターン」であるということだ。

　なお，負債コストが株主資本コストよりも低いことから，資本構成を変化させ，負債をより多く活用することによりWACCを低下させることができると考えてしまうかもしれない。しかし，企業が負債を活用すると，負債と株主資本はそれぞれ，よりリスクが高まる。結果として，債権者と株式投資家は高いリスクに対応した高いリターンを期待することになるため，WACCが下がるとはいえないのである。このことは資本構成の詳細に関する次章で議論する。

Part 4
Financing Decisions

- This part deals with financing activities of a company, covering funding capital from outside, and returning cash to outside.

- The first two chapters explains various patterns of financing and how debt financing influences the financial performance and the value of a company.

- The later chapter discusses payout activities of a company such as dividend payments and share repurchases along with its possible effects on the financial performance and the value of a company.

Chapter 11   Financing and Company Value

Chapter 12   Optimal Capital Structure

Chapter 13   Payout Policy

第4部
資本政策

★★★★

- 企業の財務活動に関する議論を行う第4部では，企業が外部から資金を調達することと，企業が外部に資金を返還することの両方を議論する。

- 前半の2つの章は企業のさまざまな資本調達手法について学び，負債による資金調達が財務業績や企業価値にどのような影響を及ぼすのかを考える。

- 後半では，配当や自社株買いといった資金を還元する取組みが財務業績や企業価値にどのような影響を及ぼすのかを考える。

第11章　資金調達と企業価値

第12章　最適資本構成

第13章　資金還元

Chapter 11 Financing and Company Value

> **Points!**
> ✓ There are a variety of dissimilarities between debt and equity, and financing comes in many forms
> ✓ Debt financing amplifies the volatility of the financial performance but does not affect the value of a company in an assumed world without taxes

● Debt and Equity

When a company needs capital or cash to operate its business, it considers the best way to finance those needs. Financing options can be broadly categorized as debt and equity. Debt financing includes bank borrowing and bond issuance. We have already explained why the expected return on debt is different from the expected return on equity, and why the cost of equity is higher on a relative basis. There are various other dissimilarities between debt and equity other than their costs. Figure 11.1 summarizes the key characteristics of both.

Figure 11.1 | Characteristics of Debt and Equity

	Debt	Equity
Form of Financing	Bank Borrowing / Bond Issuance	Share Issuance (Equity Issuance / IPO)
Cost of Capital	Relatively Low	High
Redemption	At Maturity	Not Required
Periodic Payment	Usually Interest Required	Not Required
Risk	Bankruptcy	Takeover, Proxy Fight
Disclosure Requirements	Relatively Low	IR Activities, Shareholder Meetings
Ongoing Cost	Relatively Low	High

第11章 資金調達と企業価値

ポイント！

- ✓ 負債による資金調達と株主資本による資金調達にはそれぞれ特徴があり，またそれぞれの手法には細かな違いが存在する
- ✓ 負債の活用は企業の財務業績の変動性を高めるが，税金がない場合には企業価値に影響は与えない

● 負債と株主資本

事業活動を行うために資金が必要になると，どのように資金を調達すべきかを企業は考える。資金調達の形態は，負債と株主資本に大きく分類できる。負債には銀行からの借入れと社債の発行が含まれる。すでに，銀行・債権者が求めるリターンと株主が求めるリターンは異なっており，株主資本コストは負債コストより高いことを確認した。資本コスト以外にも，負債と株主資本には違いがある。図表 11.1 にその特徴をまとめている。

図表 11.1 ｜ 負債と株主資本の特徴

	負 債	株主資本
調達手法	銀行借入・社債発行	株式発行（増資・株式上場）
資本コスト	比較的低い	高い
返済	返済期限あり	期限・返済義務なし
定期的な支払い	多くの場合，利息支払いあり	義務なし
リスク	利息，元本を返済できない場合の倒産リスク	買収リスク 株主総会での議決権行使 （委任状争奪戦）
情報開示	比較的軽い	IR活動 株主総会の開催
維持コスト	比較的低い	高い

The key difference between debt and equity is that debt has a maturity. It is necessary for a company to make periodic interest payments as well as to repay the principal. A company will face bankruptcy if it cannot meet its promised interest and principal payments.

In contrast to debt, a company is not required to repay equity. Dividend payments are decided by management and are not obligatory. However, shareholders may question top management and attempt to oust them with enough shareholder proxies to win a corporate vote, if a company does not pay dividends without good reasons or if the share price remains stagnant because of poor performance. Further, a company with a stagnant share price is more likely to be the target of a hostile takeover or acquisition.

However, a company will not go bankrupt if it does not pay dividends or has a stagnant share price. Given these features of equity financing, in comparison debt financing brings greater constraints.

At the same time, equity financing has its own constraints, including the need for a company to explain how it will use cash that is raised or what its business strategy is in order to attract investors. (This is not the case for private companies where personal or private sources provide sufficient capital.) Moreover, listing on a stock exchange requires various forms of information disclosures that impose a large cost on the company. In addition to regular reporting to the stock exchange, companies issue annual reports to investors, provide earnings announcements, hold shareholder meetings, and visit investors all over the world. Exchange-listed companies have recently had to strengthen their internal control systems following corporate scandals that have occurred both within and outside Japan. It has also become necessary for listed companies to prepare detailed rules and regulations for a variety of internal operating processes.

負債と株主資本の大きな違いは，負債には返済期限があるということである。元本だけではなく，通常は定期的な利息の支払いも必要である。利息が支払えなかったり，元本が返済できないと，企業は倒産してしまう。

　負債とは異なり，株主資本は返済の必要がない。また，配当を払うことも株主総会で決めることであり，義務ではない。ただし，合理的な理由がないままに長く無配であったり，業績が振るわずに株価が低迷していると，株主は株主総会などで経営陣を厳しく問いただし，議決権の委任状争奪戦を通じて経営陣に交代を迫ることもある。また，株価の低迷している企業は，買収・乗っ取りのターゲットとして狙われやすくなる。

　しかし，配当を支払わなくとも，あるいは株価が下がったまま放置したとしても，企業は倒産することはない。そう考えると，株主資本に比べると，負債には多くの制約があることがわかる。
　一方で，株式を発行するのは手間がかかる。資金の使途や今後の事業戦略などを説明し，投資家を募らなければならない（企業の規模が小さく，親族や親しい友人からの出資だけで資金はまかなえる場合はこの限りではない）。さらに，株式を上場するとなるとさまざまな形での情報開示が必要となり，またコストもかさむ。証券取引所に定期的に報告することをはじめ，アニュアルレポートといった投資家向けの冊子を作成したり，決算発表や株主総会を行ったり，海外の投資家を訪ねて経営陣が世界中を回ったりということが必要となる。特に最近では，国内外で発生した企業の倫理的不祥事の影響から，上場企業に求められる内部統制のレベルが上がっている。社内業務のさまざまなプロセスにおいて非常に細かなルール・規程を整備することが求められる。

Variation of Corporate Financing

Companies usually issue common stock. But some companies also issue preferred stock that promises preferred status. For example, no dividends will be paid on the common stock until the dividends on the preferred stock have been paid, and preferred shareholders have a prior claim on a company's assets when it is liquidated. (Instead, preferred stock usually does not carry voting rights.) Some companies have different classes of common stock. Alphabet (the holding company of Google) split its stock in April 2014 creating two classes of shares, one with voting rights and the other without. Both shares are traded in the stock exchange market. More recently in 2016, Under Armour, a sports apparel company did a similar split.

Debt also comes in many forms. Aside from a fixed interest debt or bonds, there is a floating interest rate debt for which the interest rate is revised periodically during the repayment period. There are a lot of variation of debt issues such as callable bonds which an issuing company has the option to buy them back before maturity at a specified price. Subordinated debt is a loan or security that ranks below other debts with regard to claims on assets or earnings. In the case of default, creditors who own subordinated debt are paid only after all senior debt holders are paid in full. Therefore, subordinate debt is closer to equity.

A convertible bond locates between equity and debt, giving the holder the right to exchange the bond for a predetermined number of stocks at certain times before the bond maturity. The convertible bond is a combined security of a common corporate bond and option discussed in chapter 16.

It is advisable that a company match the cash flows associated with financing with cash flows generated from operations in order to minimize the risk of default. A company committing money in a long-term project should rely on equity finance or long-term debt. A company operating globally and earning foreign currency denominated cash flows, should raise funds in the foreign currency. A mature company promising stable cash flows can utilize debt, but a fast growing company is more relevant to issuing convertible bonds.

● さまざまな資金調達手法

通常の株式は普通株と呼ばれる。普通株に優先して配当が支払われたり，企業が清算した場合に残った財産を優先的に受け取れる等，投資家にとって権利内容が優先的になっているのが優先株式である（その代わりに，優先株式の保有者は議決権を制限されるのが一般的である）。優先株式ではないが，複数の種類の株式を発行する企業もある（日本では優先株式のような権利関係が普通株と異なっている株式を種類株式と呼ぶ）。最近ではグーグルの持ち株会社であるアルファベットや，スポーツ用品メーカーのアンダーアーマーなどが普通株式を議決権のある株式とない株式に分割し，それぞれの株式は証券取引所で取引されている。

負債にもさまざまな種類がある。固定金利だけではなく，返済途中に定期的に金利が見直される変動金利の負債もある。また，満期前に企業が決められた価格で返済できる繰上償還条項付債券や，一般の債権者よりも債務弁済の順位が劣る劣後債などもある。劣後債の投資家は，会社が清算した場合に他の債権者への支払いをすべて終えたあとに，債務を返済される立場になる。そのため劣後債は，負債の一種ではあるものの，株式により近いといえる。

株式と負債の中間にあたるものが転換社債である。転換社債は，社債でありながら，投資家が決められた数の株式に債券を転換できる権利のついた社債であり，通常の社債と，第16章で紹介するオプションが組み合わさった資産といえる。

企業は，債務不履行のリスクを低減させるために，調達する資金にかかわるキャッシュフローを，企業が事業活動において生み出すキャッシュフローとできるだけ一致させる必要がある。企業が携わる投資案件が長期にわたるのであれば，株式か長期負債で資金調達するのが望ましいし，海外に投資をして他国通貨建てのキャッシュフローを得るのであれば，その通貨で資金調達をするほうがいい。また，安定的なキャッシュフローを生み出す成熟した企業は通常の負債で資金調達すべきだが，成長企業はより転換社債のほうが望ましい場合も多い。

⦿ Capital Structure Doesn't Matter

How does a company's choice of capital structure change its market value? The answer is related to taxes. However, to keep things simple, we will begin by ignoring taxes.

The value of a company is determined by its generation of cash flows. These cash flows are produced through business activities, which are unrelated to the sources of financing. The value of the business is unchanged as long as the same amount of capital is employed regardless of whether it is in the form of debt or equity. Therefore, the financing mix or financing choice does not affect the underlying value of the company. The value of the company or the sum of the present value of all cash flows is likened to the size of a pizza, and financing is likened to how the pizza is sliced. The size of the pizza is independent of how it is divided, or sliced. The capital structure only impacts how the pizza is sliced and is irrelevant to the size of the pizza itself.

Figure 11.2 | **Capital Structure Does Not Affect Company Value**

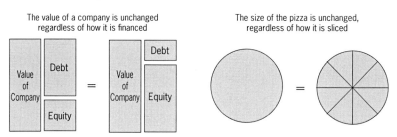

This concept was proven by two Nobel Prize winners, Franco Modigliani and Merton Miller, and is called the Modigliani-Miller (MM) Theorem. This theorem states that the value of a company is unaffected by how the company is financed and that the value of a company cannot increase by changing the mix of the financing.

企業の資本構成は意味がない？

　資金調達の違いによって企業の価値はどう変わるのだろうか。この議論には実際には税金が大きく関わってくるが，議論を単純にするためにまずは税金がない状態から考えよう。

　企業価値は将来的に生み出されるキャッシュフローによって決まる。キャッシュフローは企業の事業活動から生み出されるが，その元手となる資金をどこから調達しようが，事業活動には関係ない。すべて負債で調達しようが，すべて株主資本で調達しようが，同じ金額を使用して行った事業の価値は同じだからである。そう考えると財務活動である資金調達手段は基本的には企業価値とは関係がないことがわかる。このことはよくピザにたとえられる。企業価値，つまり企業のキャッシュフローの現在価値の合計がピザの大きさであり，それをどのように分けるのかが財務活動である。どのようにピザを切り分けたとしても，ピザそのものの大きさが変わるわけではない。資本構成は，企業価値というピザをどう分けるかということだけであって，ピザそのものの大きさには関係ないということである。

図表11.2 ｜ 資金調達で変わらない企業価値

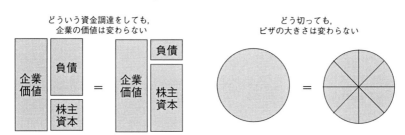

　以上の内容は，ノーベル経済学賞を受賞したフランコ・モジリアーニとマートン・ミラーによって論証されており，その頭の文字を取ってMM理論と呼ばれている。企業価値は，企業の資金調達とは独立しており，企業は資本構成を変更することによって企業価値を高めることはできないということである。

Debt Changes Business Performance

Capital structure does not affect the value of the company. However, a change in the capital structure can change a company's financial performance (see Figure 11.3).

Let's begin by considering a scenario in which a company does not utilize debt. A company needs 10,000 in capital to conduct its business. Supposing a share price of 100, the company would issue 100 shares and its total market value of equity would be 10,000. Its earnings are 1,500, resulting in an earnings per share of 1,500 / 100 = 15. Shareholder return would be 15%: investors purchase a share with a value of 100 and receive earnings of 15.

Now, let's consider a case in which the same company utilizes debt to conduct the same exact business. Again, the company needs capital of 10,000; however, in this case it borrows 5,000 and raises 5,000 in equity. Supposing the same share price of 100, the company would issue 50 shares.

Assuming a 10% interest rate on debt, earnings after interest would be 1,000, resulting in earnings per share of 1,000 / 50 = 20. The shareholder return would increase to 20%: investors purchase a share with a value of 100 and receive earnings of 20.

Figure 11.3 | Debt Changes Business Performance

	No Debt	Debt
Number of Shares	100	50
Price	100	100
Market Capitalization	10,000	5,000
Debt	0	5,000
Market Value	10,000	10,000
Earnings	1,500	1,500
− Interest		500
Earnings after Interest	1,500	1,000
Earnings per Share	15	20
Return on Investment	15%	20%

● 負債によって変わる業績

資本構成によって企業価値は変わらないが、資本構成が変化すると企業の業績は変化する（図表11.3）。

まず負債がない場合を考えよう。ある会社が事業を行うために10,000の資金が必要だとする。株価100とすると株式を100株発行することになり、株式時価総額は10,000である。利益は1,500なので、1株あたり利益は1,500÷100 = 15である。株主は100という株価の資産（株式）に投資して15の利益を得るので、投資の利益率は15%となる。

次に負債を活用して同じ事業を行い、全く同じ業績が上がる場合を考える。同じ事業を行うので、必要な資金はやはり10,000である。ただし、負債で5,000を調達し、5,000を株式で調達する。株価は前回と同様の100で、50株を発行することになる。

負債の利率を10%とすると、金利を支払った後の利益は1,000となる。1株あたり利益は1,000÷50 = 20と計算できる。株主は100の投資をして20の利益を得るので、投資の利益率は20%となる。

図表11.3 ｜ 負債によって変わる業績

	負債がない会社	負債がある会社
株数	100	50
株価	100	100
株式時価総額	10,000	5,000
負債	0	5,000
企業価値	10,000	10,000
利益	1,500	1,500
－金利		500
金利後利益	1,500	1,000
1株あたり利益	15	20
投資利益率	15%	20%

Effect of Debt Leverage

The company in Figure 11.3 is assumed to record profits. But what if the company records losses? Figure 11.4 shows the earnings per share and the return on investment when earnings are negative 1,000. Both the earnings per share and the return on investment are lower if the company employs debt compared to no debt.

Figure 11.4 | Debt Changes Business Performance (loss)

	No Debt	Debt
Number of Shares	100	50
Price	100	100
Market Capitalization Capitalization	10,000	5,000
Debt	0	5,000
Market Value	10,000	10,000
Earnings − Interest	− 1,000	− 1,000 500
Earnings after Interest	− 1,000	− 1,500
Earnings per Share	− 10	− 30
Return on Investment	− 10%	− 30%

Figures 11.3 and 11.4 illustrate that profits, losses and shareholder returns (positive as well as negative) increase when a company utilizes debt. Debt amplifies profits and losses. It resembles the effect of a lever, and so is referred to as "leverage" (also called debt leverage or financial leverage).

Excessive leverage is frequently the cause of crisis for companies. Leverage works well to generate more profits when a company achieves solid results, but it can also wreak considerable damage when performance is poor. Leverage increases the volatility of a company's performance and increases the risk as well. The additional risk is called financial risk.

● 負債によるレバレッジ

　図表 11.3 の例は利益が計上されていたが，損失が出ている場合を考えてみよう。図表 11.4 は利益がマイナスの 1,000（損失が 1,000）だった場合の 1 株あたり利益と投資利益率を表わしている。負債がない場合に比べ，負債がある場合のほうが 1 株あたり利益，投資利益率ともに低くなっていることがわかる。

図表 11.4　負債によって変わる業績（損失の場合）

	負債がない会社	負債がある会社
株数	100	50
株価	100	100
株式時価総額	10,000	5,000
負債	0	5,000
企業価値	10,000	10,000
利益	−1,000	−1,000
−金利		500
金利後利益	−1,000	−1,500
1 株あたり利益	−10	−30
投資利益率	−10%	−30%

　これらの 2 つの図表の例からわかるように，企業が負債を活用すると，利益を計上している場合にはさらに利益が高まり，損失を計上している場合にはその損失が膨らむ。負債は利益，損失を増幅させるのである。このことが「てこ」の活用のように見えることから，「レバレッジ」効果という。

　企業が危機に陥るときは，レバレッジを効かせすぎていたということが原因ということが多くある。レバレッジは業績が黒字の場合には非常に効率的に利益を上げることができるが，業績が赤字の場合のダメージも大きい。レバレッジは企業の業績の変動性を大きくし，企業のリスクを高める。この増分のリスクは財務リスクと呼ばれる。

Please note that the total return attributed to shareholders and creditors (interest payments and earnings after interest) are constant regardless of whether debt is utilized or not. The value of a company does not change because the total amount of earnings or cash flows does not change, although the distribution of them changes. Therefore, leverage does not create value; rather, it only impacts the slicing of value.

Let us think about it from another perspective. Figure 11.5 demonstrates the example from Figure 11.3 from an investor's perspective. The return on a single share of the company without debt is 15% and is increased to 20% with the use of debt. An investor can also attain the same effect of leverage that can be employed by a company.

An investor can borrow money from a bank to invest in shares. In this case let's assume the investor purchases a single share for 100 and then invests an additional 100 using funds that he/she borrowed from the bank, so that he/she now owns 2 shares. The total return from two shares would be $15 \times 2 = 30$, from which he/she would make interest payments on the borrowings.

If an investor can borrow money with the same interest rate as the company (in theory, the single interest rate should be applied to everyone since it would be invested in the same business bearing the same degree of risk), then the interest rate would be 10% and the interest payment would be 10. Subtracting the interest payments from the earnings, the investor's net earnings would be 20 and the return on investment would be 20%. Thus, an investor can achieve the same rate of return as the company by employing leverage.

ここで，負債を活用しようがしまいが，企業が株主と債権者に提供するリターンの合計額（金利の額と金利支払い後の利益の合計額）は変化していないことに注意してほしい。利益，キャッシュフローの分配は変わるもののその合計額が変わらないのであれば，企業価値は変化しない。レバレッジは価値を生み出すものではなく，やはり価値をどう切り分けるのかということでしかないのである。

　もうひとつ別の面から考えてみよう。図表11.5は図表11.3の事業の例を投資家の立場から見たものである。負債がない企業に1株投資した場合の利益率は15%であったが，負債を活用することにより20%となった。この効果は企業が負債を活用したためだが，同じことは投資家によっても可能なのである。

　投資家は自ら借入れを行い，自分の資金と合わせて事業に投資することもできる。この例では，投資家が1株に投資するためには100という資産が必要だが，さらに100借り入れることにより，投資家は2株に投資することができるようになる。2株からの利益は15 × 2 = 30であり，そこから借り入れた資金の金利を支払うことになる。

　投資家が企業と同じ金利で借入れをすることができれば（理論的には同じ事業に投資するのであれば，リスクは同じであるから，誰が借りても利率は同じになるはずである。これが，資本市場が効率的に正しく機能している，という状態である），金利は10%の10である。株式投資からの利益から利息分を差し引いた投資家の利益額は20，利益率は20%となる。企業が負債を活用した場合の利益率と同一の利益率を投資家独自でも達成できるのである。

Figure 11.5 | Leverage by an Investor

	Buy 1 Share	Buy 2 Shares with Borrowing
Investment	100	200
— Borrowing	0	100
Net Investment	100	100
Earnings on Share	15	30
— Interest	0	10
Net Earnings	15	20
Return on Investment	15%	20%

A company's financial results can be altered by the use of leverage; however, through personal leverage, an investor can achieve the same results. If a company pursues a strategy that can be replicated by investors on their own, then the strategy does not create value.

図表 11.5　投資家によるレバレッジ

	1株に投資する場合	借入れして2株に投資する場合
株式投資額	100	200
－借入れ	0	100
純投資額	100	100
株式投資からの利益	15	30
－金利	0	10
純利益	15	20
投資利益率	15%	20%

　企業が負債を活用することで業績は変わるが，同じことは投資家でもできるということだ。誰でも同じことができるのならば，その活動が価値を生み出すことはないのである。

Chapter 12 Optimal Capital Structure

> **Points!**
> - Debt increases the cost of equity due to financial risk
> - Utilizing debt initially increases the value of a company due to the tax saving effect, but excessive usage of debt decreases the value of a company due to the financial distress cost
> - It is very difficult to find where the optimal capital structure or debt ratio is

● Capital Structure and Cost of Capital

Consider the relationship between debt, company value and the cost of capital. Consider an unlevered company (company U) and a levered company (company L), both of which produce constant earnings and will maintain the same profitability in the future. Company U has no debt, and company L has debt of 1,000. Suppose that both companies conduct the same business, use the same assets, and produce exactly the same profits.

Because we assume constant earnings, we can assume the company requires ongoing investments to recover the depreciation of its assets (net investment is zero); therefore, profits are equal to cash flow (FCF). In addition, since profits and the cash flows are to be constant in the future, we can apply a perpetuity formula for valuation.

The interest rate on debt, or the cost of debt (r_d), is assumed to be 5%. Both companies produce the same profits and cash flows of 300 (see Figure 12.1). Because both companies operate the same business, the cost of capital (the cost of total assets, r_a) for both companies are identical at 10%. Given these assumptions, the value of companies U and L would both be 300 / 10% = 3,000.

第12章 最適資本構成

> **ポイント!**
> - 負債を活用すると，財務リスクの影響により企業の株主資本コストは上昇する
> - 負債の活用は，節税効果の影響を通じて企業価値を増加させるが，過度な負債の活用は倒産コストの増大を通じて企業価値を低下させる
> - 最適資本構成は存在するが，それがどこであるのかは難しい問題である

● 資本構成と資本コスト

負債と企業価値，および資本コストの関係を数値例で見ていこう。同じ利益率で同じ利益を将来的にも上げ続ける企業U（レバレッジを行っていない）と企業L（レバレッジを行っている）を想定する。企業Uは負債のない会社であり，企業Lは負債を1,000活用しているが，企業Uと企業Lは全く同じ事業を全く同じ資産を使用して行っており，全く同じ利益を上げているとする。

将来の業績が一定だというこの前提においては，減価償却費で資産が目減りする分だけ補修的に投資を行うことになるから（すなわち，純投資額がゼロ），利益とキャッシュフロー（FCF）が同額になる。また，将来的に利益・キャッシュフローの額が変わらないため，永久年金式が活用できる。

負債にかかる金利，すなわち負債コスト（r_d）は5%とする。利益およびキャッシュフローは300と同じである（図表12.1）。両社は全く同じビジネスを行っていることから，資本コスト（企業の資産全体にかかるコスト，r_a，aはassetを意味する）も同一であり，10%とする。すると，企業Uおよび企業Lの価値は300÷10%＝3,000となる。

Figure 12.1 | Cash Flow for Company U and Company L

	U	L
Profit	300	300
Interest Expense = CF to Debt		50
Net Income = CF to Equity	300	250
Total CF to Capital Providers	300	300

Company L utilizes debt of 1,000, so the value of equity for L is 2,000. With the perpetuity formula, the cost of equity (r_e) for company L would be 12.5%:

$$\text{Value of Equity} = 2,000 = \frac{250}{r_e}$$

The value and risk of the two companies are identical; however, company L's cash flows to equity shareholders are more volatile so the financial risk that equity shareholders bear increases. As a result, the cost of equity increases.

Figure 12.2 illustrates this relationship. The capital structure does not affect the value of the company; and r_a, the WACC in this case, is constant. Only the cost of equity changes. It increases because financial risk is increased due to leverage.

Figure 12.2 | Capital Structure, Company Value, and the Cost of Capital

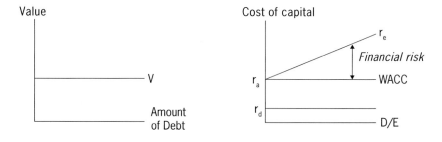

図表 12.1　企業 U と企業 L のキャッシュフロー

	U	L
利益	300	300
支払利息＝債権者への CF		50
純利益＝株主への CF	300	250
資金提供者への CF 合計	300	300

企業 L は負債（D）を 1,000 活用しているから株式の価値（E）は 2,000 となる。また，企業 L の株主資本コスト（r_e）は，以下の永久年金式により 12.5% と計算される。

$$株式の価値 = 2,000 = \frac{250}{r_e}$$

事業そのものは同じなので，企業価値もリスクも同一だが，株主のキャッシュフローの取り分はレバレッジにより変動性が高まるため，企業 L の株主の負う財務リスクは高まる。そのため株主資本コストが大きくなるのである。

この関係を示したのが図表 12.2 である。企業の資本構成は企業価値に影響を与えず，また，r_a，すなわち WACC は一定のままだ。株主資本コストだけが変化し，レバレッジによる財務リスクの増大の影響を受け上昇していく。

図表 12.2　企業の資本構成と企業価値，資本コスト

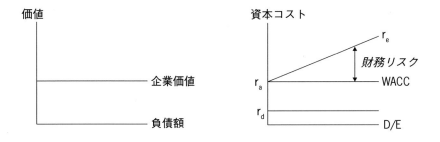

Rearranging the formula of WACC, the cost of equity can be expressed in the following way. The cost of equity in this case is calculated to be 12.5%, using the numbers in the example above.

$$r_a = \frac{D}{D+E} r_d + \frac{E}{D+E} r_e$$

$$r_e = r_a + \frac{D}{E}(r_a - r_d)$$

$$12.5\% = 10\% + \frac{1,000}{2,000}(10\% - 5\%)$$

Tax Contributes to Company Value

So far, we ignored the discussion of taxes; however, in practice companies must pay taxes. When a company employs debt and pays interest, the profits subject to corporate tax decrease and tax payments are reduced. As a result, the value of the company will increase. This is referred to as the "tax savings effect" or the "interest tax shield."

Using the example of companies U and L, let's consider the value of the companies when profits are taxed at a rate of 40%; r_a and r_d are unchanged, 10% and 5%, respectively (Figure 12.3).

Figure 12.3 | Tax Contributes to Company Value

	U	L
Profit	300	300
Interest Expense = CF to Debt		50
Profit Before Tax	300	250
Tax	120	100
Net Income = CF to Equity	180	150
Total CF to Capital Providers	180	200
Tax Savings Effect		20

WACC の式を変形すると，株主資本コストは以下のように表わされ，先ほどの数値を代入すると，やはり 12.5% と計算される。

$$r_a = \frac{D}{D+E} r_d + \frac{E}{D+E} r_e$$

$$r_e = r_a + \frac{D}{E}(r_a - r_d)$$

$$12.5\% = 10\% + \frac{1,000}{2,000}(10\% - 5\%)$$

● 税金が企業価値に与える影響

ここまでは税金がないという前提の中で説明をしてきたが，実際には企業は税金を支払う必要がある。企業が負債を活用し，支払利息を支払うと，その分課税対象となる利益が少なくなり，支払う税金が少なくて済む。そのため，企業の価値は高まる。このことを負債の節税効果と呼ぶ。

企業 U と L の数値例を引き続き使用し，企業の利益に対して 40%（税率，T）の税金が発生する場合の企業価値を考えよう。r_a は 10%，r_d は 5% と変わらない（図表 12.3）。

図表 12.3 ｜ 税金が企業価値に与える影響

	U	L
利益	300	300
支払利息＝債権者への CF		50
税前利益	300	250
税金	120	100
純利益＝株主への CF	180	150
資金提供者への CF 合計	180	200
節税効果		20

Company U pays taxes of 120, which is 40% of the profit before tax of 300; so the net income or cash flow to equity shareholders is 180. On the other hand, company L pays interest on debt of 50 and pays taxes of 100, which is 40% of the profit before tax of 250. The net income of company L is 150. However, the cash flows that a company provides to investors are not limited to the net income but also include interest payments to debt holders. Total cash flows available for capital providers generated by company L comprise the net income of 150 plus the interest payment of 50. In total, cash flows are 200, which is 20 greater in comparison to company L. This is the tax savings effect.

The tax savings effect increases as a company utilizes more debt. The left chart of Figure 12.4 illustrates the relationship between company value and leverage. The diagonal line reflects that the borrowing increases the company's value due to the tax savings effect.

The value of company U is calculated to be 180 / 10% = 1,800. On the other hand, the value of company L is greater as a result of the tax savings. Since company L is assumed to produce a sustainable level of profits, its interest payments and tax savings would be constant going forward. Therefore, the value of the interest tax savings would be:

$$\frac{D \times r_d \times T}{r_d} = D \times T = 1{,}000 \times 40\% = 400$$

(It is also calculated as the increase in cash flows of 20, that are due to the use of debt, divided by r_d, 20/5%=400.)

Hence the value of company L is:

The value of company U + PV of the tax savings = 1,800 + 400 = 2,200

企業 U は，税前利益 300 に対する 40% にあたる税金 120 を支払うため，税引後の純利益＝株主へのキャッシュフローは 180 となる。一方で，負債を使用しているため 50 の利息を支払う企業 L は，税前利益が 250 であり，税金はその 40% である 100 となる。企業 L の純利益は 150 である。しかし，企業が投資家に対して提供できるキャッシュフローは株主に対する利益だけではなく，銀行あるいは債権者に対する利息も含まれる。企業 L が資金提供者にもたらすキャッシュフローは税後利益の 150 に支払利息の 50 を加えた 200 となり，企業 U に比べて 20 だけ増加している。これが節税効果である。

　節税効果は企業が負債を使用するに従って大きくなる。企業の価値と負債の関係を表わすと図表 12.4 の左図のようになる。右上がりの直線は，企業が負債を使用するにつれて，節税効果が増加し企業価値が高まっていくことを示している。

　企業 U の価値は，180 ÷ 10% = 1,800 となる。一方，企業 L の価値は節税効果の影響で増加する。企業 L の業績は今後も継続していくことから，企業 L が支払う利息も一定であり，税金を引き下げる効果も継続する。そのため支払利息による節税効果の価値は永久年金式により以下のように計算できる。

$$\frac{D \times r_d \times T}{r_d} = D \times T = 1{,}000 \times 40\% = 400$$

（負債によって増加したキャッシュフロー 20 を r_d で割っても同じ値となる。20 ÷ 5% = 400。）

　そのため，企業 L の価値は以下のようになる。

$$企業 U の価値 ＋ 節税効果 ＝ 1{,}800 ＋ 400 ＝ 2{,}200$$

Figure 12.4 | Effect of Tax Savings

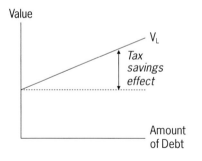
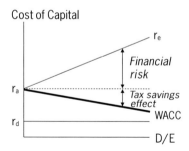

Since company L has debt of 1,000, the value of equity is 1,200. The cash flows to equity are 150, so the cost of equity would be 12.5% with the perpetuity formula:

$$\text{Value of Equity} = 1{,}200 = \frac{150}{r_e}$$

Without debt, the cost of equity is 10% and equal to the cost of all assets (r_a). As seen earlier, the cost of equity for company L has increased to 12.5%, corresponding to the increased risk due to the use of leverage. The cost of equity is increased by the amount of financial risk due to leverage.

When tax is considered, as we discussed in chapter 10 WACC is expressed as:

$$\text{WACC} = \frac{D}{V} \times (1-T) r_d + \frac{E}{V} \times r_e$$

Using our example, the WACC of company L is calculated as:

$$\frac{1{,}000}{2{,}200} \times (1-40\%) \times 5\% + \frac{1{,}200}{2{,}200} \times 12.5\% = 8.18\%$$

This reflects how the WACC of company L declines due to the tax savings effect.

図表 12.4 | 節税効果の影響

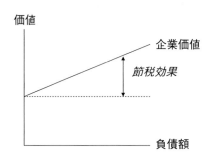
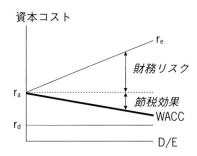

企業Lの負債は1,000だったので，株式の価値は1,200である。株式へのキャッシュフローは150なので，株主資本コストはやはり以下の永久年金式により12.5％と計算される。

$$株式の価値 = 1,200 = \frac{150}{r_e}$$

負債がない場合は株主資本コストは企業トータルの資本コストr_aと同じ10％だったわけだが，企業Lの株主資本コストは負債を活用することによりリスクが高まるので，先に見たように12.5％に上昇する。レバレッジによる財務リスクの分だけ株主資本コストが高くなるのである。

また，税金を加味した場合，WACCの式は第10章で見た通り

$$WACC = \frac{D}{V} \times (1-T) r_d + \frac{E}{V} \times r_e$$

となるから，数値を式に当てはめると，企業LのWACCは

$$\frac{1,000}{2,200} \times (1-40\%) \times 5\% + \frac{1,200}{2,200} \times 12.5\% = 8.18\%$$

と計算される。企業LのWACCは負債の導入により，節税効果分低下していることが表われている。

Costs of Financial Distress

Leverage can increase the value of a company; however, there is a limit. Costs related to financial distress come into play when a company utilizes too much debt. When a company faces financial distress, business activities are constrained. A company may not be able to procure raw materials or capital equipment and may not be able to sell its products or services. Additionally, employees may become distracted and unmotivated. The costs of financial distress depend both on the likelihood of distress and on the magnitude of the costs encountered if distress occurs.

The value of a company initially increases due to the tax advantages as the company takes on debt. However, the cost of financial distress grows more substantial as the debt burden increases. Hence, the overall value of the company is:

Value of Company = Value of all equity financed
+ Present value of tax savings
− Present value of the costs of financial distress

Figure 12.5 | Optimal Capital Structure

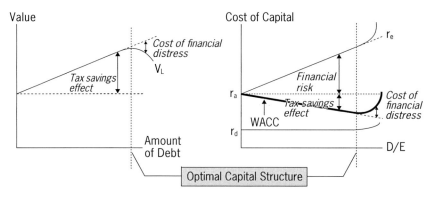

The increase in value due to the tax savings effect could be offset due to financial distress costs. In the same manner, the WACC of the company would decline due to the tax savings effect but would rise at some point due to the increase in financial

企業の倒産コスト

　実際には，負債を活用することによって企業価値が高まるのはある程度までであり，負債を際限なく活用すればいいというわけではない。企業が負債比率を高めすぎると倒産リスクが生じる。倒産が近づくと企業は事業活動を継続することが困難になるからである。原料や資材が購入できなくなったり，販売活動も難しくなる。従業員のモチベーションも下がるだろう。このような倒産に直面する確率とそれにより発生する悪影響全体が倒産コストとしてとらえられる。

　企業価値は，節税効果により負債の活用とともに上昇していく。しかし，ある一定の点から倒産コストが発生しそのコストは負債比率とととともに大きくなっていく。つまり，企業価値は以下のように表わされる。

　　　　企業価値＝負債のない場合の企業価値
　　　　　　　　＋節税効果の現在価値
　　　　　　　　－倒産コストの現在価値

図表 12.5　最適資本構成

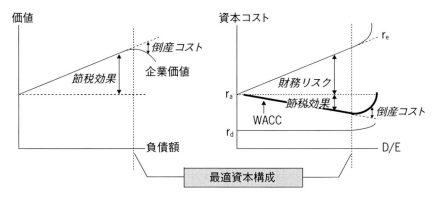

　節税効果により増大していく企業の価値は，倒産コストの影響で減少する。同様に，節税効果の影響により低下する WACC は，倒産コストの影響で上昇する。その結果，図表 12.5 にみられるように企業価値が最大となり，WACC

distress costs. As a result, there is an optimal point that maximizes the value of a company while minimizing the WACC, as seen in Figure 12.5. That point is called the optimal capital structure.

Theory and Practice for Financial Choices

The theory behind the financial choices that explain the optimal capital structure is known as "trade-off theory" and is called this because there is a trade-off relationship between the value of tax savings and the value of financial distress costs.

An alternative theory is the "pecking-order theory," which states that a company prefers to issue debt rather than equity if internal financing is insufficient. It is called this based on the idea that there is a pecking order with regards to financing choices. Pecking-order theory is based on the notion of information asymmetry and that the top management of a company knows more about their company's future prospects, risks and values than outside investors do.

Suppose that the share price of a company is 100 yen, but the top management of that company believes that the true value is 120 yen. In this case, would top management decide to issue shares? The answer is no because they would not want to sell shares worth 120 yen for 100 yen. What if they think the true value is 80 yen? In this case, they would be inclined to issue shares because selling shares worth 80 yen for 100 yen is a good deal. This indicates that issuing shares may reflect management's lack of confidence in the company's share price or in its future. The theory suggests that a company would postpone issuing shares and instead would rely on debt issuance when it needs additional cash to avoid the negative signaling effect.

が最小となる点が生じる。ここが企業の最適資本構成である。

◉ 資金調達を巡る理論と実際

　節税効果と倒産コストを考え，そのバランスの中で最適な資本構成を示す資金調達の理論が「トレード・オフ理論」である。企業が負債を増やせば節税効果の影響で価値は高まるが，一方で倒産コストが発生して価値が下落するため，両者にはトレード・オフがあることからこの名称がついている。

　もう1つ有名な理論は「ペッキング・オーダー理論」と呼ばれるもので，これは企業が資金調達が必要になった場合，まずは負債によって調達を行い，その後に最後の手段として株式による資金調達を行うという理論である。資金調達には「突っつく順番」があるということである。この理論は企業経営者のほうが，外部の投資家よりも企業の将来性，リスクおよび価値をよく知っているという，情報の非対称性を前提としている。

　たとえば，ある企業の現在の株価が100円であるのに，この企業の経営者は本来の株価は120円だと考えているとする。この場合，経営者は株式を発行するだろうか。120円であるはずの株式を100円で売り出したいとは思わないだろう。逆に，経営者が本来の株価は80円だと考えていたらどうか。80円の株式を100円で発行できれば得なので，株式を発行したくなると考えられる。このことから，企業が株式を発行することは，経営者の自信の欠如を示すことになり得るということである。このために，企業は資金を必要としても，株式による調達をなるべく行わず，まずは負債によって資金調達を行うと，この理論では考える。

In practice, it is very difficult for companies to find an optimal capital structure or debt ratio. However, there is general agreement with regards to what industries are better suited for low and high debt ratios. Figure 12.6 summarizes this:

Figure 12.6 | Business Characteristics and Preferable Debt Ratio

Debt Ratio	
High	Low
Cash Cow	High Operational Risk
Regulated	Start-up
Holding Many Tangible Assets	

A cash cow business is one that produces consistent cash flows. Businesses such as these that can easily service debt can take advantage of the benefit of tax savings. Regulated businesses are not likely to have problems making fixed payments because their profits are generally stable, so they can pursue the available tax advantages. Companies with a high reliance on tangible assets can generally have high debt ratios because they could sell assets to make payments if faced with financial difficulty.

On the other hand, it is not advisable for start-up ventures or businesses with high operational risk to rely on debt that require fixed cash payments. If companies with unpredictable profit and cash flows raise money in the form of debt, the risk of bankruptcy can be high. That is one reason why emerging equity markets, such as the Mothers market established by the Tokyo Stock Exchange, are important and function to provide sufficient funds to small- and mid-sized companies that exhibit greater volatility.

For a long time in Japan, it has been a prevailing idea that zero debt is the most preferable strategy. Zero debt is in fact optimal for maximizing accounting profits (net income). However, it is not optimal in the context of value creation and finance. A zero debt strategy does not maximize the value of a company.

企業価値を最大化する最適資本構成が負債比率何パーセントなのかということは実際には非常に難しい問題である。それでも，事業の特性に応じて負債比率を高くしたほうがいいのか，あるいは低くしたほうがいいのかに関しては，一般的に図表 12.6 のようにいわれている。

図表 12.6 ▏事業特性と一般的に望ましい資本構成

負債比率	
高	低
金のなる木 規制産業 有形固定資産多い	事業リスク高い ベンチャー

　金のなる木はキャッシュが安定的に生み出される事業である。このような事業においては負債を抱えても問題なく，ある程度，節税効果を狙っていくことができる。また，規制産業は業績が安定しているため固定利払いにも支払いが滞ることはあまりなく，やはり節税効果を狙っていくことができるだろう。有形固定資産が多い企業も，もし支払いが滞ったとしても資産を売って支払いにあてることができると考えられ，一般的には負債比率が高くてもよいといわれている。

　反対に，事業リスクが高かったり，また起業後間もないベンチャーなどは定期的な固定利払いが要求される負債に頼るのは望ましくない。業績が安定しない中で負債による資金調達を行えば，倒産のリスクが極めて高くなる。そのため，東証マザーズのような新興株式市場がベンチャーや事業の安定しない中小企業向けの資金供給源として重要視されているのである。

　なお，日本では長らく，無借金の状態が経営上望ましいという考えが支配的だった。確かに，会計利益（純利益）を最大化するためには，無借金の状態が最も望ましい資本構成といえる。しかし，価値創造，ファイナンスの観点からはこの限りではない。企業価値を最大化する最適資本構成は無借金の状態ではないからである。

Chapter 13 Payout Policy

> **Points!**
> - ✓ A company returns or pays out cash to investors, such as through dividends and repurchasing shares
> - ✓ Payout policy neither creates nor destroys value but the signaling effect can affect the value of a company
> - ✓ Shareholders special benefit plans are very popular in Japan

● Dividends

Dividends are the means of returning the cash generated by a company to its shareholders. When a company earns profits, it may distribute them to its shareholders in the form of dividends. Dividends neither create nor destroy value because they are essentially just the movement of cash.

Assume that a company with a value of $1,000,000 issues 100,000 shares, each with a price of $10. When the company pays $1 per share as a dividend, $100,000 flows to shareholders. As a result, the value of the company is reduced to $900,000 and the share price will drop to $9. However, the funds held by each shareholder are the total of the share with a value of $9 and the dividend payment of $1. The cash transfer does not influence value; so the dividend policy is irrelevant to value.

● Share Repurchases

There is another mechanism for companies to return cash to shareholders. Share (stock) repurchases occur when a company buys its own shares back from shareholders. After Japanese law lifted a ban on treasury shares in 2001, many companies have implemented share repurchases in Japan.

第13章 資金還元

> **ポイント！**
> ✓ 企業は配当支払いや自社株買いといった形で投資家に資金を返還する
> ✓ 資金還元は企業価値に中立であるがシグナルの影響は無視できない
> ✓ 株主優待制度は日本では人気が高い

● 配 当

　配当は企業が生み出した価値を株主に還元する手法の1つである。企業は利益をあげ，株主に分配する。この分配される利益が配当である。配当自体は単なる資金の移動であるため，価値を創造したり，あるいは破壊したりするものではない。

　ここに企業価値が1,000,000ドルで100,000株発行する企業があったとする。株価は10ドルと計算できる。この企業が1株あたり1ドルの配当を行うとすると，100,000ドルが企業から流出し投資家にわたる。すると，企業の価値は900,000となるため株価は9ドルに下がる。しかし，投資家の取り分は9ドルの株式と1ドルの配当をあわせた10ドルであり，配当前と変わらない。このように，現金が移動するだけなので，価値は増減しない。配当政策は価値に影響を与えないのである。

● 自社株買い

　企業の資金還元にはもう1つの方法がある。一度発行した株式を買い取る自社株買いである。日本では2001年に「金庫株」制度が解禁されて以降，多くの企業が実施している。

While dividends result in payments to all shareholders uniformly, share repurchases represent payments to a limited number of shareholders. Both are similar in that they are forms of cash payment to shareholders. Therefore, share repurchases are also value neutral.

Let's revisit the company with a value of $1,000,000, 100,000 shares and a share price of $10. Assuming the company repurchases 10,000 shares, the company would pay out $100,000, and the value of the company would be reduced to $900,000 after completing the repurchase. The number of shares would decrease to 90,000, so the share price would remain unchanged at $10. Shareholders who do not participate in the share repurchase would continue to hold shares with a value of $10; shareholders who sell shares would receive $10 per share in cash. The total funds held by the shareholders remain uniform.

⊙ How Do Companies Decide on Payout ?

Given that returning cash to the investors or payout is seen as value neutral, how does a company decide on the amount of dividends or buyback? Payout imposes cash outflows on the company and the company must have sufficient cash in order to make the payments. Thus, payouts should be based on cash demands in the context of how many attractive investment opportunities exist.

In this context, attractive opportunities mean those with a positive NPV. When a company is presented with a number of positive NPV opportunities, the company should use its cash for investment and should forego a dividend or share repurchase. If a company undertakes the positive NPV investments instead of paying dividends, the value of the company will increase, leading to a rise in the share price by an amount greater than the foregone dividend payment. If the company has a strong desire to pay dividends despite having positive NPV projects, the company will have to finance the dividend payments by raising capital.

配当が株主全員に対して一律に現金を返すのに対し，自社株買いは一部の希望者のみに返すという違いはあるが，企業が現金を返すということに違いはない。したがって，自社株買いも価値には中立である。

配当の説明で使用した，企業価値が 1,000,000 ドルで 100,000 株発行する会社の例で確認しよう。株価は 10 ドルであり，この会社が自己株式 10,000 株を買い戻すとする。企業が支払う金額は 100,000 ドルなので，企業の価値は 900,000 となる。自社株購入により株数は 90,000 に減っているから，株価は 10 ドルで変わらない。自社株買いに応じなかった投資家は 10 ドルの株を保有したままであり，自社株買いに応じて株式を売却した投資家は現金 10 ドルを得ている。いずれにしても投資家の取り分は変わらない。

● 資金還元の決定規準

　資金還元が価値に中立だとすれば，企業は何を基準に配当額・自社株買い額を決めるべきなのであろうか。株主に資金還元を行うということは，その分企業から現金が出ていくということだから，資金還元を行うためには現金に余裕が必要だということである。資金還元は資金需要，つまりどれだけ企業に魅力的な投資案件が存在するのかとの見合いで判断すべきなのである。

　ここで言う魅力的な投資案件とは，NPV がプラスの投資案件という意味である。もし NPV がプラスの投資案件が多数あるのであれば，配当や自社株買いなどせずに投資すべきある。NPV がプラスの投資を行えば，理論上企業価値は高まり，結果として資金還元額以上の株価の上昇がもたらされる。このことは，NPV がプラスの投資があり，その投資に資金を振り向けなければならない状況において，どうしても配当をしたいのであれば，配当と同時に新たに資金調達すべきだということを意味している。

Conversely, when a company has only negative NPV investment opportunities, the company should not use its cash for investments but instead should pay dividends or buy back its own shares. Investing in negative NPV projects would destroy value and, theoretically lead to a decline in the share price.

Dividend payments and share repurchases are less relevant to growing companies with large numbers of attractive investment opportunities, and more relevant to mature companies suffering from a lack of investment opportunities.

It became a popular topic of conversation in 2012 when Apple announced that it would resume dividend payments for the first time since 1995 and that it also planned to repurchase shares. Dividend decisions reflect the cash demands and growth potential of a company, so dividend-related announcements often create big discussions.

◉ Dividend Signaling

Because a dividend is not a mandatory payout, the decision to increase or decrease dividends reaches investors as a signal that indicates the condition and prospects of a company. Companies handle dividend announcements carefully because of this signaling effect.

When a company increases dividends, for example, what do investors think? As stated above, unlike the interest payments from borrowing, a company is not obligated to pay dividends. Deciding to increase dividends indicates that top management is confident in its future performance. This is positive dividend signaling.

On the other hand, increasing dividends may imply that future growth opportunities are exhausted because top management does not need cash for future investments. This is negative dividend signaling.

逆にNPVがマイナスの投資案件しかなければ，投資などせず配当や自社株買いをすべきである。NPVがマイナスの案件に投資することは価値の毀損であり，理論上株価の下落をもたらすためである。

つまり，有益な投資機会を多数もつ成長企業においては，資金還元を行う意味はない一方で，有益な投資機会がそれほどない成熟企業においては，資金還元が有効なのである。

1995年から無配を続けていたアップルが2012年3月に配当の再開と自社株買いを発表すると大きな話題となった。これらが話題となるのは配当が企業の資金需要と成長可能性を反映していると考えられるからである。

配当のシグナル

配当額はあらかじめ決まっているものではないため，その増減の意思決定が企業の状態を示すシグナル（情報）として投資家に届く。シグナルは企業の意図どおりとならないことがあるため，配当の意思決定と発表に企業は非常に慎重になることが多い。

たとえば，ある企業が配当を増額（増配）する場合，投資家はこの企業の状態をどのように考えるだろうか。前述のように配当は支払利息と異なってその支払いが義務付けられているわけではない。これをあえて増加させるということは，将来的な業績見通しが明るく，経営陣の自信が表われているともいえる。これが配当の「良いシグナル」である。

一方で配当を増額するということは，その分資金が不要だと経営陣が考えていることを意味するから，成長機会の枯渇を反映しているのかもしれない。これが配当の「悪いシグナル」である。

Decreasing dividends carries the same positive/negative signaling in the reverse directions. Dividend signaling is tricky because it does not always go as planned.

Japanese companies have traditionally taken a stable dividend policy, paying the same amount of dividends regardless of the level of profits. More recently, however, an increasing number of companies are paying dividends that are linked with profits or setting payout ratio targets.

○ Share Repurchase Signaling

Share repurchases send signals to investors similar to those indicated by dividend increase announcements. They provide an additional signal about the value of the shares. It is assumed a company would not buy an overpriced stock, even if it is its own. Therefore, buying back shares implies that top management judges the current share price to be undervalued, and the decision to buy back its own shares conveys a strong message that the current share price is cheap. The implicit message of share repurchase signaling may be received favorably and so be a factor in driving up share price.

○ Share Repurchases Do Not Affect Share Price

Share repurchases decrease the number of shares traded in the market. Decreasing the number of shares can improve the financial measures of the company on the whole. For example, earnings per share would increase because net income would not change while the number of the shares decreases. Since share repurchases compress equity on the balance sheet, ROE would also increase, as does ROA, after share repurchases. However, unlike changes in other financial measures, it should not always raise the share price.

配当を減額する場合には増額と逆に，やはり正負両方のシグナルが出る。配当のシグナルは，なかなか思いどおりにならないために厄介なのである。

日本企業は伝統的に一定額の配当をするという安定配当を行ってきた。しかし，最近では利益に連動して配当をする企業，たとえば配当性向（利益の何パーセントを配当するのかという割合）を目標あるいは目安にする企業が増えてきている。

● 自社株買いのシグナル

自社株買いを行うと，増配と同じシグナルが発生し投資家に届く。加えて，自社株の場合にはさらに強いシグナルがある。自社の株式であったとしても，もし割高だったら企業は購入しないはずである。そのため，自社株買いを行うということは，その企業の経営陣が自社の株価が割安だと判断していると考えることができるのである。自社株買いには，今の株価が割安だという強いメッセージがこめられる。この暗黙のメッセージが「よいシグナル」となって，自社株買いの決定が株価の上昇要因となることがみられる。

● 自社株買いしても株価は変わらない

自社株買いを行うと市中に出回る企業の株数が減る。実はこの影響で企業の財務数値は軒並み改善する。たとえば，EPSは1株あたりの利益だが，自社株買いを行うからといって利益が減るわけではないため，株数が減れば上昇する。自社株買いをすればB/S上の株主資本が小さくなるのでROEは上昇する。またB/Sそのものも小さくなるのでROAも上昇する。このように財務数値は改善するが，だからといって必然的に株価が上昇するわけではない。

Figure 13.1 illustrates the financial condition of a company before and after the share repurchase. The market value of the company is 100 shares × 200 = 20,000. The company records earnings of 1,000, so EPS would be 1,000 / 100 shares = 10. The PER is the share price of 200 / EPS of 10 = 20.

Figure 13.1 | Effect of Share Repurchases on a Company's Value

Market Value	20,000	Earnings	1,000
Number of Shares	100	EPS	10
Share Price	200	PER	20
Share Repurchase Amount	2,000		
Number of Shares	10		
Share Price	200		
Market Value after Repurchase (correct)	18,000	Earnings	1,000
Number of Shares	90	EPS	11
Share Price	200	PER	18
Market Value after Repurchase (incorrect)	20,000	Earnings	1,000
Number of Shares	90	EPS	11
Share Price	222	PER	20

Suppose that the company decides to repurchase 10 shares and pays cash to acquire its shares from the market. Given the current price of 200, the company would pay 10 shares × 200 = 2,000. Therefore, the value of the company after the share repurchase would be 18,000, subtracting the cash payment of 2,000 from the original value of 20,000. The remaining number of shares would be 90 and the share price after repurchase would be calculated as 18,000 / 90 = 200, which is unchanged from the initial share price.

図表 13.1 は自社株買いを行う前と後における企業の状況を示した例である。ある 100 株を発行している企業の株価が 200 だったとする。企業価値は 100 株 × 200 ＝ 20,000 である。利益は 1,000 であり，EPS は 1,000 ÷ 100 株 ＝ 10 である。PER は株価 200 ÷ EPS10 ＝ 20 倍である。

図表 13.1　自社株買いの企業価値への影響

企業価値		20,000	利益	1,000
	株数	100	EPS	10
	株価	200	PER	20
自社株買い		2,000		
	株数	10		
	株価	200		
自社株買い後の企業価値（正）		18,000	利益	1,000
	株数	90	EPS	11
	株価	200	PER	18
自社株買い後の企業価値（誤）		20,000	利益	1,000
	株数	90	EPS	11
	株価	222	PER	20

　この企業が 10 株の自社株買いを行うとする。自社株買いは，市場に流通している株式を買い取ることなので，企業はお金を支払う。現在の株価は 200 なので，この企業は自社株買いを行うために 10 株 × 200 ＝ 2,000 の現金を支払うはずである。したがって，自社株買いを行った後の企業価値は，自社株買い前の企業価値 20,000 から，現金支払額の 2,000 を差し引いた 18,000 となるはずである。自社株買いによって株数が 10 株減少し，90 株になっているので，株価は 18,000 ÷ 90 ＝ 200 であり，変化しない。これが正しい計算である。

However, if you subscribe to the notion that the relationship of "PER × EPS = Share Price", as introduced in chapter 2, then you might draw the wrong conclusion, as depicted at the bottom of Figure 13.1. When the company repurchases its shares, the number of shares outstanding decreases to 90, so EPS would actually increase: 1,000 / 90 shares = 11.111. This is correct so far. Multiplying the increased EPS by a PER of 20, you may conclude that the share price after repurchase would be 222. It appears that the share price has drifted upward, but this is incorrect. If the share price goes up to 222, then the value of the company would be 90 shares × 222 = 20,000, unchanged from before the repurchase. This implies that the cash expenditure used for repurchasing shares is ignored. In reality, the share price would not change despite the improvement in EPS.

The PER is determined as a result of the relationship between share price and EPS, rather than a factor to determine the share price. When the company repurchases its shares, EPS improves; and keeping PER constant, it seems that the share price moves up based on the relationship of "PER × EPS = Share Price". However, the share price does not automatically go up even if EPS increases, as the PER is not constant but variable.

しかし，第2章で確認した，「PER × EPS ＝株価」という関係に固執すると，図表13.1の一番下のような間違った結論を導いてしまう。自社株買いを行うと，株数は10株減少し90株になる。すると，EPSは1,000 ÷ 90株＝ 11.111となる。ここまでは正しい。上昇したEPSにPER20倍を掛けると222となる。株価は上昇するように見えるがこれが誤りである。もし，株価が222となっているとしたら，企業価値は90株× 222 ＝ 20,000となり，自社株買いを行う前と変わらない。これでは，自社株を購入するために支払った現金の影響が全くないことになってしまう。たとえEPSが改善したとしても，株価は変化しないのである。

　PERは株価とEPSの関係から結果として算出される数値であり，PERが株価を決めているわけではない。企業が自社株買いを行うとEPSは上昇するため，PERが一定と考えると，「PER × EPS ＝株価」という関係から，株価は上昇するように見える。しかし，EPSが上がったからといって，自動的に株価が上がるわけではない。PERは結果であって，株価を決める要因ではないからである。この場合ではPERは一定ではなく，変化する。

⬤ Share Issuance Does Not Affect Share Price

When a company issues new shares, the number of shares outstanding increases; however, the share issuance would not affect the share price. Figure 13.2 shows the effect of share issuance on a company's value. Suppose that the company repurchasing shares issues 20 new shares with a current price of 200, as illustrated in Figure 13.1. The company raises cash by 20 shares × 200 = 4,000. Therefore, the value of the company after the share issuance would be 22,000, which reflects the cash raised of 4,000 plus the value after repurchases of 18,000.

The number of shares would be 110 and the share price after the share issuance would be calculated as 22,000 / 110 = 200, which is unchanged. However, while the share price remains unchanged, contrary to share repurchasing, new share issuance weakens EPS. Again, if you are mistaking the relationship of "PER × EPS = Share Price", then you may incorrectly assume that the share price would decline to 164, by multiplying EPS of 9.09 by the PER of 18.

Figure 13.2 | Effect of Share Issuance on a Company's Value

Market Value		18,000	Earnings	1,000
Number of Shares		90	EPS	11
Share Price		200	PER	18
Equity Issue		4,000		
Number of Shares		20		
Share Price		200		
Market Value after Equity Issue (correct)		22,000	Earnings	1,000
Number of Shares		110	EPS	9
Share Price		200	PER	22
Market Value after Equity Issue (incorrect)		18,000	Earnings	1,000
Number of Shares		110	EPS	9
Share Price		164	PER	18

● 増資でも株価は下がらない

　自社株買いと逆に，増資する場合には，発行する株数が増加するが，同様に株価に変化を与えない。図表 13.1 で自社株買いを行った企業が，現在の株価 200 で 20 株の増資を行うとする（図表 13.2）。増資により 20 株× 200=4,000 の現金を調達する。したがって，増資後の企業価値は，増資前の企業価値 18,000 から，調達額の 4,000 を加えた 22,000 となるはずだ。

　増資によって株数が 20 株増加して 110 株になっているので，株価は 22,000 ÷ 110 = 200 であり，変化しない。自社株買いと全く逆で，増資によって EPS は下がるが，株価が下がらない。しかし，やはり「PER × EPS = 株価」という関係に固執すると，株数が増加した結果下落した EPS 9.09 に PER18 倍を掛けて，株価は 164 に下がるように見えてしまう。

図表 13.2　増資の企業価値への影響

企業価値		18,000	利益	1,000
	株数	90	EPS	11
	株価	200	PER	18
増資		4,000		
	株数	20		
	株価	200		
増資後の企業価値（正）		22,000	利益	1,000
	株数	110	EPS	9
	株価	200	PER	22
増資後の企業価値（誤）		18,000	利益	1,000
	株数	110	EPS	9
	株価	164	PER	18

There are numerous analyst reports and newspaper articles suggesting that a share repurchase guarantees an increase in share price. The "PER×EPS = Share Price" formula is popular because it is easily understood; however, it is frequently misapplied.

◉ Share Price Impact of Signaling

Neither share repurchases nor new share issuance affects share prices by themselves. However, if they impact and change investors' expectations, then the share price may be influenced. In this scenario, it is "signaling" that may be the factor changing investor expectations and the share price.

Conversely, new share issuance has the opposite signaling effect to that of share repurchases. Logic suggests that a company should issue new shares when its share price is over-valued. So, the decision to issue shares may signal that top management considers the company's shares to be overpriced. If investors interpret the company's decision as this signal, then the share price could decline.

However, it is also possible that a new share issuance reflects good investment opportunities and a corresponding drive to invest in the company. The share price may rise under this scenario.

Signaling can change investor expectations and lead to positive or negative share price movements. Further, inappropriate pricing of share repurchases or the share issuances may affect the share price. If shares are repurchased at an overvalued price, or if shares are issued with an undervalued price, the share price would likely decline. And, conversely, if shares are repurchased at an undervalued price, or if shares are issued with an overvalued price, the share price would likely rise.

In summary, share repurchases and new share issuances can serve as a trigger to move the share price, but such movements are due to the change of investors expectation based on signaling or due to mispricing, rather than to improvements of financial measures such as EPS.

新聞・雑誌の記事やアナリストによるレポートでも，自社株買いをすることによって株価上昇が望まれるといったことが，しばしば書かれる。「EPS × PER ＝株価」の式はわかりやすく，また覚えやすいため広く使われているが，間違った使われ方も多いため注意が必要である。

● シグナルによる株価の変化

自社株買いや増資を行ったことだけでは株価に影響はない。しかし，自社株買いや増資によって投資家の期待に変化が生じる場合には，株価も変化する。先ほどの自社株買いのシグナルは投資家の期待に変化を与える1つの要素である。

増資にもシグナルはある。シグナルも自社株買いと逆である。増資は企業が株を売るということなので，企業からすれば株価が高いときに行いたい。そのため，増資は株価が割高であるというシグナルとなりえ，投資家がこのようなシグナルを受け取り，企業が現在の自社の株価が高いと判断しているから増資すると考えれば，株価は下落するかもしれない。

ただし，増資が企業の旺盛な投資意欲を反映しているととらえられれば，株価は上昇することも考えられる。

このようなシグナルが株主の期待に変化を与え，株価を上下させることはありえる。また，自社株買いや増資の際の価格設定も株価変動の要因となる。自社株買いを割高な価格で行ったり，増資を割安な価格で行ったりすれば株価の下落要因となるし，自社株買いを割安な価格で行ったり，増資を割高な価格で行ったりすれば株価の上昇要因となる。

自社株買いや増資によって株価が変化するとすれば，このようなシグナルなどの影響による投資家の期待の変化や売買価格の影響などによってであり，EPSなどの財務指標の見かけ上の改善が原因ではないのである。

⬤ Shareholder Special Benefit Plans

Shareholders special benefit plans have become very popular in Japan. More than 1,500 Japanese companies, accounting for about 40% of all listed companies, implement such plans. Under such plans, a retail company may provide shareholders with gift coupons that can be used in its stores. Food or home product manufacturers may send an assortment of its own products out once or twice a year. Railway and airline companies may issue special discount tickets to its shareholders. Some companies offer rice coupons, which are not relevant to their main business, and some include donation programs toward environmental protection efforts.

Offering special benefit plans to shareholders is another type of payout policy. Giving gift coupons and discount tickets is viewed as the transformation of the future profits of the company, and providing rice coupons imposes a cost on the company, which is financially the same as a company paying a dividend.

Special benefit plans are not common outside of Japan. They are rarely seen in the United States, where the majority of shareholders prefer cash dividends to gifts.

It is logical for a company to distribute wealth in a way that is most desirable to the investor, which is generally in cash. However, many Japanese companies implement special benefit plans to encourage shareholders to hold stocks for the long term, and to encourage their shareholders to become customers and their customers to become shareholders.

Financial investment magazines often publish feature stories about such plans, and as a result, large numbers of people purchase stock in those companies with special benefit plans. However, it is risky for an investor to make investment decisions based solely on being able to participate in these plans. The plans can be changed or abolished at any time. In addition, investors should not forget the primary risk of equity, which is that prices can change and the original purchase price is not secure.

● 株主優待制度

　日本企業においては株主優待制度が盛んであり，1,500社以上の企業，上場企業の約4割が株主優待を実施している。この制度により，小売業が自社の店舗で使用できる商品券を，食品や生活製品関連企業が自社製品の詰め合わせなどを半年か1年に1度株主に贈る。また，鉄道会社や航空会社は乗車券・特急券や航空券がそれぞれ割引となる株主優待券を発行している。本業と全く関係のないお米券を提供したりする例や，最近では，環境保全活動などへの寄付を株主優待のメニューに加える企業もある。

　株主優待制度を提供することも株主への資金還元の一種といえる。自社の商品券や割引券は将来の企業の利益の一部を株主に渡しているものだし，自社の商品に関係のないお米券はその分のお金を企業が負担しているのだから，経済的には配当と同じと考えられる。
　株主優待制度は日本以外の国では一般的ではない。米国でもまれにあるが，商品よりも現金で配当してほしい，という声のほうが強い。
　株主への資金還元は，最も使い勝手のいい現金，つまり通常の配当で行うほうが合理的ではある。それでも多くの日本企業が株主優待制度を導入するのは，株主に長期保有を促したり，商品券などの活用によって既存顧客の株主化および既存株主の顧客化を狙ってのことであろう。

　投資関連の雑誌が株主優待の特集を組むことも多く，この制度を目当てに株式を購入する投資家も少なくない。しかし，投資家が株主優待制度のみを投資の判断材料とすることには，大きな危険が伴う。株主優待は突然廃止・変更されることもある。また，なによりも価格が変動し，元本が保証されていないという株式本来のリスクを忘れてはならない。

Part 5
Hedging Risk and Derivatives

- This part studies the risks associated with unexpected events which the company running international business will confront, and how to deal with them.

- We start with a discussion about a foreign exchange, and then cover derivatives to hedge the risk with respect to the price movements of various assets.

- The next chapter introduces several types of derivatives such as forward contracts, futures contracts, and swaps. The final chapter features options, whose payoff is unique.

- Option valuation is a complex subject. A spreadsheet to estimate the value of an option is available online for anyone who would like to learn more.

Chapter 14   Foreign Exchange and Cross-border Investments

Chapter 15   Futures and Swaps

Chapter 16   Options

第5部
リスクヘッジとデリバティブ

★★★★★

- 第5部では，国際的にビジネスを展開する企業が直面する，コントロールが不可能なイベントに伴うリスクとそれらへの対処の仕方について学ぶ。

- 最初の章で外国為替を議論し，その後資産の価格変動のリスクをヘッジする手法としてデリバティブをカバーする。

- 先物取引，オプション，スワップなどさまざまなデリバティブについて紹介したのちに，最後にリターンが特徴的なオプションについて学ぶ。

- オプション価値の議論は複雑だが，興味のある人のためにはオプション価値の算定フォーマットを用意している。

第14章　外国為替と海外投資

第15章　先物取引とスワップ

第16章　オプション

Chapter Foreign Exchange and Cross-border Investments

> **Points!**
> ✔ Foreign currency risk can be hedged with the forward exchange rates
> ✔ The forward exchange rates in the market are determined with the interest rate differentials between the currencies
> ✔ The foreign investment project should be separately evaluated from the arbitrary forecast of the exchange rate in the future

○ Foreign Exchange Rates

Companies operating globally must take into account currency risk because foreign exchange rate fluctuations can affect financial performance.

Foreign exchange rates are readily available online, including websites like Yahoo Finance and Bloomberg. An exchange rate shows the price of a unit of the domestic currency in terms of foreign currencies, or the price of a unit of foreign currencies in terms of the domestic currency.

In Japan, exchange rates for Japanese yen are usually expressed as the number of yen equivalent to a unit of foreign currencies. Most exchange rates for U.S. dollar are expressed as the number of another currencies equivalent to 1 dollar except for the euro and the British pound.

The exchange rate for immediate delivery is known as the spot rate of exchange.

第14章 外国為替と海外投資

> **ポイント！**
> - ✓ 為替リスクは先物為替レートを活用することによってヘッジが可能である
> - ✓ 先物為替レートは国内外の金利差によって決まる
> - ✓ 海外の投資案件の判断は，為替の主観的な予測とは切り離して行うべきである

● 為替レート

　国際的に事業展開を行う企業では，多かれ少なかれ外国為替が業績に影響を与えるため，為替に対するリスクを認識しておく必要がある。

　外国為替レートはYahoo！ファイナンスやBloomberg等多くのホームページにおいて容易に入手可能である。為替レートは自国の通貨1単位が他国の通貨でいくらの価値をもつのか，または他国の通貨1単位が自国の通貨でいくらの価値をもつのかを表わす。

　通常，日本円の為替レートは，他の通貨の1単位に対して円がいくらであるのかが表わされる。米国ドルの場合はドル1単位に対して他国の通貨がどれだけの価値をもっているのかを表わすことが多いが，ユーロとポンドに対してはそれぞれ1ポンド，1ユーロが何ドルなのかと表わされることが多い。

　なお，現在の為替レートのことをスポットレートといい，また通常為替レートとはこのスポットレートのことをさす。

Figure 14.1 | **Foreign Exchange Rates**

Euro – US Dollar	1 Euro =	1.17 US Dollar
US Dollar – Japanese Yen	1 US Dollar =	111.12 Japanese Yen
British Pound – US Dollar	1 British Pound =	1.31 US Dollar
Euro – Japanese Yen	1 Euro =	129.50 Japanese Yen
British Pound – Japanese Yen	1 British Pound =	145.59 Japanese Yen
US Dollar – Chinese Yuan	1 US Dollar =	6.83 Chinese Yuan
US Dollar – Hong Kong Dollar	1 US Dollar =	7.85 Hong Kong Dollar
US Dollar – Singapore Dollar	1 US Dollar =	1.36 Singapore Dollar
Dollar Indian Rupee	1 US Dollar =	68.74 Indian Rupee

Source : Bloomberg website as of July 30, 2018

○ Change in Exchange Rates

Figure 14.1 shows the exchange rates in July, 2018, the yen/dollar exchange rate was 111.1 yen = 1 dollar($). When the value of the domestic currency appreciated, the amount of domestic currencies to buy one unit of a foreign currency decreases. The yen/dollar exchange rate hovered around 100 yen per dollar from 2013 to 2014. In 2018, you need more yen to buy 1 dollar than in 2013 and 2014. The amount of yen on the exchange rate increases from 100 to 111, this is an increase in yen required to exchange for 1 dollar, therefore the yen has depreciated, or the dollar has appreciated.

In the present day, most countries implement a floating exchange rate system. Meaning, the exchange rates fluctuate every day. Therefore, a company using foreign currencies for its transactions is subject to the risk that cash flows in the home currency may vary. In order to fix the profit or the cost for those transactions, derivatives including forward contracts, as introduced next, can be used.

図表 14.1 為替レート

ユーロ-ドル	1 ユーロ=	1.17 ドル
ドル-円	1 ドル=	111.12 円
ポンド-ドル	1 ポンド=	1.31 ドル
ユーロ-円	1 ユーロ=	129.50 円
ポンド-円	1 ポンド=	145.59 円
ドル-中国元	1 ドル=	6.83 中国元
ドル-香港ドル	1 ドル=	7.85 香港ドル
ドル-シンガポールドル	1 ドル=	1.36 シンガポールドル
ドル-インドルピー	1 ドル=	68.74 インドルピー

出所：2018 年 7 月 30 日時点　Bloomberg ホームページのデータを抜粋して加工

為替レートの変化

　図表 14.1 では 2018 年 7 月における円ドルの為替レートが 1 ドル 111.1 円であることが示されている。自国通貨の価値が高まると，他国の通貨を 1 単位買うために必要な自国の通貨が少なくなる。2013 年から 2014 年にかけて円ドルの為替レートは 1 ドル 100 円近辺で推移していた。2018 年においては当時と比べて 1 ドルを買うためにより多くの円が必要ということである。1 ドル 100 円から 111 円と円の額面は増加しているが，1 ドルと交換するために必要な円が増えたわけであるから，円の価値は下落している（円安，ドル高になっている）のである。

　現在はほとんどの国が変動為替制度を適用しているため，為替レートは日々変動している。そのため企業が他国の通貨によって取引を行う場合には，自国通貨建てのキャッシュフローが変動するリスクが生じる。そのような海外での個別の取引において，利益やコストを固定するには，この後説明する先物為替予約を含むデリバティブを活用することが有効である。

○ Hedging Risk with Forward Contracts

For example, a company in the U.S. purchases a piece of machinery from a Japanese company. The machinery will be delivered in 1 year, costing 100 million yen. The yen/dollar spot exchange rate is supposed to be 100yen=$1. If the exchange rate is unchanged the dollar denominated cost is 1 million. However, if the exchange rate in 1 year changes to 90yen=$1, the dollar cost will be 1.11 million(100 million/90), and if the exchange rate changes to 110yen=$1, the dollar cost will be 0.909 million(100 million/110).

A forward exchange contract or a foreign exchange forward contract is an arrangement that two parties agree to exchange two designated currencies with the specified exchange rate at a specific time in the future. The forward contracts are a useful tool to hedge currency risk.

The exchange rate at a future date is called the forward exchange rate. The forward exchange rate is not usually the same as the spot exchange rate. Recall the case of the U.S. company, suppose the forward rate in 1 year is 105yen=$1. If the company enters into a forward contract with a bank to buy yen 1 year from now, it can lock in the dollar cost today at 0.952 million (100 million/105). The company does not pay anything immediately but just promises to pay in the future. The actual transaction will occur in 1 year when the company pays $0.952 million to the bank, and the bank pays in exchange 100 million yen, which will be used for the payment to the Japanese company.

Hedging the foreign exchange risk lets a company concentrate on its own business because usually companies are not experts at forecasting future exchange rates. Fortunately, arranging forward contracts are not so difficult or costly.

◉ 先物為替予約によるリスクヘッジ

たとえば米国企業が日本から設備を購入することを想定しよう。設備は1年後に引き渡され、その価格は1億円であるとする。現在の為替レートは1ドル100円であったとしよう。1年後も為替レートが変化しなければドルベースでの設備のコストは1,000,000ドルとなる。しかし1年後の為替レートが1ドル90円となった場合、ドルベースでの設備のコストは1,111,111ドルとなる（1億円÷90円）。一方で、1年後の為替レートが1ドル110円であれば、ドルベースでの設備のコストは909,090ドルになる（1億円÷110円）。

先物為替予約は、このような為替変動リスクを回避するために将来の特定の期日に、特定の通貨を、特定の為替レートで受け渡す約束をする取引である。

将来の為替レートのことを先物為替レートといい、先物為替レートは現在のスポットレートよりも高いこともあれば安いこともある。先ほどの例では、仮に1年後の先物為替レートが1ドル105円であり、このレートで円買いドル売りの為替予約を銀行と行うと、1億円÷105円＝952,000ドルに、ドルベースでの支払いコストを固定することができる。為替予約を行ったとしても現時点において何か支払いが発生するわけではなく、現時点では支払いを約束するだけである。支払いが発生するのは約束した1年後であり、1年後に銀行に952,000ドルを支払うことで1億円が入手でき、これを設備の購入代金にあてればよい。

普通の企業は、為替レートを予測することを専門に行っているわけではないのだから、為替のリスクをヘッジすることは企業が本業に集中するためにも有効である。幸いなことに、為替予約のコストはそれほど高くない。

Setting Forward Exchange Rates

The forward exchange rates in the market are determined with the interest rate differentials between the currencies. The difference in interest rates in two currencies is reflected in the difference between the forward and the spot exchange rates of the two countries. This relationship is known as interest rate parity. Interest rate parity assumes that if the forward rates are imbalanced, there exists opportunities for arbitrage transaction (or arbitrage opportunities where you can earn riskless return from an imbalance in the price), and that the forward rate will be naturally adjusted to eliminate such opportunities.

$$\frac{1 + \text{Interest rate}_{yen}}{1 + \text{Interest rate}_{\$}} = \frac{\text{Forward rate}_{yen/\$}}{\text{Spot rate}_{yen/\$}}$$

Suppose you are an investor in Japan with 1 million yen to invest for 1 year. Assuming the risk-free rate in Japan is 2% and it is 5% in U.S., with the spot rate being 100yen=$1 and the forward rate is 98yen=$1. You have two riskless investment opportunities. You can get 1,020,000 yen in 1 year if you simply invest in a risk-free asset in yen, Alternatively, you can convert your 1,000,000 yen into $10,000 with the spot rate, and investing risk-free asset in dollars. In 1 year, you will have $10,500, and convert it back into 1,029,000 yen with the forward rate ($10,500×98). Your riskless return for the later alternative is 2.9%, which is higher than the risk-free rate in Japanese yen and there is an arbitrage opportunity.

● 先物為替レートの決定

　先物為替レートは市場において国内外の金利の差によって決まる。2国間の金利の差の比率が為替のスポットレートと先物レートの比率に反映されるのである。これを金利平価という。金利平価は，先物レートが不均衡であると，金利による裁定機会（価格差を利用して無リスクで利益を得る機会）が発生してしまうため，これらが生じないように為替の先物レートが調整されることを前提にしている。

$$\frac{1+金利_{円}}{1+金利_{ドル}} = \frac{先物レート_{円/ドル}}{スポットレート_{円/ドル}}$$

　たとえば現在，日本の投資家が，1年間投資する資金を100万円有しているとしよう。日本円のリスクフリー・レートが2%，米ドルのリスクフリー・レートが5%，現在のスポットレートは1ドル100円とする。そして1年後の先物レートが98円であったとしよう。ここで投資家は2つのリスクフリー投資の方法を有することになる。1つは100万円をそのまま無リスク資産に投資をすることにより，1年後に102万円を得るという方法である。もう1つは100万円を現在の為替レートにより10,000ドルに変え，ドルで無リスク資産に投資する方法である。1年後には投資額は10,500ドルとなり，これを1年後の先物レートで円に交換すると，投資家の資産は10,500ドル×98＝102.9万円になる。投資家は無リスクで2.9%のリターンを得ることになり，これは日本円のリスクフリー・レートの2%よりも大きい。このような場合には裁定の機会が生じることになる。

Figure 14.2 | Interest Rate Parity

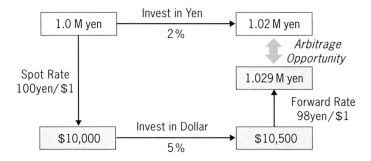

If investors find the opportunity to get a higher return from an alternative, a number of investors will rush toward the 1 year forward rate of 98yen=$1. Converting 1 dollar into 98 yen means selling 1 dollar and buying 98 yen, increasing demand for yen and leading to yen appreciation in the forward market. Ultimately the forward exchange rate will converge on 97.14yen=$1 where the arbitrage opportunity disappears.

Foreign currency dealers set the forward exchange rates by watching the difference between the interest rates in different currencies.

Interest Rate Parity and Purchasing Power Parity

Interest rate parity expects that the currency with a higher interest rate will be depreciated in the future (the dollar in the previous case), and the currency with lower interest rate will be appreciated in the future (the yen in the previous case). As chapter 3 stated, the real interest rate excludes the effect of inflation from the nominal interest rate. In other words, the nominal rate consists of the real rate and the inflation rate.

$$1 + \text{Real interest rate} = \frac{1 + \text{Nominal interest rate}}{1 + \text{Inflation rate}}, \text{ accordingly}$$

$$1 + \text{Nominal interest rate} = (1 + \text{Real interest rate}) \times (1 + \text{Inflation rate})$$

図表 14.2 金利裁定

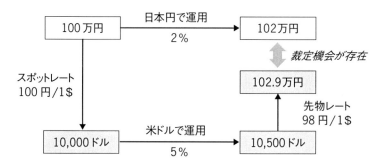

ドルに変換して投資を行うほうが高いリターンを得られることがわかっているのであれば，多くの投資家が1ドル98円という1年後の先物為替レートに殺到する。1ドルを98円に交換するとは，1ドルを売って98円を買うということであり，円買いの注文が増えるということだから，先物市場における円の価格が上昇する。先物為替レートは裁定機会が消える（裁定取引から利益が上げられなくなる）1ドル97.14円で均衡する。

実際には，為替ディーラーは2国間の金利の差に注目して先物の為替レートを決定している。

● 金利平価と購買力平価

金利平価によれば，金利が相対的に高い通貨（上記の例ではドル）は将来的には割安になり，金利が相対的に低い通貨（上記の例では円）は将来的に割高になっていく。第3章において，名目金利からインフレの影響を取り除いたものが実質金利であることを確認した。つまり，名目金利は実質金利とインフレ率とで構成されている。

$$1 + 実質金利 = \frac{1 + 名目金利}{1 + インフレ率}$$ すなわち，

$$1 + 名目金利 = (1 + 実質金利) \times (1 + インフレ率)$$

In summary, the interest differentials relate the inflation differentials, and when the real interest rates are identical, the differences of interest rates are completely subject to the differences of the inflation. (The real interest rates between any countries should be the same because capital flows to where returns are highest as long as it can flow without any barriers. However, it may not be the case if the government considerably controls or intervenes in the transfer of funds or the interest rates.) Inflation is the rise of prices of goods and shows the decline of the purchasing power of the currency. Therefore, it is reasonable to conclude the currency with higher inflation will devalue in the long run.

The purchasing power parity or PPP is a theory stating that the cost of living in different counties should be equal and inflation differentials will be adjusted by changes in exchange rates. PPP suggests when you can buy the same hamburger for $3 in U.S. and 300 yen in Japan, the fair exchange rate is 100yen=$1. In reality, PPP does not hold all the time because of the costs and possibilities of transportation as well as tariffs and taxes. However, it is understood that the exchange rates are determined with the purchasing power of each currency.

Since the inflation rates are linked to the interest rates, PPP is consistent to the interest rate parity.

A popular reference from a business magazine publisher, the Economist exhibits "The Big Mac Index" which compares the prices of a Big Mac in a number of countries. (http://www.economist.com/content/big-mac-index)

このことは，金利差はインフレ率の差が関係しており，特に実質金利が2国間で同一であるならば，金利の差はすべてインフレ率の差によって説明されることになることを示している（国をまたいだ資本の移動が阻害されない状況であれば，資本は金利の高いところに移動するため，長期的には実質金利はどの国においても一致するはずである。ただし，政府が資金の移動や金利を管理したり介入する場合にはこの前提は成立しない）。インフレーションとは物価の上昇であり，通貨の購買力の低下を意味するから，インフレ率が相対的に高い国の通貨は長期的には価値が下がっていくことは妥当である。

　為替レートの決定要因の1つとされる購買力平価は，どの国においてもモノの値段は同一であり，通貨の購買力を表わすインフレ率の違いは為替レートの変動によって相殺されるという説である。購買力平価によれば，同じハンバーガーが米国で3ドルで，日本で300円で売られているのであれば，適正な為替レートは1ドル100円となる。現実世界では，輸送費や税金・関税，保管と移動の可否などの関係で購買力平価が完全に成立する場合は多くはないが，為替は各国の通貨の購買力によって決定されることは直感的にも理解できる。
　インフレ率の高さは高い金利に結び付いているので，購買力平価の考え方は金利平価とも整合している。
　なお，エコノミスト誌は各国のビッグマックの値段を比較したビッグマックインデックスを定期的に発表している。
（http://www.economist.com/content/big-mac-index）

◯ Coping with Competitive Advantages

When the foreign exchange rates influence the competitive advantages of a company, a company should cope with the risks more substantially and strategically hedge them through operating and financing activities, not limited to fixing the cost of each transaction.

For example, Japanese car makers export to U.S. an automobile with the price tag of 2,000,000 yen. It is sold for $20,000 in U.S when 100yen=$1. But suppose the yen appreciates to 70yen=$1, the price of the car will be as high as $28,571 (=2,000,000/70) in the U.S., possibly leading to a significant decline of export sales. A measure to hedge the risk includes manufacturing cars in the region close to where they are for sale. Japanese car makers built factories in the U.S. and produced cars to be sold there, which is one way to hedge the currency risk.

If you cannot change the place of the operation, hedging with financing activities can be considered an effective alternative. For example, Swiss luxury watch makers will not redeploy their production bases outside Switzerland because "Swiss-made" is an important competitive advantage and moving out of the nation will damage their brand value. Alternatively, they can hedge the currency risks by utilizing foreign denominated debts. Suppose they borrow money in dollars. When the Swiss franc appreciates, the value of the interest payments and the redemption in dollars will be discounted, this will offset some of the loss from the decrease of export sales.

● 競争優位性に及ぼす影響への対処

　為替レートは企業の競争優位性にも影響を与えることがある。この場合には個別の取引のコストを固定するだけではなく事業活動や財務活動を通じた，より本質的，戦略的なリスクヘッジが必要となってくる。

　たとえば日本企業は自動車を生産し米国に輸出している。価格が2,000,000円の自動車は，為替レートが1ドル＝100円の時，ドルベースでの価格は20,000ドルである。しかし，円高が進み1ドル＝70円になった場合，ドル建てでの自動車の価格は28,571ドル（＝2,000,000円÷70円）と高額になるため，自動車の輸出売上が大きく落ち込む可能性がある。このようなリスクをヘッジするための1つの手段は，製品を販売する場所により近いところで生産を行うことである。日本の自動車メーカーが世界最大の市場である米国に工場を建設し，そこで生産を行うのは為替リスクヘッジの一例である。

　事業を行う場所を移動できない場合には，資金調達によってリスクをヘッジすることも考えられる。たとえばスイスの高級腕時計の会社が為替リスクをヘッジするために生産拠点を海外に移すことは考えにくい。生産をスイスで行っていること自体がブランドであり重要な競争優位性であるため，生産拠点を移動することは企業にとって大きな損失となるからである。このような場合の為替ヘッジとしては，他国通貨建てでの資金調達を行うことが考えられる。借入れをドルで行っていれば，スイスフランの価値が高くなった場合には，ドル建ての金利の支払いや元本の返済が割安になる。これにより，スイスフラン高による輸出売上の減少分をある程度緩和することができる。

Investment Decisions for Cross-border Projects

Basically, the decision-making criteria for a cross-border investment with foreign currency is the same as for domestic investments. Accept a positive NPV project and reject a negative NPV project.

The cash flows generated by foreign investments are commonly in the foreign currency, you should use the forward exchange rates to convert all foreign denominated cash flows into the domestic currency and use the cost of capital in the domestic currency to discount them.

Figure 14.3 shows an example of a chemical manufacturer in the U.S. and examines how it constructs a plant in Japan. Suppose the risk-free rate in U.S. and in Japan are 2%, and 0.5%, respectively, and the spot exchange rate is 100yen=$1. The discount rate or the cost of capital for the investment in dollars is assumed to be 10%.

Figure 14.3 | Investment Decisions for Cross-border Projects

	0	1Y	2Y	3Y	4Y	5Y
Cash flow (millions of yen)	−500	100	150	200	250	300
Forward Exchange rate Yen to the dollar	100.00	98.53	97.08	95.65	94.25	92.86
Cash flow (millions of dollars)	−5	1.015	1.545	2.091	2.653	3.231
PV of CF	−5	0.923	1.277	1.571	1.812	2.006
NPV (millions of dollars)	2.588					

The forward exchange rates in 1 year are available in the market or various websites, but the rates in the more distant future are not usually quoted. The forward rates, however, can be easily derived based on the interest rate differential in the two currencies, and you do not have to forecast the forward rates in an arbitrary manner.

● 海外の投資案件の評価

　投資の意思決定基準は，他国の通貨で行う国際的な案件であっても基本的には国内の評価プロセスと同じである。NPV がプラスであるならば投資を行い，マイナスであれば行わない。

　海外で行われる投資から生じるキャッシュフローは，通常は他国通貨建てであるから，それらの予測されるキャッシュフローを先物為替レートを用いて自国の通貨建てに変換し，自国通貨建ての資本コストを使って現在価値に割り引けばよい。

　図表 14.3 は，米国の化学メーカーが日本に製造拠点を設立することを検討している例である。米国のリスクフリー・レートは 2%，日本のリスクフリー・レートは 0.5% とする。また現在における為替レートは 1 ドル 100 円である。ドルベースでのこの投資案件の割引率，資本コストは 10% とする。

図表 14.3　海外の投資案件の評価

	0	1年度	2年度	3年度	4年度	5年度
キャッシュフロー（百万円）	−500	100	150	200	250	300
先物レート　円/1ドル	100.00	98.53	97.08	95.65	94.25	92.86
キャッシュフロー（百万ドル）	−5	1.015	1.545	2.091	2.653	3.231
キャッシュフローの現在価値	−5	0.923	1.277	1.571	1.812	2.006
NPV（百万ドル）	2.588					

　1 年後程度の先物為替レートは市場やインターネットでも入手可能だが，遠い将来のものは発表されていない。しかし，2 国間の金利差に基づく先物為替レートは簡単に計算が可能であり，企業は将来の為替レートを恣意的に予測する必要はない。

The forward rate for year 1 is calculated as the current (spot) exchange rate × (1 + yen risk-free rate) / (1 + dollar risk - free rate), therefore, 100 × 1.005 ÷ 1.02 = 98.53 yen/$. The forward rates for each year are calculated similarly (98.53 × 1.005 ÷ 1.02 = 97.08 for year 2). The dollar cash flows converted with the forward rates are discounted at 10% of the dollar cost of capital to get NPV.

Foreign investment should be separately assessed from the forecast of the exchange rate in the future. It is illogical for a company to accept a worthless project according to the particular view about the future exchange rate. If a company forecast the future rate and is confident of it, it should pursue a profit with investing (or speculating) on the currency directly rather than mixing it with other projects regarding business activities.

The NPV of foreign projects can be calculated alternatively as discounting the cash flows in the foreign currency at the foreign cost of capital, calculating NPV in the foreign currency, then converting the foreign NPV into the home currency with the spot exchange rate. This approach does not require an estimate of the future exchange rates. Instead it requires to estimate the foreign cost of capital. Both approaches will derive identical calculation results and judgement when the same assumptions are given.

1年後の先物為替レートは，現在の為替（スポット）レート×（1＋日本のリスクフリー・レート）÷（1＋米国のリスクフリー・レート）で計算でき，100 × 1.005 ÷ 1.02 ＝ 98.53 円である。2年目以降の先物為替レートも同様に計算がなされる（2年目は 98.53 × 1.005 ÷ 1.02 ＝ 97.08）。これらの先物為替レートを使用して変換されたドル建てのキャッシュフローを 10％のドル建ての割引率を用いて NPV を計算する。

　投資を行うか行わないかの決定は，企業の将来の為替レートの予測とは切り離すべきである。本来行うべきではない投資であるのにかかわらず，主観的な為替予測に基づいて投資を行うという意思決定をするのは本末転倒である。もし企業やマネジメントが将来の為替予測を行い，それに自信があるのであれば，事業活動における投資案件を活用するのではなく，直接的に為替レートへの投資（というよりも投機）によって利益を狙うべきである。

　海外での投資案件の評価は，他国通貨建てのキャッシュフローをそのまま他国通貨ベースの資本コストで割り引き，他国通貨建ての NPV を計算したうえで，最後に現在の為替レートによって自国通貨建ての NPV に変換する方法でも行うことができる。このアプローチは将来の為替レートを使用する必要がなくなるが，その代わりに他国通貨建ての資本コストを予測することが必要になるので，プロセスが簡便になるわけではない。どちらの方法でも，前提が同じであれば計算結果と意思決定は同一になる。

Chapter 15 Futures and Swaps

> **Points!**
> - There are several types of derivatives such as forward contracts, futures contracts, swaps and options
> - The underlying asset of derivatives varies from currencies, stocks, to commodities, oil, metals, and a lot of companies use these to hedge risks
> - Forwards and futures are contracts to buy or sell assets in the future and a swap is a series of them

● Approaches to Hedge Risks and Derivatives

Hedging external risks such as the unexpected movement of raw material costs, retail prices, foreign exchange rates or interest rates, relieves managers of uncontrollable factors and enable them to focus on the original mission, value creation through the business operation. Using appropriate risk hedging strategy makes business planning and execution simpler

There are various approaches to hedge risks. It is one way to possess flexibility in the operations with dispersing plant locations and procurement channels and building manufacturing lines to assemble multiple items. Also buying an insurance policy against unfavorable events is another way to hedge risk. Then, a company may effectively use derivatives to fix the price or costs, and to limit losses in operations.

Derivatives are financial contracts whose payoffs are reliant on the price of the other financial instruments or commodities. There are several types of derivatives such as forward contracts, futures contracts, swaps and options. The financial instrument or commodity on which a derivative's price is based is referred to as the underlying asset.

第15章 先物取引とスワップ

> **ポイント！**
> - ✓ デリバティブには先物取引やスワップ，オプションなどがある
> - ✓ デリバティブの対象は通貨・株式から農作物，原油，金属などさまざまなものがあり，多くの企業がデリバティブをリスクヘッジの手法として用いている
> - ✓ 先渡・先物取引とは将来の取引の約束であり，将来の一連の取引の約束を束ねたものがスワップである

● リスクのヘッジ方法とデリバティブ

　原料や小売価格，あるいは外国為替レートや金利の予期できない変動といった，外部的なリスクをヘッジすることにより，経営者は自らコントロールできない要素から開放され，本来の使命である事業経営を通じた価値創造に注力することができるようになる。適切なリスクヘッジは事業計画の立案と遂行を容易にする。

　リスクヘッジの管理の仕方にはさまざまなものがある。製造拠点や部品調達の場所を分散させることや，1つの製造ラインで複数の商品を製造できるようにすることにより，事業活動に柔軟性をもたせることもリスクヘッジの1つである。また，単純に好ましくない状況に対して保険をかけておくこともあり得る。そして，デリバティブを活用して価格や費用を固定化，損失を限定化することも有効である。

　デリバティブとは，ある商品や資産の価格に依存して価格が決定する派生商品である。デリバティブには先渡取引，先物取引，スワップ，オプションなどの種類がある。派生のもととなる商品・資産のことを原資産と呼ぶ。

Forward Contracts

A forward contract (or forward) is the contract to buy or sell a specified amount of an asset at a specified price on a specified future date. You can lock in a price for a future transaction with forwards. Since a forward contract is the agreement of a future transaction, neither money nor assets change hands when a futures contract is entered into.

The detailed conditions including the specification and the quantity of a commodity as well as a delivery arrangement is determined on a negotiation basis between parties on a forward contract. The most active trading in forwards are foreign exchange forwards as previously introduced. For example, making a table reservation or booking a trip is a kind of forward contracts.

Futures Contracts

Similar to forwards, a futures contract (or futures) is the contract to buy or sell a specified amount of an asset at a specified price on a specified future date. Futures are traded by a number of investors on a futures exchange. They are standardized for quality and quantity to facilitate trading. Promising to buy the underlying asset at a later date is called buying futures or a long position in a futures contract, and promising to sell it at a later date is called selling futures or a short position in a futures contract. The price at which the participants in a futures contract agree to transact at on the settlement date is called a future price.

● 先渡取引（先渡契約）

　先渡取引は，将来の特定の期日に，特定の価格で，特定の商品を，特定の数量売買する契約である。先渡契約を結ぶことにより，契約者は売買価格を固定することができる。なお先渡取引は将来の取引の合意であるから，現金や商品の受け渡しは合意時点では発生しない。

　先渡取引は，商品の仕様や数量，受渡しの方法や時期などの細かい条件が，売買の当事者間で決定される相対取引である。先渡契約が最も活用されているのは，すでに説明した為替取引（為替予約）である。身近な例では，ホテルや旅行会社に予約をすることも，先渡取引の一種といえる。

● 先物取引（先物契約）

　先物取引は先渡取引と同様に，将来の特定の期日に，特定の価格で，特定の商品を，特定の数量売買する約束という性質を持つ。しかし，取引が金融商品市場において行われる点が異なる。先物は多くの投資家に市場で取引されるため，標準化された商品単位で売買する約束をすることになる。なお，将来において商品を買う約束をすることを「先物を買う」「ロング・ポジション」，売る約束をすることを「先物を売る」「ショート・ポジション」という。また，将来における取引価格は先物価格と呼ばれる。

◉ Characteristics and Mechanics of Future Trading

The underlying asset in a futures contract could be commodities such as wheat, sugar, rice, corn, metals such as gold, silver, copper, or aluminum, natural resources including gas and crude oil, in addition, currencies, interest rates and financial securities are included. Futures traded on markets are standardized and highly liquid.

The futures contract is held at a recognized exchange through a brokerage firm like a securities company or a commodity trading firm. Unlike a common securities transaction, a futures contract requires the transaction in the future and nothing is exchanged immediately. The exchange acts as mediator between the parties to ensure the execution of the transaction. You need to find a reliable counterparty for a forward contract, but the futures exchange guarantees the credibility of the transaction for a futures contract.

On the other hand, futures investors are required by the exchange to put a deposit to absorb the potential loss beforehand, this is known as margin. Since a futures contract waits for payment until its maturity, you can enter into a large transaction with margin. In the case your loss due to price fluctuations reaches a certain level, putting additional margin to cover the loss is required (called maintenance margin). A brokerage firm monitors future prices and the necessity of additional margin based on a daily settlement.

Different from a forward contract which the underlying asset will be delivered and received in principle, most futures contracts do not result in actual delivery. You must negotiate with other party to dissolve a forward contract, while you can close your position easily for a futures contract before expiration with entering the opposite type of trade (reversing trade, a sell order will close a long position, and a buy order will close a short). The difference between the future price of a long position and a short position will be made up or received when closing the position.

● 先物取引の特徴

　先物取引の対象となる商品・資産（原資産）にはさまざまなものがある。小麦，砂糖，米，とうもろこしなどの農作物，金，銀，銅，アルミニウムのような金属，あるいはガスや原油のような天然資源に加え，各国の通貨，金利，株式などの金融証券なども含まれる。市場で取引がなされる先物取引は，取引の単位が標準化されており流動性が高いという特徴がある。

　先物取引は，証券会社や商品取引業者を通じて取引所において行われる。先物取引は将来における取引の実行を要求するものだが，通常の株式の取引のようにその場で取引が行われない。そのため，将来の取引を確実に実行させる仕組みと役割を取引所が担うのである。相対取引である先渡取引では，信頼できる相手を選ぶ必要があるが，先物取引の場合は取引所が取引の信頼性を担保してくれる。

　その代わりに，投資家は証拠金と呼ばれる，取引から発生する損失を吸収するための預託金を差し入れる。先物取引では，決済期日までは代金を支払う必要がないため，投資家は証拠金を差し入れるだけで大きな取引が可能になる。しかし，先物価格が変動した結果，一定の水準以上の評価損が発生した場合は，投資家は証券会社から新たな証拠金（追加証拠金）を要求される。証券会社は毎日先物価格の変動を把握しており，日々の評価損益に基づいて追加証拠金の必要性をチェックしている。

　なお，先渡取引では，期限日に現物の取引を行うことが原則だが，先物取引のほとんどは実際の商品の取引は行われない。先渡取引においては，契約を解消する場合には，相手方と交渉しなければならないが，先物取引では，取引の期日前に，反対売買（買い手が売る契約を，売り手が買う契約を行うこと）によって取引を解消することができるからである。取引の解消にあたっては，先物買いの価格と先物売りの価格の差額を支払うまたは受け取ることにより決済を行う。

Hedging with Forward and Futures

The price of corn depends on the climate of the year. A corn farmer will suffer a loss from a decline of corn price if the weather is unfavorable. Suppose a corn farmer hopes to sell corn for $5 per bushel and is concerned about a potential decline in the price of corn. If the future price of corn is $5, the farmer can fix the selling price in the future at $5 by selling corn futures.

If the price of corn climbs upward in the future, the farmer benefits more from actual sales proceeds of corn while the future contracts lose money. The profit will be offset by a loss and the farmer will be the same situation as corn is sold for $5. Conversely, if the price of corn falls, the farmer suffers a loss from actual sales proceeds while the future contracts make a profit, offsetting the loss.

Figure 15.1 | **Hedging with Forward and Futures**

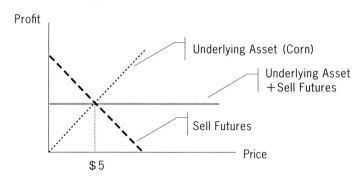

The farmer has the alternative to find a credible buyer and conclude a forward contract. However, selling futures available in exchange markets enable the farmer to hedge the risk of price fluctuations more easily.

● 先渡，先物によるリスクヘッジ

とうもろこしの価格はその年の天候によって変動し，とうもろこし農家は価格が下落すると損失を被ってしまう。たとえば，とうもろこし農家がブッシェル（穀物の単位）あたり5ドルでとうもろこしを売りたいと考えているが，将来の値下がりを懸念しているとする。現在の先物価格が5ドルであったとすると，農家はとうもろこしの先物を売ることにより，将来のとうもろこしの販売価格を事実上固定化できる。

将来においてとうもろこしの価格が上昇する場合，実際の取引からの利益は大きくなるが，一方で先物取引では損失が発生している。利益と損失を相殺すると結局とうもろこしを5ドルで売った場合と状況は同じになる。反対にとうもろこしの価格が下落する場合，実際の取引からは損失が発生しても，先物取引からの利益があるため，やはり利益と損失は相殺される。

図表15.1 ┃ 先渡，先物によるリスクヘッジ

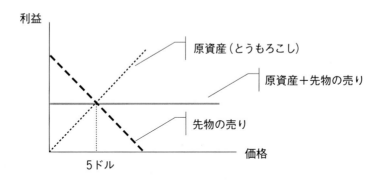

とうもろこし農家は独自で信頼できる売り先を見つけ，5ドルで売るという先渡契約を結ぶこともできる。しかし，売り先を探さずとも，市場で取引されている先物を売ることで同様のリスクヘッジは可能である。

Swaps

A swap is the arrangement by two counterparties to exchange one stream of cash flow for another and can be considered as a nexus of forward or futures contracts. Similar to forwards and futures, swaps work for hedging risks.

Swaps are frequently used to exchange floating interest rates with fixed rates, called interest rate swaps. Suppose a company having floating rates debt is concerned about a potential increase in the interest rates going forward. It is preferable for the company to fix the cost before the interest rates rise. In this case, the company could issue new debt with fixed interest rates and redeem the current floating debt, but it will be costly. Alternatively, the company can utilize swaps to reform the debt with floating to fixed rates. The company enters into the swap agreement with a financial institution such as a bank, paying fixed interest rates in exchange for receiving floating rates.

Figure 15.2 shows the image of the arrangement. The company's payment to creditors (arrow ①) is countered by the receipt of floating rates from the financial institution (arrow ③), and the cash flows left after the arrangement then there will be fixed rate payments to the financial institutions (arrow ②).

Figure 15.2 | **Interest Rate Swaps**

● スワップ

　スワップとは相手先と一連のキャッシュフローを交換する取引である。先渡・先物取引を複数束ねたものということもできる。先渡・先物取引と同様に，価格や金利の変動リスクをヘッジするために使用される。

　スワップは変動金利と固定金利を交換する際によく使用される（金利スワップ）。たとえば，変動金利での負債を抱えている企業が，今後金利が上昇するリスクを認識しているとする。企業としては，金利が上昇する前に金利にかかわるコストを固定してしまうほうが望ましい。この場合，企業は新たに固定金利の負債を発行し，現存する変動金利の負債を返済することもできるが，借り換えにはコストがかかる。その代わりに，企業はスワップを活用することにより，現存の変動金利の負債を固定金利の負債に実質的に再構成することが可能である。銀行のような金融機関との間で，固定金利を払う代わりに変動金利を受け取るスワップ契約を結ぶのである。

　図表15.2はこのスワップ契約のイメージを示している。企業の債権者への変動金利の支払い（矢印①）は金融機関からの変動金利の受け取り（矢印③）とキャンセルされるので，差し引きでのキャッシュフローは金融機関への固定金利の支払い（矢印②）のみとなる。

図表15.2 ｜ 金利スワップ

○ Currency Swaps

Currency swaps allow companies to exchange a series of payments in one currency for a series of payments in another currency. Swaps therefore are used to hedge the risk of foreign exchange rate fluctuations or to reduce financing costs in a foreign currency.

For example, a U.S. company considers borrowing yen to finance its operation in Japan. The company has a high profile in the U.S. and can raise cash with the low interest rate there. But it is not well known in Japan and cannot enjoy the low interest rate.

The company might issue bonds in the U.S and enter into a swap with a swap dealer (usually a financial institution) to convert the dollar denominated debt into the yen denominated debt. The company provides the dollar funds raised from the bond issue to the swap dealer and receives a yen loan. The dealer pays the interest on the dollar fund, and the company pays the interest on the yen loan. The interest payments to bond holders from the U.S. company are funded by the swap dealer. At maturity the principals of the loan will be returned to original holders.

On the other hand, the swap dealer can arrange a similar but inverse scheme, providing a dollar loan in exchange for receiving yen funds, with a Japanese company which would like to raise money in dollars but cannot enjoy the low interest rate (well known in Japan but not in U.S.).

Figure 15.3 shows the cash flows of the currency swap. Both the U.S company and the Japanese company can transform their loans from in the domestic currency to the foreign currency.

● 通貨スワップ

　通貨スワップはある特定の通貨の一連のキャッシュフローと，他の通貨の一連のキャッシュフローを交換する取引である。為替レートの変動に対するリスクをヘッジするためや，他国通貨建ての資金調達コストを低減させるために使われる。

　たとえば，米国の企業が日本で事業展開をするために日本円での借入れを検討しているとする。この企業は米国においては知名度が高く，米国においてドル建てで借入れを行う場合は，低金利での調達が可能である。しかし，日本においてはそれほど知名度が高くないことから，日本で借入れを行う場合には低金利を享受できないとする。

　そこで，この企業は米国において社債を発行したうえで，このドル建ての負債を円に変えるために金融機関とスワップ取引を行うことが考えられる。企業は調達したドル資金を金融機関に提供し，代わりに円資金を受け取る。金融機関はドル資金に対応した金利を企業に支払い，企業は円資金に対応した金利を金融機関に支払う。米国企業が調達したドル資金の金利支払いの費用は金融機関から提供されるので実際の負担はない。一方で金融機関から受け取った円資金に対しては金融機関に金利を支払う。満期においては，調達した資金の元本はそれぞれ元の所有者に戻すことになる。

　金融機関は，米国ドル建てで資金調達をしたいが低金利での調達ができない日本企業（日本では知名度が高いが，米国では知名度が低い企業）に対して，円建て資金を受け取る代わりにドル建ての資金を提供して同様のスキームを組むことができる。

　図表15.3はこのスワップ取引での資金の流れを表わしている。米国企業と日本企業はともに自国通貨建ての負債を，他国通貨建てに変換できている。

Figure 15.3 | Cash Flows from Currency Swaps

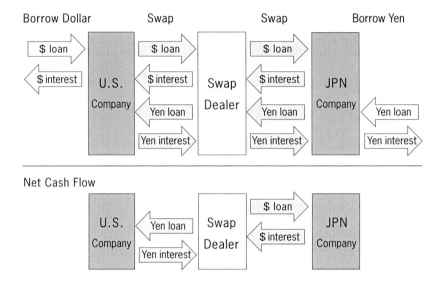

It might be difficult for a company to find another party for swaps (the U.S. company finds the Japanese company in the example), but a swap dealer takes the role as an intermediary making a swap arrangement accessible for many companies.

図表15.3 通貨スワップのキャッシュフロー

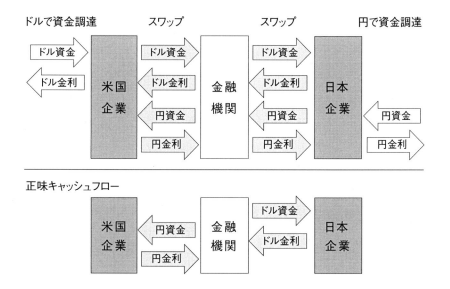

　金融機関ではなく，企業が独自にスワップの最終相手先を（上記の例では米国企業が日本企業を）探すことは難しいが，金融機関が仲介することによって取引は容易に可能である。

Chapter 16 Options

> **Points!**
> - ✓ An option is a right not obligation, so the value of an option cannot be negative
> - ✓ An option offers a leverage effect to amplify the return, and functions as an insurance to limit loss
> - ✓ The value of an option increases as the price of an underlying asset becomes more volatile

○ What Are Options

Options are rights to buy or sell a financial asset or commodity (the underlying asset) at a specified price (the exercise price or the strike price) in a specified period. A call option gives its holder the right to buy an asset for an exercise price on or before an expiration date, and a put option gives its holder the right to sell an asset for an exercise price on or before an expiration date. Since options are rights, buyers of options or holders have no obligation to exercise them. On the other hand, sellers of options or writers have obligation to meet the request when options are exercised. A call seller has the obligation to sell the asset, and a put seller has the obligation to buy the asset.

Figure 16.1 | Rights and Obligations of Options

	Buyer	Seller
Call Option	Right to buy asset	Obligation to sell asset
Put Option	Right to sell asset	Obligation to buy asset

第16章 オプション

> **ポイント!**
> - ✓ 権利であって義務ではないオプションの価値はマイナスにはならない
> - ✓ オプションには利益を増幅させるレバレッジとしての機能と，損失を限定する保険としての機能が内在している
> - ✓ オプションの価値は原資産の価格の変動性が増大すると高まる

● オプションとは

　オプションとは商品や資産などをある期間内においてあらかじめ決められた価格で売るあるいは買う権利である。この権利行使の対象となる商品や資産が原資産である。決められた価格のことを行使価格という。コール・オプションは満期日またはそれ以前に行使価格で資産を買う権利である。プット・オプションは満期日またはそれ以前に行使価格で資産を売る権利である。コール・オプション，プット・オプションともに権利であるため，オプションの買い手つまり保有者は行使する義務はない。一方で，オプションの売り手（ライターともいう）には，オプションを行使された場合にそれに応える義務が発生する。コール・オプションの売り手であればその資産を売る義務が，プット・オプションの売り手であればその資産を買う義務が発生する。

図表 16.1　オプションの権利と義務

	買い手	売り手
コール・オプション	資産を買う権利	資産を売る義務
プット・オプション	資産を売る権利	資産を買う義務

The option exercised only on its expiration date is referred to as a European option. An option which is exercised on or before the date is referred to as an American option. These names are unrelated to the region where they are traded or issued.

○ Payoff to Option Buyer

The payoff of an option when it is exercised is determined with the price of an underling asset and the exercise price. For example, a call option on the stock with an exercise price of $100 becomes profitable when the stock price exceeds $100. Suppose the stock price is $110, the right to buy the shares worth $110 for $100 yields a profit of $10. The profit generated by the option is 20 if the stock price rises to $120. Conversely, if the stock price comes short of $100, the option is not profitable. However, the option is a right not obligation, so you can leave it unexercised and avoid a loss, even if the share price remains around $80 or even $1. The value of an option cannot be negative. (The left in Figure 16.2)

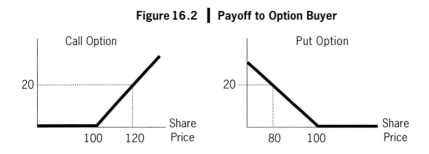

Figure 16.2 | Payoff to Option Buyer

Figure 16.2 also shows the payoffs of a put option with an exercise price of $100. When the share price falls below the exercise price like $80 or $90, the put option is profitable because the option holder can sell the cheap stocks for a higher price. Conversely, if the stock price exceeds the exercise price, the put option which is the right to sell the stock with cheaper price is not profitable. However, the put holder is not required to exercise the option, so the value of option cannot go below zero.

満期日のみに権利の行使が可能なオプションはヨーロピアン・オプションと呼ばれ，満期日以前であればいつであっても行使が可能なオプションのことはアメリカン・オプションと呼ばれる。なお，これらの名称はオプションが発行・取引される地域とは関係がない。

● オプションの買い手の利益

オプションが行使されたときの利益は原資産の価格と行使価格によって決まる。たとえば，原資産が株式で行使価格が 100 ドルのコール・オプションであれば，株価が 100 ドルを上回る場合に利益が発生する。株価が 110 ドルになった場合，110 ドルの価値の株式を 100 ドルで購入する権利は，10 ドルの利益を生み出す。株価が 120 ドルであるならば，オプションの利益は 20 ドルである。一方で，株価が 100 ドルに満たない場合にはオプションの利益はゼロである。ただし，オプションは権利であって義務ではないため，仮に株価が 80 ドルあるいは 1 ドルだとしても権利を行使しない限り損失は発生しない。オプションの価値はマイナスにはならないのである（図表 16.2 左）。

図表 16.2 ｜ オプションの買い手の利益

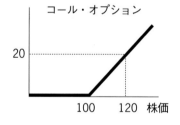
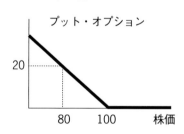

図表 16.2 は，行使価格が 100 ドルのプット・オプションの利益も示している。株価が 80 ドル，90 ドルと行使価格を下回った場合には，より高い 100 ドルという価格で売ることができるため，オプションは利益を生み出す。反対に株価が行使価格を上回る場合には，安い価格で売る権利であるプット・オプションからは利益は生じない。しかし，損失が発生してしまう権利行使を行う義務はないため，オプションの価値はゼロより小さくはならない。

In summary, a call option benefits when the current share price exceeds the exercise price, and a put option benefits when the current share price falls below the exercise price, and the value of options cannot be negative.

● Payoff to Option Seller

Figure 16.3 shows the payoff to the option seller with an exercise price of $100. The figures of the payoffs to sellers are inversed of the payoffs to buyers. The seller's loss is the buyer's gain, and vice versa. A call seller is subject to an unlimited loss when the share price increases, and a put seller will be exposed to significant loss when the share price declines.

Figure 16.3 | Payoff to Option Seller

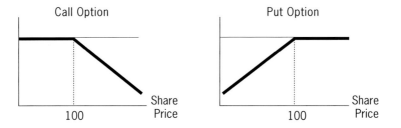

● In the Money vs. Out of the Money

The option which will make a profit if it is exercised immediately is called an "in the money" option. In the case of the call option on a stock, if the current stock price is higher than the exercise price, the option is "in the money". The put option whose exercise price is higher than the current stock price is "in the money". An "in the money" option has an intrinsic value.

まとめると，コール・オプションでは株価が行使価格を上回った場合，プット・オプションは株価が行使価格を下回った場合に利益が発生する。ただし，オプションの価値はマイナスにはならない。

● オプションの売り手の利益

図表 16.3 は，行使価格 100 ドルのオプションを売った場合の利益を表している。オプションの売り手の利益のイメージはオプションの買い手の利益と上下正反対である。オプションの売り手の損失はオプションの買い手の利益であり，その逆も然りである。コール・オプションの売り手は株価が上昇していった場合に無制限に損失を被る可能性があり，プット・オプションの売り手は株価が下落していった場合に損失が大きく膨らむ。

図表 16.3 ｜ オプションの売り手の利益

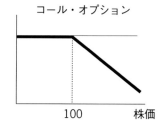
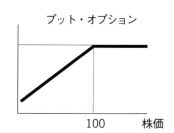

● イン・ザ・マネーとアウト・オブ・ザ・マネー

現時点でオプションを行使した場合に利益が発生するオプションのことをイン・ザ・マネー・オプションと呼ぶ。株式のコール・オプションであれば，株価が行使価格よりも高い場合がこれにあたる。プット・オプションの場合は，株価が行使価格よりも低い場合がイン・ザ・マネー・オプションである。イン・ザ・マネー・オプションのみがオプションの本質的な価値（本質価値）をもつ。

The option which will not make a profit if it is exercised immediately is called "out of the money". Also, the option whose exercise price is equal to the current stock price is called "at the money".

● Profit for Options Trade

The cost to purchase options are not free, so the profit generated by the option trade is not the payoffs of options. Recall the call option with the exercise price of $100, and suppose it is sold for $15. The price of the option is also known as the option premium. Although the call will produce a gain when the stock price exceeds $100, the option holder cannot make a profit until the share price exceeds $115 because he/she pays the initial cost of $15. $115 is the break-even share price for the option transaction in this example.

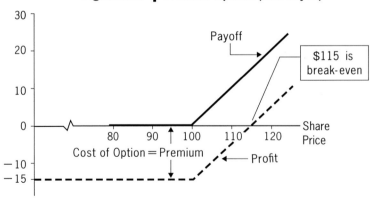

Figure 16.4 | Profit for Options (Call Buyer)

反対に，現時点においてオプションを行使した場合に利益が発生しないオプションのことを，アウト・オブ・ザ・マネー・オプションという。また，行使価格と現在の資産の価格が一致しているオプションのことをアット・ザ・マネー・オプションと呼ぶ。

● オプション取引の損益

　オプションを購入する費用はただではないため，オプション取引における全体の損益はオプションが生み出す利益とは同じにならない。先程の行使価格が100ドルのコール・オプションが15ドルで売られているとする。なお，オプションの価格のことをオプションのプレミアムと呼ぶ。このコール・オプションは株価が行使価格の100ドルを超えたときに利益を生み出すが，オプションを購入するために15ドル支払っているため，オプションの買い手は株価が115ドルを超えない限り利益を得ることができない。115ドルが損益分岐点の株価となる。

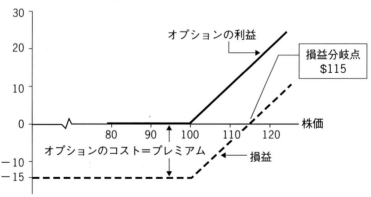

図表16.4 ┃ オプション取引の損益（コールの買い手）

第16章　オプション

A call seller starts to suffer a loss when the share price exceeds the exercise price of $100, but he/she gets $15 as initial proceeds from selling the option. Therefore, total profit is positive before the share price hits $115.

Figure 16.5 | Profit for Options (Call Seller)

```
       |
    15 |- - - - - - - - - -,
       | Cost of Option = Premium  `,
     0 |_____|_____`_____ Share Price
                          100   `115
                                  `.
                                    `. Profit
                                      `.
                                        `. Payoff
```

● Options vs. Stock Investments

A call holder makes a profit when the share price goes up, so investing in a call is an alternative strategy to investing in equity or a stock.

Compare the returns of an option investment with a stock investment. Suppose at the money call option that matures in 1 year with the exercise price of $100 is sold for $10. The risk-free rate is assumed to be 2%. Consider the following three strategies for investing a sum of $10,000. A: investing entirely in stocks, B: investing entirely in call options (buying 1,000 calls), C: buying 100 calls and investing the remaining in government bonds yielding the 2% risk-free return.

The upper table in Figure 16.6 simulates the value of three strategies a year later, according to the change in the share price. The lower table shows the returns of each simulated result.

また，コール・オプションの売り手は株価が 100 ドルの行使価格を上回ると損失が発生しはじめるが，オプションを売ることによって先に 15 ドルを手に入れている。そのため株価が 115 ドルまで上昇しない限りは，全体の損益はプラスである。

図表 16.5 ｜ オプション取引の損益（コールの売り手）

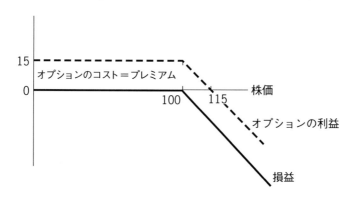

● オプションと株式投資の比較

コール・オプションの買い手は，株価が上昇すると利益が得られるため，コール・オプションへの投資は，株式を直接購入することの代替的な投資戦略となりうる。

オプションへの投資のリターンを株式への投資のリターンと比較してみよう。行使価格が 100 ドルで 1 年満期のアット・ザ・マネー・コール・オプションが 10 ドルで購入できるとしよう。リスクフリー・レートは 2% とする。投資資金は合計 10,000 ドルであるとし，以下のような 3 つの投資戦略を考える。A：10,000 ドルすべてで株式投資を行う。B：10,000 ドルすべてで 10 ドルの価格のコール・オプションを 1,000 オプション購入する。C：1,000 ドルでコール・オプションを 100 購入し，残りの 9,000 ドルを 2% の利益を生み出す国債に投じる。

図表 16.6 の上段は，3 つの投資戦略の 1 年後の投資の価値を，株価の変化にあわせてシミュレーションしたものである。下段はそれぞれの投資の価値に応じたリターンを表わしている。

Figure 16.6 | Value and Return of Investments with Options

Value of Investment ($)

Share Price	50	60	70	80	90	100	110	120	130	140	150
A. Stock	5,000	6,000	7,000	8,000	9,000	10,000	11,000	12,000	13,000	14,000	15,000
B. Call Options	0	0	0	0	0	0	10,000	20,000	30,000	40,000	50,000
C. Call + Bonds	9,180	9,180	9,180	9,180	9,180	9,180	10,180	11,180	12,180	13,180	14,180

Rate of Return (%)

Share Price	50	60	70	80	90	100	110	120	130	140	150
A. Stock	−50	−40	−30	−20	−10	0	10	20	30	40	50
B. Call Options	−100	−100	−100	−100	−100	−100	0	100	200	300	400
C. Call + Bonds	−8	−8	−8	−8	−8	−8	2	12	22	32	42

The value of strategy A changes according to the change of the share price and the return of it is identical to that of the share. The strategy B is worthless if the stock price is lower than the exercise price, but the return rises rapidly when the stock price become higher than the exercise price. For example, 9% share price appreciation from $110 to $120 will results in a sharp rise on the return from 0% to 100%. Lastly, the value of strategy C will not be lower than $9,180 underpinned by the government bonds and their risk-free returns even if the share price is lower than the exercise price of the call options.

Figure 16.7 | Return Diagram of Investments with Options

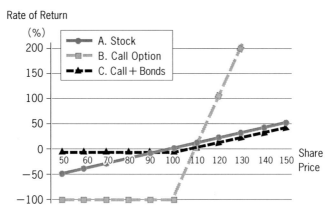

図表16.6 オプションを活用した投資資産の価値とリターン

投資の価値（ドル）

株価	50	60	70	80	90	100	110	120	130	140	150
A. 株式	5,000	6,000	7,000	8,000	9,000	10,000	11,000	12,000	13,000	14,000	15,000
B. コール・オプション	0	0	0	0	0	0	10,000	20,000	30,000	40,000	50,000
C. コール＋国債	9,180	9,180	9,180	9,180	9,180	9,180	10,180	11,180	12,180	13,180	14,180

リターン（％）

株価	50	60	70	80	90	100	110	120	130	140	150
A. 株式	−50	−40	−30	−20	−10	0	10	20	30	40	50
B. コール・オプション	−100	−100	−100	−100	−100	−100	0	100	200	300	400
C. コール＋国債	−8	−8	−8	−8	−8	−8	2	12	22	32	42

　株式に全額投資をするAは株価の変動に伴って投資の価値が1対1で変化し，株価のリターンと同様のリターンを投資から得ることになる。コール・オプションに全額投資をするBは，株価が行使価格を下回る場合は投資の価値はゼロであるが，株価が行使価格を上回るとリターンは急激に大きくなっていく。たとえば株価が110ドルから120ドルに9％上昇しただけでBのリターンは0％から100％に急上昇する。最後にオプションと国債を組み合わせたCはオプションの行使価格に株価が達しない場合でも国債とそのリターンがあるため投資の価値が下支えされており，9,180ドル未満にはならない。

図表16.7 オプションを活用した投資のリターン

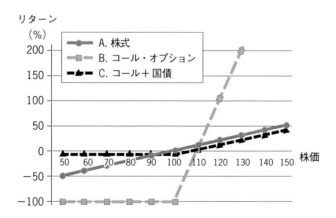

第16章　オプション

As demonstrated, an option offers a leverage effect which amplifies the return. Also, due to the feature that the value of an option will not be negative, you can pursue a higher return securing the minimum value of investment when you combine options with safer financial assets such as government bonds.

○ Hedging Risk with Options

Consider a company sells a product. The financial performance of the company is subject to price fluctuations of the product, the decline of the price affects the profit of the company negatively.

How can you use options to hedge the risk? You can buy or sell a call or a put option, namely you have four usages of options; selling a call, buying a call, selling a put, or buying a put. Which is the most effective way for hedging the risk?

The answer is buying a put. If you hold a put you can sell the product for a specified exercise price even if the price declines. With a put option, you can hedge the risk with respect to the price fluctuation and stabilize the financial performance. The strategy of having an asset combined with a put option that guarantees minimum proceeds is known as a protective put (strategy).

Figure 16.8 | Hedging Risk with Options (Protective Put)

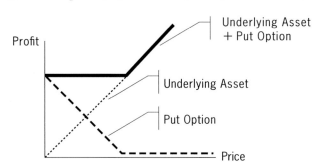

このようにオプションにはリターンを急激に大きくするレバレッジとしての機能がある。また，価値がマイナスにはならないという特性により，国債のような安全な資産と組み合わせると，最低額の投資価値を確保しつつ高いリターンを狙うことも可能である。

オプションによるリスクヘッジ

ある商品を売っている企業を考えてみよう。商品価格の変動はこの企業の業績に大きな影響を与える。当然だが，商品の価格が下落すれば企業の利益は減少することになるだろう。

このリスクをヘッジするために，オプションを活用することを検討しよう。オプションにはコールとプットがあり，それらを買うことと売ることができる。つまり，コールの売り，コールの買い，プットの売り，プットの買い，の4つの方法を取りうる。このうちどれがリスクヘッジに有効であろうか。

ここで有効なのは，売る権利を保持するプットの買いである。プット・オプションを保有していれば，商品価格が下落した場合でも，あらかじめ決められた価格で商品を売ることができる。そのため価格変動のリスクをヘッジでき，利益を安定させることができるからである。なお，原資産とプット・オプションを組み合わせて最低限の売却価格ラインを確保するこの投資戦略はプロテクティブ・プット（戦略）と呼ばれる。

図表 16.8 オプションによるリスクヘッジ（プロテクティブ・プット）

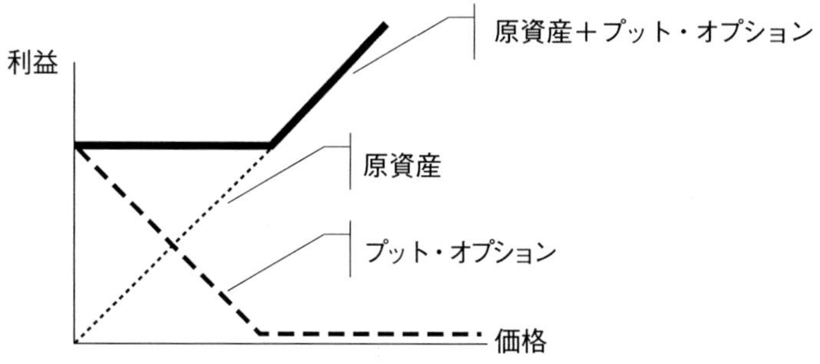

Option Values

The value of an option consists of the intrinsic value which corresponds to the profit if it is exercised immediately, and the time value which corresponds to the probability to move the price of assets before the maturity date.

Figure 16.9 shows the price of call options (option premium) with a January 2019 expiration on Apple stock in October 2017 when Apple stock was selling for $157.

Figure 16.9 | Prices of Call Options on Apple

Exercise Price	Premium	Exercise Price	Premium
120	41.1	170	12.35
130	33.7	180	9.25
140	26.8	190	6.95
150	21.05	200	5.1
160	16.3	250	1.2

Source: Derived from Yahoo! Finance

The price of the call with an exercise price of $120 was $41.1. Considering the price of the stock at the time was $157, this call option is "in the money", having the intrinsic value which generates profit of $37 (= 157 − 120) if it was exercised immediately. The difference between the intrinsic value of $37 and the option price of $41.1 is attributed to the time value.

Then look at the price of another call with an exercise price of $250. It costed $1.2. This call is an "out of the money" option, having no intrinsic value. Nevertheless, the option is valuable ($1.2) reflecting the time value of the option.

The price of the call with an exercise price of $160, which was close to the stock price at the time of $16.3, displaying a noticeable time value. As described, a time value of an option will be maximized when the option is "at the money".

● オプションの価値

オプションの価値は，オプションがその時点において行使された場合の利益である本質価値と，満期までの間にその資産の価格が変動する可能性に対応した時間価値とからなる。

図表16.9は2017年10月において，1年3カ月後の2019年の1月に満期を迎えるアップルのコール・オプションの価格（プレミアム）を表わしている。アップルのこの時点の株価は157ドルであった。

図表16.9 アップルのコール・オプション価格

行使価格	オプション価格	行使価格	オプション価格
120	41.1	170	12.35
130	33.7	180	9.25
140	26.8	190	6.95
150	21.05	200	5.1
160	16.3	250	1.2

出所：Yahoo! Financeから抜粋して加工

行使価格が120ドルの場合のコール・オプションの価格は41.1ドルである。当時の株価は157ドルであるためこのオプションはイン・ザ・マネーであり，この時点でオプションを行使した場合の本質価値は157－120ドル＝37ドルである。これとオプション価格の41.1ドルとの差分が時間価値である。

また，行使価格が250ドルのオプションの価格は1.2ドルである。このオプションはアウト・オブ・ザ・マネーであり本質価値はゼロである。それにもかかわらず，オプションの価値は時間価値が反映されて1.2ドルとなっている。

さらに，この時点の株価に近い行使価格160ドルのオプションの価格は16.3ドルと時間価値は極めて大きくなっている。このように，オプションの時間価値はアット・ザ・マネーの状態で一番大きくなる。

● Determinants of Option Value

Figure 16.10 summarizes the determinants of option value and their impacts.

Figure 16.10 | Determinants of Option Value and Influences on Value

When the Factor Increases	The Value of a Call Option	The Value of a Put Option
Underlying Price (Stock Price)	Increase	Decrease
Exercise Price	Decrease	Increase
Volatility	Increase	Increase
Time until Expiration	Increase	Increase (in most cases)
Risk-free Rate	Increase	Decrease
Dividend Yield	Decrease	Increase

Let us begin with a call option. We have seen the value of a call option increases as the price of an underlying asset (the current stock price in case of a stock) increases. Then, because the lower exercise price makes the profit of an option bigger, the value of a call option decreases as the exercise price increases.

It is interesting that the higher the volatility or the standard deviation of the underlying asset price, the higher the option is valued. For illustration, Figure 16.11 shows the profits of the two call options with the exercise price of $100 on the stocks whose price at maturity varies from $50 to $150 and from $80 to $120, respectively. Suppose the five outcomes occur with equal probability. The call option on the high volatility stock will reach a state of "in the money" when the share price is $125 and $150, producing gains. The average payoff will be $15 $(=(0+0+0+25+50)/5)$. On the other hand, the average payoff of the call option on the low volatility stock will be $6 $(=(0+0+0+10+20)/5)$.

● オプションの価値に影響を与える要因

図表 16.10 は，オプションの価値に影響を与える要因と，それぞれの影響について整理している。

図表 **16.10** ｜ オプション価値の決定要因と影響

以下の要因の増加	コール・オプションの価値への影響	プット・オプションの価値への影響
原資産価格（株価）	プラス	マイナス
行使価格	マイナス	プラス
原資産価格の変動性	プラス	プラス
満期までの期間	プラス	（多くの場合）プラス
金利（リスクフリー・レート）	プラス	マイナス
配当利回り	マイナス	プラス

まず，コール・オプションから確認していこう。原資産の価格（株式であれば株価）が上昇すれば，コール・オプションの価値は高まることはこれまでみた通りである。また，行使価格は低いほうが利益が大きくなるから，行使価格が高ければコール・オプションの価値は低下する。

原資産価格の変動性（標準偏差）が大きいとオプションの価値は高まることは興味深い。説明のためにここで例を用いて説明しよう。図表 16.11 は，満期日における株価が 50 ドルから 150 ドルの範囲で変動すると予想される株式と，80 ドルから 120 ドルの範囲で変動すると予想される株式の 2 つがあったとして，それぞれに行使価格が 100 ドルのコール・オプションを保有する場合の利益を表わしている。なお，5 パターンある株価のうちどれになるのかの確率は同一とする。変動性が大きい株式の場合は，株価が 125 ドルと 150 ドルになった場合にオプションはイン・ザ・マネーとなり，コール・オプションから利益が発生する。平均的な利益は 15 ドルである（0+0+0+25+50）÷ 5 = 15)。一方で，変動性が小さい株式の場合，コール・オプションの平均的な利益は 6 ドルである（0+0+0+10+20）÷ 5 = 6)。

Figure 16.11 | **Volatility and Payoffs of Option (Exercise Price : $100)**

High Volatility Stock						Average Payoff
Stock Price	50	75	100	125	150	
Option Payoff	0	0	0	25	50	15

Low Volatility Stock						Average Payoff
Stock Price	80	90	100	110	120	
Option Payoff	0	0	0	10	20	6

As demonstrated in the figure, the price of a high volatility stock is more likely to be higher than the exercise price by a large margin, so the call option is more valuable. The price of a volatile stock can drop significantly as well, but the payoff generated by an option cannot be negative, therefore the possibility that the price can rise alone affects the value of a call option.

In previous chapters, we have discussed the present value of an asset whose volatility of the return is high, namely a high-risk asset, will be further discounted. However, the higher volatility contributes to the value of an option because the payoffs generated by an option when the price of an underlying asset move upward and downward are asymmetry.

Next, the longer the remaining time before expiration or maturity is, the more valuable a call option is, because there is more time for an unexpected event allowing the option go in the money.

In addition, the call options value rises when the interest rate rises. The option might not be exercised immediately, so an option holder can invest the funds and get the return from other opportunities before exercising the option. The return from it will be higher when the interest rate rises. Also, it can be said a higher interest rate leads to a higher discount rate, lowering the present value of the exercise price or the future payment, therefore, increases the value of a call.

図表16.11 株価変動とオプションの利益（行使価格：100ドル）

株価変動が大きい株式						平均利益
株価	50	75	100	125	150	
利益	0	0	0	25	50	15

株価変動が小さい株式						平均利益
株価	80	90	100	110	120	
利益	0	0	0	10	20	6

　このように，変動性が高い株式であるほど株価が行使価格を大幅に上回る可能性が高くなるため，コール・オプションの価値は高まるのである。株価の変動性が大きいと，大きく値下がりする場合もありうるが，オプションからの利益はマイナスにならないため，株価が大きく上昇する可能性のみがコール・オプションの価値に影響を与えているのである。

　これまで，リターンの変動性，すなわちリスクが高い場合，その資産の現在価値は低くなることを学んできた。しかしながら，オプションの場合は，利益が資産価格の上昇場面と下落場面で非対称であるため，資産価格の変動性が高い価値に結びつくという特性をもつのである。

　次に，満期までの期間が長ければ長いほど株価に影響を与える予期しない出来事が起こる余地が増え，このことはオプションがイン・ザ・マネーの状態になるチャンスを増加させるため，コール・オプションの価値は上昇する。

　さらに，金利が高くなるとコール・オプションの価値は上昇する。オプションを行使するのは現在とは限らないため，行使の際に必要となる資金は行使までの間は運用できる。そのため，金利が高ければその分高いリターンを得ることができるからである。また，金利が高いことは割引率の上昇を通じて将来の支払額である行使価格の現在価値を低くすることになるため，コール・オプションの価値は高くなるともいえる。

Lastly, the call option value on the stock depends on a dividend yield. Because a share price is decreased by the amount of a dividend payment, dividends decrease the value of a call.

○ Put Option Value

A put option generates profit when the price of an underlying asset is lower than the exercise price, so the value of a put option increases as the price of an underlying asset decreases and the exercise price increases. The higher volatility of the underlying asset price increases a puts value the same as a call.

An increase in interest rate lowers the present value of the exercise price. Therefore, decreases the value of a put. Because a share price is decreased by the amount of a dividend payment, dividends increase the value of a put option on a stock.

It is not simple to understand the effect of time before expiration on a put. Similar to the case of a call option, a put option with a longer life is more valuable because there is more time for an unexpected event making the option go in the money. On the other hand, the longer the time before maturity is, the lower the present value of the exercise price is. Therefore, there is a decrease in the value of a put. The time before expiration has two opposite effects on a puts value, but in general, the value of a put option with a longer life is higher than one with a shorter life.

最後に，特に株式の場合は，株式の配当利回りもコール・オプションの価値に影響を与える。配当を支払う分，原資産価格である株価は下がるため，配当はコール・オプションの価値を下落させる。

● プット・オプションの価値

プット・オプションは，行使価格を原資産価格が下回る場合に利益が発生するので，行使価格の上昇と原資産価格の下落が価値のプラス要因となる。変動性の大きさはコール・オプションと同様にプラス要因である。

金利の上昇は，行使価格の現在価値の下落につながるので，プット・オプションの価値にマイナスに働く。また，配当利回りの上昇は株価の下落要因であるので，株式のプット・オプションの価値を高める。

満期までの期間に関しては単純ではない。一面では，コールと同様に，期間が長ければ長いほど株価に影響を与える予期しない出来事が起こる余地が増えるため，プット・オプションの価値は上昇する。一方で，満期までの期間が長いと，行使価格の現在価値は下落し，これはプット・オプションの価値にマイナスの影響を与える。このようにプラス・マイナスの両面の影響があるが，多くの場合は満期までの期間が長いほどプット・オプションの価値は高くなる。

○ Black-Scholes Model

Black-Scholes Model including all factors above is widely used to calculate the price of an option.

The formula designed by Fischer Black and Myron Scholes is extremely complex and is beyond the scope of this book, but the simple Microsoft Excel spreadsheet requiring six inputs to value an option is available online. If you are interested to learn more, go to the website:

https://www.biz-book.jp/isbn/978-4-502-30201-5

Figure 16.12 | **Image of Black-Scholes Model Spreadsheet**

INPUTS		OUTPUTS	
Stock Price	200	d1	0.8107
Exercise price	180	d2	0.6607
Standard deviation (annual)	0.30	N (d1)	0.7912
Maturity (in years)	0.25	N (d2)	0.7456
Risk-free rate (annual)	0.03	Call Option Value	24.6463
Dividend yield (annual)	0.01	Put Option Value	3.8007

● ブラック・ショールズ・モデル

オプションの価値を評価するモデルとして広く使われているブラック・ショールズ・モデルは，上記の要因をすべて含んでいる。

フィッシャー・ブラックとマイロン・ショールズによって考案されたブラック・ショールズ・モデルの計算式は極めて複雑である。そのため本書では説明しないが，6つの項目を入力することでオプション価値が算出できるマイクロソフト Excel ベースのファイルを用意している。興味のある方は以下のウェブページからダウンロードできる。

https://www.biz-book.jp/isbn/978-4-502-30201-5

図表 16.12 ブラック・ショールズ・モデル計算ファイルのイメージ

入力項目	
原資産価格（株価）	200
行使価格	180
原資産価格の変動性(標準偏差(年率))	0.30
満期までの期間（年）	0.25
リスクフリー・レート（年率）	0.03
配当利回り（年率）	0.01

計算結果	
d1	0.8107
d2	0.6607
N (d1)	0.7912
N (d2)	0.7456
コール・オプションの価値	24.6463
プット・オプションの価値	3.8007

Postface

Describing the same things in two different languages is surprisingly difficult. A usable phrase in one language does not always exist in another language, or it requires more than one sentence to express subtle nuances conveyed by one word in another language. With full understanding that even carrying the text side-by-side in both Japanese and English will not provide perfect bilingual material, this book tries to complete the textbook with sufficient precision and readability in two languages.

In order for a textbook to be understandable, presenting a great number of real cases, numerical examples, and exercises is effective. But I have had to give up that due to space limitations. I apologize that I need to leave supplementary explanation to an instructor using this book as a text in a lecture. I also would like the readers including students to understand that I let you try to access real data related to what is written in this book.

This book is based on what I teach at Temple University Japan Campus (TUJ). I wish to express my gratitude to TUJ and its Director of International Business Studies, William J. Swinton who led me to this new journey. I am greatly indebted to Professor Nobuya Takezawa (Rikkyo University) and my former colleagues at Stern Stewart, the consulting firm focusing on corporate finance who inspired me to learn corporate finance and stimulated my intellectual curiosity. Finally, I appreciate the productive support regarding English expression provided by Timothy C. Amburn, a TUJ student with outstanding academic results.

I would be more than happy if this book could help a lot of people advance their knowledge of corporate finance and polish their English or Japanese language skills.

Akashi Hongo

あとがき

　2つの言語で全く同じことを語るのは思いのほか難しいものです。ある言語で便利な言い回しが他の言語にはなかったり，1つの単語がもつ微妙なニュアンスを別の言語で語るためには1行以上の文章が必要だったりするからです。日英バイリンガルといっても，完全な対訳は不可能なのは百も承知なのですが，それでも誤りなくわかりやすく，日本語としても英語としても成立する教科書に仕上げることにトライしたのが本書です。

　わかりやすい教科書にするためには，多くの例，数値，計算演習を含むことが効果的なのですが，バイリンガル書籍の本書では最低限に絞っています。本書を講義で使用いただく先生方にはその点の補足をゆだねることになりますがご了承ください。また，読者の皆さんにも，よりたくさんのリアルなデータへのアクセスを皆さん自身にお任せしてしまうことをご了承いただければと思います。

　本書の内容は私がテンプル大学において担当している内容がもとになっています。その機会をいただき，新たなキャリアの道を開いてくれたテンプル大学と，国際ビジネス学科ディレクターのウィリアム J. スウィントン氏にまずお礼を申し上げます。そして，ファイナンスの面白さをお教えいただいた立教大学の竹澤伸哉先生と，企業財務コンサルティング会社スターンスチュワート時代の仲間に感謝したいと思います。また，本書の英語表現に関しては，テンプル大学の優等生ティモシー アンバーン君のすばらしいアシストを得ました。ご協力に感謝いたします。

　最後に，本書が，ひとりでも多くの方のコーポレートファイナンスに関する知識の向上と，英語（あるいは日本語の）のブラッシュアップの助けとなることを，心から願っています。

本合暁詩

Index／索引

■ A～C ■

Accounts Payable ……………………… 50
Accounts Receivable ……………… 42, 50
American Option ……………………… 268
Annuity ………………………………… 76, 104
Apple …………………………………… 218
Arbitrage Opportunity ……………… 240
At the Money ………………………… 272, 280
Bank …………………………………… 22
Bank Borrowing ……………………… 182
Bankruptcy …………………………… 182
Beta, β ………………………………… 136, 142, 166
Big Mac Index ………………………… 244
Black-Scholes Model ………………… 288
Bond …………………………………… 70, 182
Book Value …………………………… 42, 48, 172
B/S, Balance Sheet ………………… 38, 42
Bubble Economy ……………………… 36
Callable Bond ………………………… 186
Call Option …………………………… 282
Capital ………………………………… 22
Capital Gain …………………………… 116
Capital Investment …………………… 50
Capital Structure ……………………… 170, 188
CAPM, Capital Asset Pricing Model …… 142, 143, 172, 173
Cash Flow ……………………………… 26, 48
Commercial Bank ……………………… 32
Common Stock ………………………… 186
Consol Bond …………………………… 74
Convertible Bond ……………………… 186
Corporate Bond ……………………… 22, 80
Correlation …………………………… 150, 156
Correlation Coefficient (ρ) …… 148, 152, 166

Cost of Capital ………………………… 168
Cost of Debt ………………………… 170, 172, 178
Cost of Equity ……………………… 170, 178, 200
Costs of Financial Distress ………… 208
Coupon ………………………………… 70
Coupon Rate ………………………… 70
Covariance …………………………… 148, 166
Credit Rating ………………………… 80
Credit Rating Agency ………………… 80
Credit Risk …………………………… 80
Credit Risk Premium ………………… 172
Creditor ……………………………… 22
Currency Risk ………………………… 246
Currency Swap ……………………… 262

■ D～F ■

DCF, Discounted Cash Flow ………… 98
DDM, Dividend Discount Model …… 86, 88
Debt …………………………………… 24, 182
Debt Capital …………………………… 22
Debt Leverage ………………………… 192
Depreciation ………………………… 50
Derivative …………………………… 32
Discount Factor ……………………… 64
Discount Rate ………………………… 64, 94, 172
Diversification Effect ………………… 132, 148
Dividend ……………………………… 22, 116, 184, 214, 286
Dividend Yield ………………………… 116, 282
Dot-com Bubble ……………………… 36
Dow Jones Industrial Average ……… 124
Earnings Forecast …………………… 30
Efficient Frontier of Risky Asset …… 160
Efficient Frontier with Risk-free Asset … 162
Efficient Market Theory ……………… 36
EPS, Earnings per Share …… 46, 47, 88, 89,

220, 221, 224, 225
Equity ······ 24, 182
Equity Capital ······ 22
Equity per Share ······ 48
Equivalent Annual Annuity ······ 106
European Option ······ 268
Exercise Price ······ 266, 282
Expected Return ······ 62, 72, 94, 100, 118, 130, 142, 152, 168
FCF, Free Cash Flow ······ 50, 94
Financial Institution ······ 32, 34
Financial Leverage ······ 192
Financial Market ······ 32, 34
Financial Risk ······ 200
Fixed Asset ······ 42
Floating Exchange Rate ······ 236
Forecast Period ······ 108
Foreign Exchange Rate ······ 234
Forward Contract (or Forward) ······ 238, 254
Forward Exchange Contract ······ 238
Forward Exchange Rate ······ 238, 240
Forward Rate ······ 250
Future Price ······ 254
Futures Contract (or Future) ······ 254
FV, Future Value ······ 60, 62

■ G～I ■

Government Bond ······ 122
Growth Rate ······ 88, 90
High Yield Bond ······ 82
Implied Growth Rate ······ 92
Income Gain ······ 116
Income Statement ······ 38, 40
Industry Beta ······ 140
Inflation ······ 68
Inflation Rate ······ 242
Initial Cash Expenditure ······ 94
Insurance Company ······ 34

Interest ······ 22, 116
Interest Payment ······ 184
Interest Rate Swap ······ 260
Interest Tax Shield ······ 202
In the Money ······ 270, 280
Intrinsic Value ······ 270, 280
Inventory ······ 42, 50
Investment Bank ······ 32
Investment Grade ······ 82
Investment Opportunity Set ······ 154
Investors Shareholder ······ 22
IRR, Internal Rate of Return ······ 98, 100, 101

■ J～L ■

Junk Bond ······ 82
Leverage ······ 192, 200, 206, 278
Levered Company ······ 198
Liability ······ 42
Linear Regression ······ 138
Liquidation Value ······ 110
Long Position ······ 254

■ M～O ■

Maintenance Margin ······ 256
Margin ······ 256
Market Capitalization ······ 28, 30, 46
Market Portfolio ······ 164
Market Risk ······ 132, 138
Market Risk Premium ······ 126, 142
Market Value ······ 42, 48, 172
Maturity ······ 184
Modigliani-Miller (MM) Theorem (MM 理論) ······ 188, 189
Monthly Return ······ 142
Multiple ······ 48
Mutual Fund ······ 32, 34
Net Income ······ 40, 46
Net Investment ······ 52

293

Net Working Capital ····· 50
Net Worth ····· 42
Nikkei Average (Nikkei 225) ····· 124
Nominal Interest Rate ····· 68, 242
NOPAT, Net Operating Profit After Tax ··· 50, 51
NPV, Net Present Value ····· 94, 96, 97, 100, 101, 217, 250, 251
OCF, Operating Cash Flow ····· 52
Operating Profit ····· 40
Optimal Capital Structure ····· 210
Option ····· 266
Option Premium ····· 272
Out of Money ····· 272, 280

■ P ～ R ■

Payback Period ····· 102
PBR, Price to Book value Ratio ····· 46, 47, 92, 93
Pecking-Order Theory ····· 210
Perpetuity ····· 74, 76, 88
Perpetuity Formula ····· 74, 84, 110, 198, 206
Perpetuity Value ····· 110
Perpetuity with Growth Formula ····· 78, 84, 88, 110
PER, Price Earning Ratio ····· 46, 47, 90, 91, 224, 225
Plowback Ratio ····· 88
P/L, Profit and Loss Statement ····· 40
Portfolio ····· 34, 128, 134
PPP, Purchasing Power Parity ····· 244
Preferred Stock ····· 186
Present Value Factor ····· 64
Principal ····· 22, 70, 184
Protective Put ····· 278
Put Option ····· 266, 286
PV, Present Value ····· 26, 60, 62, 66
R^2乗 ····· 139
Real Interest Rate ····· 68, 242

Risk ····· 118, 122
Risk Premium ····· 122, 142
Risk-free Rate ····· 122, 142, 172, 240, 250, 274
ROA, Return on Assets ····· 44, 220, 221
ROE, Return on Equity ····· 44, 88, 89, 90, 91, 92, 93, 220, 221
R-square ····· 138

■ S ～ U ■

Security ····· 22, 32
Shareholders' Equity ····· 42
Shareholders Special Benefit Plan ····· 230
Share Issuance ····· 182, 226
Share Price ····· 30, 46, 86, 224
Share (Stock) Repurchases ····· 214, 220
Sharpe Ratio ····· 164
Short Position ····· 254
Signal ····· 218, 220
Signaling ····· 228
Signaling Effect ····· 218
SML, Security Market Line ····· 146
Speculative Grades ····· 82
(Spot) Exchange Rate ····· 250
Spot Rate ····· 234, 240
Standard & Poor's Composite Index (S&P 500) ····· 124, 125, 164, 165
Standard Deviation ····· 120, 130, 148, 152, 156, 166
Stock Market Index ····· 124
Strike Price ····· 266
Subordinated Debt ····· 186
Sunk Costs ····· 112
Sustainable Growth Rate ····· 92
Swap ····· 260
Systematic Risk ····· 132
Tax Savings Effect ····· 174, 202, 204
Tax Shield ····· 50
Terminal Value ····· 108

Time Value	280
TOPIX, Tokyo Stock Price Index	124, 125, 136, 137, 164, 165
Total Shareholder Return	116
Toyota Motor	136, 144, 176
Trade-off Theory	210
Underlying Asset	256, 266, 282
Unique Risk	132, 138
Unsystematic Risk	132

■ V～Z ■

Value of Company	24, 26, 28, 188, 200, 210, 222
Value of Debt	28
Value of Equity	28
Value of Option	280
Variance	120, 130, 152, 156
Voting Right	22
WACC, Weighted Average Cost of Capital	170, 171, 178, 179, 202, 203, 206, 207, 209, 210
Working Capital	50
Yield to Maturity	72
Zero Debt	212

■ あ 行 ■

アウト・オブ・ザ・マネー	273, 281
アット・ザ・マネー	273, 281
アップル	219
アメリカン・オプション	269
アンシステマティック・リスク	133
インカムゲイン	117
イン・ザ・マネー	271, 281
インプライド成長率	93
インフレーション	69
インフレ率	243
売掛金	43
売掛債権	51
運転資本	51
永久年金	75, 77
永久年金式	75, 85, 89, 111, 199, 207
営業 CF	53
営業利益	41
永続価値	111
オプション	267
オプションの価値	281
オプションのプレミアム	273

■ か 行 ■

買掛債務	51
回帰分析	139
回収期間法	103
格付機関	81
加重平均資本コスト	171
価値倍率	49
株価	29, 31, 47, 87, 225
株価指数（株式インデックス）	125
株価収益率	47
株価純資産倍率	47
株式	23
株式時価総額	29, 31, 47
株式の総合利回り	117
株式発行	183
株主	23
株主価値	29
株主資本	23, 25, 43, 183
株主資本コスト	171, 179, 201
株主資本利益率	45
株主優待制度	231
借入れ（借り入れる）	23, 183, 195
為替予約	239
為替リスク	247
為替レート	235
元本	23, 71, 185
企業価値	25, 27, 29, 189, 201, 209, 223
議決権	23

期待リターン ……63, 73, 95, 101, 119, 131, 143, 145, 153, 169	
キャッシュフロー……………………27, 49	
キャップエム………………………………143	
キャピタルゲイン………………………117	
共分散……………………………………149, 167	
銀行…………………………………………23, 33	
金融機関…………………………………33, 35	
金融市場…………………………………33, 35	
金利スワップ……………………………261	
金利平価…………………………………241	
クーポン……………………………………71	
クーポンレート……………………………71	
繰上償還条項付債券……………………187	
月次リターン……………………………143	
減価償却費…………………………………51	
現在価値…………………………27, 61, 63, 67	
現在価値係数………………………………65	
原資産………………………………257, 267, 283	
行使価格…………………………………267, 283	
購買力平価………………………………245	
効率的市場仮説……………………………37	
高利回り債…………………………………83	
コール・オプション……………267, 283	
国債…………………………………………123	
固定資産……………………………………43	
個別リスク………………………………133, 139	
コンソル債…………………………………75	

■ さ 行 ■

債券…………………………………………23, 71	
債券格付……………………………………81	
債権者………………………………………23	
在庫…………………………………………43, 51	
最終利回り…………………………………73	
裁定機会…………………………………241	
最適資本構成……………………………211	
財務リスク………………………………201	

先物為替予約……………………………239	
先物為替レート……………239, 241, 251	
先物取引…………………………………255	
先渡取引…………………………………255	
サステイナブル成長率……………………93	
産業別ベータ……………………………141	
時価…………………………………43, 49, 173	
時間価値…………………………………281	
シグナル……………………………219, 221, 229	
自社株買い………………………………215, 221	
市場ポートフォリオ……………………165	
市場リスク………………………………133, 139	
市場リスク・プレミアム……………127, 143	
システマティック・リスク……………133	
実質金利…………………………………69, 243	
資本…………………………………………23	
資本構成…………………………………171, 189	
資本コスト………………………………169	
シャープ・レシオ………………………165	
社債…………………………………23, 81, 183	
ジャンク債…………………………………83	
種類株式…………………………………187	
純資産………………………………………43	
純投資額……………………………………53	
証券会社……………………………………33	
証券市場線………………………………147	
証拠金……………………………………257	
正味運転資本………………………………51	
正味現在価値（NPV）…………………95	
将来価値…………………………………61, 63	
ショート・ポジション…………………255	
初期投資額…………………………………95	
信用リスク…………………………………81	
信用リスク・プレミアム………………173	
スポットレート……………235, 241, 251	
スワップ…………………………………261	
清算価値…………………………………111	
成長率（g）……………………………89, 91	

節税効果	51, 175, 205
設備投資額	51
相関	157
相関係数（ρ）	149, 151, 153, 167
増資	227
総資産利益率	45
総資本利益率	45
損益計算書	39, 41

■ た 行 ■

ターミナル・バリュー	109
貸借対照表	39, 43
ダウ平均株価指数	125
棚卸資産	43, 51
追加証拠金	257
通貨スワップ	263
定率成長の永久年金式	79, 85, 89, 111
デリバティブ	33
転換社債	187
当期純利益	41, 47
投機的格付	83
倒産	183
倒産コスト	209
投資家	23
投資機会集合	155
投資銀行	33
投資信託	33, 35
投資適格格付	83
東証株価指数	125
ドットコムバブル	37
トヨタ自動車	137, 145, 177
トレード・オフ理論	211

■ な 行 ■

内部利益率法（IRR）	99
内部留保	89
内部留保率	89
日経平均株価	125
年金等価コスト	107

■ は 行 ■

配当	23, 117, 185, 215, 287
配当利回り	117, 283
配当割引モデル	87
バブル経済	37
ビッグマックインデックス	245
1株あたりの純資産	49
1株あたりの利益	221
標準偏差	121, 131, 149, 153, 157, 167, 283
表面利率	71
負債	23, 25, 43, 183
負債価値	29
負債コスト	169, 173, 179
負債の節税効果	203
普通株	187
プット・オプション	267, 287
ブラック・ショールズ・モデル	289
フリー・キャッシュフロー（FCF）	51, 95
プロテクティブ・プット	279
分散	121, 131, 153, 157
分散投資	35
分散投資効果	133, 149
ベータ	137, 143, 167
ペッキング・オーダー理論	211
返済期限	185
変動為替制度	237
ポートフォリオ	129, 135
簿価	43, 49, 173
保険会社	35
本質価値	271, 281

■ ま 行 ■

埋没コスト	113
無借金	213
無リスク資産がある場合の効率的フロンティア	163

名目金利 ……………………………… 69, 243

■ や 行 ■

有価証券 ……………………………… 23, 33
有期年金 ……………………………… 77, 105
優先株式 ………………………………… 187
ヨーロピアン・オプション …………… 269
予想期間 ………………………………… 109

■ ら 行 ■

利益予想 ………………………………… 31
リスク ……………………………… 119, 123
リスク資産の効率的フロンティア …… 161

リスクフリー・レート ……… 123, 143, 173, 241, 251, 275
リスク・プレミアム ……………… 123, 143
利息 ………………………………… 23, 117
利息の支払い …………………………… 185
劣後債 …………………………………… 187
レバレッジ ………… 193, 199, 201, 207, 279
ロング・ポジション …………………… 255

■ わ 行 ■

割引キャッシュフロー法（DCF）……… 99
割引係数 ………………………………… 65
割引率 …………………………… 65, 95, 173

About the Author

Akashi Hongo

Dr. Hongo is a Professor at Showa Women's University (SWU) and a Distinguished Scholar at Temple University, Japan Campus (TUJ). Prior to joining SWU and TUJ, Dr. Hongo was in charge of planning, accounting, human resource, legal, compliance, general affairs, international business development and supply chain management as a corporate officer at Recruit Management Solutions Co., Ltd. Dr. Hongo started his business career at Nippon Steel Co., Ltd. Then, he led value-based consulting practice in Japan and served as country representative for Stern Stewart & Co., a global consulting firm focusing on corporate finance and innovating the EVA framework. Dr. Hongo is the author of many books (in Japanese) on finance and management, including a bi-lingual (J-E) guide to financial accounting, corporate finance, and valuation. He holds a BA from Keio University, an MBA from the International University of Japan, and a Ph.D from the International Christian University.

著者略歴

本合　暁詩

昭和女子大学グローバルビジネス学部ビジネスデザイン学科教授
テンプル大学ジャパンキャンパス特別招聘教授

新日本製鐵（現日本製鉄），スターン スチュワート日本支社長，リクルートマネジメントソリューションズ執行役員等を経て現職。経営指標EVA®の導入コンサルティング，企業財務分野での企業内研修講師，研究活動に加え，事業会社における経営管理業務全般を経験。
慶應義塾大学法学部卒業，国際大学大学院国際経営学研究科修了（MBA）。国際基督教大学博士（学術）。
著書に『対訳　英語で学ぶ財務会計入門』，『対訳　英語で学ぶバリュエーション入門』，『組織を動かす経営管理』，『図解　ビジネスファイナンス〈第2版〉』（以上，中央経済社），『会社のものさし―実学「読む」経営指標入門』（東洋経済新報社）など。

対訳
英語で学ぶコーポレートファイナンス入門（第２版）

2014年９月15日	第１版第１刷発行	
2016年６月10日	第１版第３刷発行	
2019年５月１日	第２版第１刷発行	
2025年６月15日	第２版第４刷発行	

著　者　本　合　暁　詩
発行者　山　本　　　継
発行所　㈱中央経済社
発売元　㈱中央経済グループ
　　　　パブリッシング

〒101-0051　東京都千代田区神田神保町1-35
電話 03 (3293) 3371 (編集代表)
　　 03 (3293) 3381 (営業代表)
https://www.chuokeizai.co.jp

©2019
Printed in Japan

製版／文唱堂印刷㈱
印刷・製本／㈱デジタルパブリッシングサービス

※頁の「欠落」や「順序違い」などがありましたらお取り替えいた
しますので発売元までご送付ください。(送料小社負担)
ISBN 978-4-502-30201-5　C3034

JCOPY〈出版者著作権管理機構委託出版物〉本書を無断で複写複製（コピー）することは，著作
権法上の例外を除き，禁じられています。本書コピーされる場合は事前に出版者著作権管理機構
(JCOPY) の許諾を受けてください。
　　JCOPY〈https://www.jcopy.or.jp　eメール：info@jcopy.or.jp〉

好評既刊

◆組織を動かす経営管理
―経営企画のプロが教える計画・実行・モニタリングのしくみ

本合暁詩／(株)リクルートマネジメントソリューションズ経営企画部[編著]

序 章 経営管理(マネジメントシステム)の全体像／

第1章 計画策定／第2章 戦略推進・計画実行／

第3章 全社業績モニタリング／

第4章 組織・部署別業績モニタリング／

第5章 組織状態モニタリング／第6章 リソースマネジメント1:資源配分／

第7章 リソースマネジメント2:人材マネジメント／第8章 組織風土醸成

◆組織を動かす働き方改革
―いますぐスタートできる！効果的な目的・施策・導入プロセス

立花則子／本合暁詩／(株)リクルートマネジメントソリューションズ経営企画部[編著]

PartI　なぜ働き方改革を行うのか

PartII　働き方改革で何をするのか

PartIII　働き方改革をどう進めるのか

◆人事のためのデータサイエンス
―ゼロからの統計解析入門　　入江崇介[著]

Part 1　人事データ活用のイメージを具体化する

Part 2　人事データの特徴を把握する

Part 3　統計解析で人事データを活用する

中央経済社

ベーシック+プラス
Basic Plus

Let's START!

学びにプラス！
成長にプラス！
ベーシック+で
はじめよう！

いま新しい時代を切り開く基礎力と応用力を兼ね備えた人材が求められています。
このシリーズは，各学問分野の基本的な知識や標準的な考え方を学ぶことにプラスして，一人ひとりが主体的に思考し，行動できるような「学び」をサポートしています。

ベーシック+専用HP

教員向けサポートも充実！

中央経済社